EVERY ROCK A UNIVERSE

Valley of Bookcase Peak, taken at Now-I-Believe-It Peak,
photo by Wang Wusheng.

EVERY ROCK A UNIVERSE

The Yellow Mountains and Chinese Travel Writing

The first complete translation of

黃 山 領 要 錄

Huangshan   lingyao   lu

*A Record of Comprehending
the Essentials of the Yellow Mountains*

by Wang Hongdu (1646–1721/2)

Translated and introduced
by Jonathan Chaves

Floating World Editions

First edition, 2013
Published by Floating World Editions, Inc.
26 Jack Corner Road, Warren, CT 06777

Printed in the U.S.A.

ISBN 978-1-891640-70-4

Dedicated to Wang Wusheng
in memory of a wonderful journey
to the Yellow Mountains

晴雲漾朝光
虛壁響空吹
荒塗没人徑
一石一天地

Beneath clear skies, clouds burgeon with dawn light;
From deserted cliffs winds whistle through the void.
Overgrown pathways show no human footsteps;
With every rock, a whole new universe!
　　　　　　　　　　—Wu Yuan (1638–1700)

CONTENTS

ILLUSTRATIONS

Wang Wusheng photos are captioned as in his book *Celestial Realm: The Yellow Mountains of China*. Where sites are translated differently, the variant is indicated in brackets.

ACKNOWLEDGMENTS

My great love for the Yellow Mountains was born of viewing the paintings of Hongren. At one point I contemplated writing my PhD dissertation on him, a task which was later performed much more authoritatively than I could have by Jason Kuo, published as *The Austere Landscape: Paintings of Hung-jen* (Taipei: SMC Publishing Co., 1998).

I was only able to visit the Yellow Mountains in April of 2011, while serving as Visiting Scholar at Shanghai University. I am most grateful to then Dean of Liberal Arts, Professor Tao Feiya of that institution, for hosting me, and for providing me with letters of introduction to the Shanghai Library Rare Book Reading Room, the Municipal Library of Xuancheng (Anhui), and the Anhui Provincial Library and Anhui Provincial Museum in the provincial capital, Hefei. Without these, I could never have gained access to these valuable collections and consulted some of the rare—and in one case, unique—copies of Qing-dynasty books held by them.

I must also thank the Sigur Center for Asian Studies at my institution, The George Washington University, and then director Shawn McHale, for a grant that made the visit financially feasible. Professor McHale was particularly helpful in helping me to prepare for this trip, as was my colleague, Professor Donald Clarke of the Law School, whose suggestions about doing research in today's China were invaluable.

Paul Moss of the Sydney L. Moss Gallery, London, first called my attention to Wang Hongdu when he consulted with me about a painting by Wang in his collection. Through him, I further learned that Joseph Chang, then of the Arthur M. Sackler Gallery of the Smithsonian Institution, now of the Asian Art Museum in San Francisco, had told him about a marvelous book of travel essays on the Yellow Mountains written by Wang. Joseph himself provided a complete copy of the text, and I translated several representative passages. Then, in the summer of 2008, Joseph curated a wonderful exhibition of Yellow Mountains paintings, entitled "Yellow Mountain," for the Arthur M. Sackler Gallery of the Smithsonian Institution, here in Washington D.C. He made use of several of my translations in the show. His knowledge of the subject is encyclopedic, and I have learned a great deal from him. To both Paul Moss and Joseph Chang I owe an incalculable debt of gratitude.

It was through Joseph that I met Wang Wusheng, the photographic artist whose pictures of the Yellow Mountains are in a class of their own. Several of these adorned the Sackler exhibition, while I viewed many others in his stunning book *Celestial Realm: The Yellow Mountains of China* (Abbeville Press, 2006). In Shanghai, Wusheng and I immediately became fast friends. On our memorable first meeting, we became so wrapped up in conversation that we missed our stop on the Shanghai metro system—Wusheng's home stop—and when we realized it, laughed out loud like Huiyuan and his friends at Tiger Stream. But even this did not prepare me for his generous offer to accompany me to the Yellow Mountains for a full week's visit, making all necessary arrangements himself. Being guided by such a master artist to some of the most beautiful spots in the Mountains made me feel as if I had indeed ridden H.G. Wells' time machine back to the early Qing dynasty, to be led through these magical scenes by Hongren himself.

Eighteen Disciples of Buddha and Stone Bamboo Shoot Bridge,
taken at Now-I-Believe-It Peak, photo by Wang Wusheng.

TRAVELERS, MING LOYALISTS, AND PILGRIMS

Huangshan, the "Yellow Mountains" of southern Anhui Province, so-called because of their association with the mythical Huangdi, or Yellow Emperor, of high antiquity, exhibit some of the most spectacular scenery in China. And yet, although there existed an ancient cult of sacred mountains in China,[1] Huangshan was rarely visited until the mid-to-late seventeenth century, when it became a favorite pilgrimage destination for the literati.[2] The reasons for this development were partly political, partly religious, and partly aesthetic. Politically, a growing dissatisfaction with late Ming dynasty (1368–1644) governance stimulated a new increase in the age-old tradition of hermitage or reclusion amongst the literati, and then gave way to an even greater sense of disillusionment with the invasion of China by Manchu forces from the northeast, leading to the establishment of the Manchu-ruled Qing dynasty in 1644, and followed by a decades-long resistance movement of Ming loyalists.

There was only one precedent in history for such a catastrophe, the Mongol conquest of China in 1279, giving rise to the Mongol-ruled Yuan dynasty (1279–1368). As previously, reclusion was underpinned by elements from all three major religio-philosophical traditions: Confucianism, Daoism, and Buddhism, with shrines to great Confucian thinkers associated with the southern Anhui region being renovated or built from scratch, and important Buddhist temples being founded, as well as smaller hermitages for individual Buddhist monks or Daoist practitioners. Aesthetically, the rediscovery during this period of the riches of the poetry of the Song dynasty (960–1279) led to a new realism in late Ming-early Qing poetry, paralleled by a golden age of prose travel writings pioneered by the great explorer-writer, Xu Xiake (1586–1641), while an entire school of Anhui painters took inspiration from the stark and austere magnificence of the Yellow Mountains landscape. All of these trends were intertwined with each other, and came together especially in the writings of what can be considered a school of Anhui literati interested

1

in all of the "Three Perfections"—poetry, painting, and calligraphy—as well as in the religious renewal underway, especially the revival of the "School of Principle," the Cheng-Zhu branch of Neo-Confucianism considered to constitute Confucian orthodoxy. One of these men, Wang Hongdu (1646–1721/22), painter, calligrapher, poet and prose writer, is the author of a book of travel essays about the Yellow Mountains, *Huangshan lingyao lu*, or *A Record of Comprehending the Essentials of the Yellow Mountains*, written in 1696 but not actually printed until 1775.[3] This work, in terms of literary quality probably the finest on the subject, is here translated for the first time.

In Wang's book, but already in the earliest surviving gazetteer of the Yellow Mountains, the *Illustrated Classic of the Yellow Mountains* (*Huangshan tujing*) from the early eleventh century, the chief points to be visited are listed systematically and in sequence. First come the Thirty-six Peaks, thirty-six having been a magical number in both Daoism and Buddhism for centuries. Each is given its name. The same is true of the streams and waterfalls, as one would expect. But even individual rocks or rock formations, and individual pine trees, are carefully named and discussed in Wang's book. And as one peruses the profusion of travel essays and poems written about the Yellow Mountains in the late Ming to early Qing, one comes to realize that the peaks and streams, rocks and pines, all constitute points on an itinerary of what can only be called pilgrimage, comparable to the well-known points on the pilgrim's ancient *camino* to Santiago di Compostela. The literati who visited these mountains were, of course, looking for an enjoyable experience, and spent much of their time drinking wine and writing poetry with friends. But they were sure to visit *specific* places associated with the Yellow Emperor, or one of his alchemists, or some later worthy of the search for immortality.

Visits to Buddhist monasteries for talks with the monks there, or to shrines dedicated to Neo-Confucian thinkers like Zhu Xi and the Cheng Brothers, are even more obviously pilgrimage-like in their nature. And even visits that did not involve explicitly religious elements took on a ceremonial aspect. One is reminded, perhaps, of the Grand Tour of the nineteenth century, with travelers inevitably going to certain specific places. Or one might think of Dean MacCannell's famous argument in *The Tourist: A New Theory of the Leisure Class* (1976)[4] that modern tourism, of which the Grand Tour was the forerunner, has about it the feeling of what might be called a secular pilgrimage, with the travelers flocking to certain designated places as if it were *essential* to visit them.

MacCannell interestingly sees the modern tourist as a kind of pilgrim *manqué*, vaguely in search of an antidote to his alienation, of something, that is, of great value sensed to have been *lost*. One might apply this insight to the visitors to the late Ming-early Qing Yellow Mountains who were indeed trying to get back in touch with the roots of civilization itself, founded by the Yellow Emperor, and reinforced by the great Confucian masters whose roots could be traced to southern Anhui. This civilization appeared to be increasingly fragile, given the depredations of the eunuch usurper, Wei Zhongxian (1568–1627) and his henchmen in the late Ming, followed by the loss of the Heavenly Mandate to rule (*tianming*) by the Ming, not only to a new dynasty, but, for only the second time in history, to a non-Han Chinese dynasty, founded by invading Manchus. In Confucian terms, such a disaster could only have occurred through moral turpitude on the part of the leadership of the late Ming. There was a deeply felt need for a renewal of moral principles, and it was in search of such a renaissance, as if praying for it, that visitors paid their respects to the peaks and pines of the Yellow Mountains.

Xu Xiake's two trips to the Yellow Mountains took place in 1616 and 1618, early in his career as perhaps China's greatest explorer of Chinese territory. His *youji,* or "travel essays," about these journeys are typical of his *oeuvre* as a whole: the emphasis is on recording, with virtually journalistic precision and an unmistakable terseness of expression, the writer's actual itineraries, by the day and even by the hour. Actual description, although at times quite beautiful, is kept to a minimum. For example, on the seventh day of the second (lunar) month of the year (1616) of his first visit, Xu writes,[5]

> The gullies being deep and the snow thick, feeling terror with each step we took, we proceeded for five *li*, noting in a crevice of the peak to left a cave mouth through which light emerged, called the Window to Heaven. Continuing ahead, a single boulder suddenly surged upwards before us, seeming to face the cliff, and this was the Monk Seated in Meditation Upon a Rock. Another five *li* downward, and the pathway narrowed slightly, following a stream as it proceeded. Abruptly, the chaotic rocks in the torrent ahead became so haphazard in arrangement that they actually blocked our progress. After spending a long time clambering over these rocks, we came upon a crag newly formed by erosion, each sliver of which seemed on the brink of collapsing, and here at

last we recovered the path. Looking up towards the summit of the peak, we noticed a yellowish gash, with some green characters inscribed thereon which were entirely legible. This is what is known as the Heavenly Plaque, or the Placard of the Immortals … On the eighth day, we planned to penetrate to the most hidden portions of the Stone Bamboo Shoots, but we were thwarted by the weather. Heavy fog rendered the entire scene confusing. We did reach Lion Forest, when the wind blew even harder, and the fog became still thicker. I was for quickly making it to the Terrace for Refining the Elixir, so we turned towards the southwest. After three *li* we were again completely confused by the fog.

Happening upon a hermitage hut, we entered it. Rain now started to pour down, so we spent the night in this place …

This sample of Xu's prose will serve to demonstrate that here we have a dramatic move in the direction of realism. Although this term is, of course, contested, there can be no mistaking Xu's priority: to record with accuracy his actual movements and experiences on specific days and under specific meteorological conditions. The places he visits are stops on the "Grand Tour" itinerary of every pilgrim to the Yellow Mountains,

Leaf from an album of fifty views of the Yellow Mountains by Jiang Zhu, with his painting of the Placard of the Immortals, with poem and calligraphy by Wang Hongdu, currently in the Palace Museum, Beijing.

whether there is a religious undertone to the trip or not. Every one of the places named by Xu is depicted in paintings, or celebrated in poems. Wang Hongdu himself, for example, would write a poem for an album leaf painting of the Placard of the Immortals (above), from an album of fifty views of the Yellow Mountains by his contemporary, Jiang Zhu, currently in the Beijing Palace Museum. To the left of the painting, he has inscribed his poem:

> As hair grows grey, what need is there
>   to ride a "feathery chariot?"
> Open these paintings—not a single place
>   is not a paradise!
> From this day on, I will be dreaming
>   of wandering with the immortals:
> I wonder which number my name will be
>   on this Placard of the Immortals?

—Inscribed on the painting of *The Placard of the Immortals,* for Master Yunning [Jiang Zhu], by his "younger brother" Wang Hongdu

Tradition claims that the name of every traveler who visits this locale will appear among the "inscriptions" (natural markings that look like archaic writing) on the placard. Xu Xiake may have been alluding to these as well, or to an actual inscription in the same location. Wang Hongdu in his poem does what Xu refrains from doing, bringing in the Daoist-alchemical element, with his reference to a "feathery chariot" of the sort said to be pulled by phoenixes and other magical birds, and ridden on celestial journeys by immortals.

Xu Xiake is careful to present his itinerary in logical sequence, so that it was a relatively simple matter for the modern editors of his complete travel diaries to draft maps, showing the points he visited linked by a line representing his actual movement through the landscape.[6] His realistic, or even quasi-scientific, presentation of his travels through the Yellow Mountains, although it set the groundwork for the burgeoning of this theme in the late Ming to early Qing, was unique in its almost minimalistic avoidance of elaborated description. The element of realistic passage through the landscape, however, was to become crucially important in the travel prose and poetry of this period,[7] so much so, that it may be considered one of the hallmark achievements of Chinese literature at this juncture in its history.

With Xu having thus established a tendency towards realism, it was left for other writers, like Wang Hongdu, who were more interested than Xu perhaps was in literary *style* as such, to extend that realism to more elaborate descriptions. In particular, they wished to see the Yellow Mountains properly recorded and transmitted in a fully developed literary voice worthy of the noble subject. An explicit call for something of this kind can be found in the writings of a man of Xuancheng, one of southern Anhui's most ancient cultural centers, who was himself a premier poet and cultural arbiter of the day, of key importance to the circles of writers and artists interested in the Yellow Mountains, Shi Runzhang (1618–1683).[8] This is expressed in his poem "A Chant of the Yellow Mountains: Presented to Cao Binji" (*Huangshan yin: zeng Cao Binji*).[9] This important poem bears witness to the meaning of the Yellow Mountains for Shi himself, but even more interestingly lays out a virtual manifesto of what good writing about the Yellow Mountains should be like. The poem is worth translating in full:

My home is close to the sacred Yellow Mountains;
    I dream of ascending the Heavenly Capital Peak!
But alas, I've suffered from the constraints of official hat-strings:
    I'm on tiptoe, but unable to follow my wish.
When feelings come, with waxed clogs I yearn
    for trips of former springs,
Green pinewood as my hiking stick,
    may it turn into a green dragon!
Now young Cao has shown me
    his Yellow Mountains draft,
The scudding clouds and voyaging sun
    open my heart again.
Up the escarpments, eighteen thousand feet
    of climbing high!
Treading upon the vast cloud ocean,
    plucking hibiscus bloom!
Pulling at vines, clutching at creepers—
    so many make the climb,
But the Mountain Spirit, jealous of them all,
    spits forth mist and fog.

Now young Cao has gone four times
　　wandering through these peaks,
Layered cliffs, doubled gullies,
　　penetrating, morning and evening.
In exploring the mountains his sole endeavor—
　　to be the mountains' scribe:
Each and every rock and stream
　　to record and annotate.
I too once, alone, whistled loud
　　from Lotus Blossom Peak:
Mount Zhong and Mount Lu by comparison
　　were mere dots in the haze.
Xi Ho—sun's charioteer—I wished would
　　rein in his steeds,
And too I resented the absence of wine
　　to invite the Immortals to drink!
I see that you lament the past,
　　and yearn to meet Li Bo:
Ah, the glory of Immortal bones,
　　fluttering up above… !
Strive in youth to work and work,
　　to write and never stop:
Shout out loud, raise your head,
　　touch the vaulted sky!
A true man, of course you'll select your friends,
　　the ones who know your soul:
Then, where will the wine shop be
　　where we'll fall asleep, drunk, together?

Here, to begin with, Shi confers upon the Yellow Mountains precisely the title they lack, *yue* 岳 (also written 嶽), meaning "sacred peak," reserved for the *Wu yue* 五岳 or "Five Sacred Peaks" of the cardinal directions and center. These five are Mounts Tai (泰) to the east, Hua (華) to the west, Heng (恒) to the north, Heng (衡, a different character) to the south and Song (嵩) in the center. To this day, half in jest, it is said that "Once you have seen the Yellow Mountains, you needn't bother with the Five Sacred Peaks," implying as Shi does in his opening line that the Yellow Mountains by rights should be ranked with them. From this he goes on to praise the writings of "Young Cao" about the Yellow

Mountains, Young Cao being Cao Fen (born c. 1655), courtesy name Binji,[10] who had a reputation as a painter as well as a writer, and also as a craftsman active in the industry of ink-making. He was a member of a very distinguished family.[11] Some of Cao Fen's writings on the Yellow Mountains, if not all of them, appear to have survived, but important to us is Shi's way of praising them:

尋山直欲作山史; 一石一泉皆記注
Xun shan zhi yu zuo shan shi; yi shi yi quan jie ji zhu

In exploring the mountains his sole endeavor
　—to be the mountains' scribe;
Each and every rock and stream to record and annotate.

Shi could not make clearer for us this crucially important point: there is an intimate connection to the actual reality of the mountains, down to each and every individual rock, stream, pine tree, etc., and the writer's job is to record them. At the same time, the enterprise of writing about the mountains is not seen here as a mere exercise in demonstrating literary brilliance; the writer is in service to the mountains, a scribe making notes upon them. (Shi also informs us that he himself on an excursion to the Yellow Mountains had ascended as far as the top of Lotus Blossom Peak, with Heavenly Capital Peak one of the two highest in the entire range—although the primacy of one or the other was endlessly debated.)

Such an attitude toward travel writing, although never so compellingly expressed, was by no means limited to Shi Runzhang. Zhu Yizun (1629–1709), another major poet of the era and a prodigious scholar of literature, epigraphy, and numerous other subjects, in a preface to the now lost travel writings of a certain Zhu Renyuan titled "Preface to the Poems on the Western Mountains" (*Xishan shi xu*), makes this point:[12]

Travelers [to the Western Mountains] sometimes go on foot, sometimes on horseback, each using the means that suits him best. Thus the scenes they pass on their itineraries are often not precisely the same. A scholar, capable of literary composition, will compose poems to record his experiences, but this is not to show off his talent: on the contrary, the beauties of mountain and stream are such that they move a man to deep feeling, such that it is impossible to express it fully with words ..."

Ultimately, such statements reflect an ancient Chinese preoccupation with writing, not merely as a display of brilliance, but to capture something real, and therefore really worthy of expression. Liu Xie (c. 465–c.520) in one of the masterpieces of Chinese literary criticism, *The Literary Mind and the Carving of Dragons* (*Wenxin diaolong*), famously made the distinction between the false practice of "fabricating feelings for the sake of literature," vs. the legitimate one of "fabricating literature for the sake of the feelings" (*Wei wen er zao qing … wei qing er zao wen*). Zhu Yizun and Shi Runzhang, in keeping with their Confucian proclivities, are even more emphatic about the priority of capturing real experience and real feelings—and real objects such as rocks in the mountains—over mere artifice for its own sake. The actual writings of such figures as Wang Hongdu would thus avoid the two extremes of excessive minimalism, as in Xu Xiake, or excessive floweriness, as in the case of the kind of writer castigated by Liu Xie centuries ago for writing merely for the sake of showing off.

A final point should be made about what has been described here as "realism." Wang seamlessly folds into his narrative examples of clearly impossible phenomena, such as, for example, the "ball of gibbons" reported by a Buddhist monk in the section describing the Residence Where One Shouts at Rocks (see p. 116). In most such cases, Wang is careful to indicate this was *reported* by a resident of the mountains. Clearly, one has to do here with Chinese bestiary lore, parallel to that of medieval and later Europe. Such accounts are intimately interwoven with the experience of the Yellow Mountains, and their inclusion need not impugn the general realism of the text; indeed, it is in a sense an aspect of it.

Twin Bamboo Shoot Peak, taken at the Heavenly Sea,
photo by Wang Wusheng.

CONFUCIANISM AND
THE YELLOW MOUNTAINS

It is well known that the early Qing dynasty saw a full-scale revival of
the so-called Cheng-Zhu school of Neo-Confucianism, known as the
School of Principle. Scholars of the day, appalled by the fall of the Ming
dynasty to foreign (Manchu) invaders, and concluding in accordance
with Confucian historiography that the loss of the Heavenly Mandate
was a consequence of moral degeneration, sought (in the words of
Frederic Wakeman, Jr.) "an antidote…to moral relativism," and issued
a plea "to restore the absolute obligation of duties such as filial piety and
loyalty."[13] Scholars of the region of the Yellow Mountains—that is to say,
southern Anhui Province—took great pride in claiming local ancestry for
the key founders of the School of Principle in the Song dynasty: Zhu Xi
(1130–1200) and the Cheng brothers—Cheng Hao (1032–1085) and
Cheng Yi (1033–1107).[14]

The actual historicity of such claims was less important than the very
desire to make them. And not only was this a matter of local pride: beyond
saying that certain famous men traced their ancestry to the homeland of
the Yellow Mountains, the scholars were associating their region with
foundational truths or "principles" (*li*) that they considered essential if
there were to be a civilizational revival. To that end, they presided over
the renovation—one might even say the renaissance—of the prestigious
Ziyang Academy (*Ziyang shuyuan*, or Purple Yang-force Academy) which
had undergone many vicissitudes after originally being founded in honor
of Zhu Xi in the foothills of Ziyang Mountain, Shexian, late in the Song
dynasty (1246). That the renovation of this venerable institution was
not a merely local event, is demonstrated by the fact that in 1686 the
Emperor himself contributed plaques with the four large characters, *Xue
da xing tian* ("Learning that penetrates human nature and heaven") in
his own imperial calligraphy to a sister institution of the same name in
Fujian, Zhu Xi's actual birthplace, as well as to other similar institutions
in Anhui and elsewhere, including a shrine to the Cheng Brothers. These

acts were proudly praised by one of the chief cultural arbiters of the day, and the editor of Wang Hongdu's poetry, Wang Shizhen (1634–1711): "This has been a grand gesture rarely encountered in all of history."[15]

Fourteen years before the Kangxi Emperor thus put his imprimatur on the Neo-Confucian revival, in 1672, one of the major poets of the day and himself an influential cultural arbiter, especially for Anhui scholars, arrived at the Ziyang Academy to take up his prestigious appointment as Lecturer there. This was the very Shi Runzhang whose poem to Cao Fen we have studied. A native of Xuancheng, as we have seen, Shi himself wrote a long and complex poem about the significance of this appointment to him, and more importantly, the symbolic significance of the Academy itself: *Ziyang shuyuan ge* ("Song of the Ziyang Academy").[16] In a brief preface, he informs us that the birthday of Zhu Xi, the fifteenth day of the ninth month, was celebrated at the Academy by the visit of an important official, the Magistrate Master Cao, along with an entourage of local officials, who were served various delicacies in the lecture hall. Songs were sung to "record the glorious event." Cao has been identified by Zhao Hongwei of Weifang University (Shandong)[17] as Cao Dingwang (1618–1693) who served in this position from 1667–1674. (Cao was in fact the father of Cao Fen, Binji, to whom Shi addressed his poem on writings about the Yellow Mountains discussed in the previous chapter.) In a letter to Cao written after these events,[18] Shi states that he has learned that his poem has been inscribed in stone and installed in the Academy. He also describes even more explicitly than in the poem (see below) how proud he is of the fact that Zhu Xi was ultimately a son of the region. He credits Cao Dingwang with having facilitated and sponsored the renovation of the Academy, and describes the attendees at the ceremony as numbering "over one thousand persons."

The poem itself goes into considerable detail as to the youth of Zhu Xi's father Zhu Song (1097–1143) who was in fact born in Anhui. In his person, we are told, the spirit of various places in the north associated with the history of Confucian learning "came south to the riverbanks of She." He thus formed the historical link between the homeland of Confucianism in Qufu, Shandong—the birthplace of Confucius himself—and southern Anhui. He built his studio at Mount Ziyang, after which the Academy would be named, and "As night went on, in wind and rain, he studied beneath his solitary lamp / Turning pages of Zhou-dynasty classics and Confucius, books piled on his rope-bed!" Zhu Song then took up a position as official in Youxi, Fujian, where Zhu Xi was born, but "His homeland of Xin'an [the name for a section of southern Anhui encompassing Shexian, Xiuning, and several other counties of the immediate Yellow Mountains region] he never would forget!" He even named his new residence Ziyang. "The tomb of his distaff relative, old Mr. Zhu, being close at hand / The mountain moon of the old days took root deep in his heart." Here, Shi adds a prose note, "When Wengong [Zhu Song] returned from Fujian to She, he cared for Mr. Zhu's tomb; he also gave lectures in his Ziyang Hall, inscribing it with the four characters, *Jiu shi shan yue* ['Mountain moon of the old days']." Zhu Song's residence became the Ziyang Academy when Emperor Lizong (r. 1225–1264) presented a plaque with the four characters for Ziyang Academy written in his own calligraphy, as Shi informs us in another prose note.

At this stage, after relating some of the later vicissitudes of the Academy, Shi introduces the Cheng brothers into what is really an ode to the Confucian presence in southern Anhui:

> The distant ancestors of the Brothers Cheng
> > were also men of She;
> Their ancestral village of Huangdun
> > lies beside lakes and ridges.
> In flourishing ancestral shrines, on magnificent stelae
> > these lineages are inscribed:
> The fame of the ancestral villages of the Chengs and the Zhus
> > is scintillatingly grand!

At this triumphal point, Shi adds another note: "The ancestors of the Cheng Brothers were men of Huangdun in Shexian. There is a shrine to the three masters there [the two Chengs and Zhu Xi], the details of which may be found in the *Gazetteer of the Ancestral Homes of the Chengs and Zhu Xi* [*Cheng Zhu queli zhi*]." Shi is now ready to bring his poem to a close with an eloquent plea:

> When Heaven gives birth to wise men and worthies,
> > it seems to *choose* the place:
> Such remarkable prodigies continuously appearing,
> > emerging from primal chaos!
> It feels as if Confucius's dais and Yan Hui's alley
> > are near neighbors to us here,

> While Lian Stream and White Deer Grotto
>   can be viewed among our groves.
> And yet, alas! while a hundred thinkers
>   have thrived within our borders,
> The sagely ruler is far away, and somehow has tolerated
>   the withering of our Way.
> Clear and bright, the sun and stars
>   have not fallen yet to earth—
> I hope for the clearing of the weeds and brambles,
>   and return to Zhou dynasty ways!

Shi Runzhang offers here a prayer for bringing the vibrant Confucian tradition back to southern Anhui, so that it would be as if Confucius himself, and his favorite disciple, Yan Hui (who endured poverty with dignity, living in a little alleyway), were neighbors, or the teaching academies of Zhou Dunyi (1017–1073), the teacher of the Chengs, at Lian Stream, and Zhu Xi (at White Deer Grotto, his primary venue) were present in the area—as indeed had been the ancestors of the Chengs and Zhu. His fervency reaches beyond a call for a merely intellectual movement, even anticipating William Blake's (1757–1827) inspired call for bringing Christ back to England, by building "Jerusalem [i]n England's green & pleasant land," where he imagines "those feet" (of Christ Himself) "in ancient time" walked, while His "Countenance Divine" shone "forth upon our clouded hills."[19] In both cases we are confronted with a voice that is nothing less than prophetic in intensity.

Shi's poem attracted attention, and several other Anhui poets wrote poems of their own "echoing" his. One excellent example is by Xu Chu (1605–1676), a close friend and associate of many of the key figures associated with the Yellow Mountains, most notably the greatest of the Anhui School of painters, Hongren (1610–1664). He also associated with Wang Shizhen. [20]

The great significance of Zhu Xi in the history of Confucian thought was of course matched by that of the two brothers, Cheng Hao and Cheng Yi, who laid the foundation for the School of Principle. Just as Ziyang Academies and shrines were erected or renovated to commemorate Zhu Xi, shrines to the brothers also became renewed pilgrimage destinations during this period. One particularly significant example is a visit paid to one of them by Zha Shibiao (1615–1698), famed today along with Hongren as one of the two greatest Anhui master painters.[21] Two years after Zha's death, in 1700, a printed edition of his poetry was issued, titled *Writings Preserved from the Hall for Planting Books* (*Zhongshutang yigao*), which includes a subsection of "Poems inscribed on paintings" (*Tihua shi*). A copy of this rare book is in the collection of the Shanghai Library, which also holds an even rarer unpublished MS of Zha's, "Draft MS of the Poetry of the Mountain Man of Plum Valley" (*Meihe shanren yincao,* 梅壑山人吟草), Meihua being a sobriquet of Zha's. It contains a poem not included in the printed edition, recording a pilgrimage made by Zha to a shrine to the Cheng brothers, whose precise location is not indicated but which was almost certainly in southern Anhui. (Chinese text is given for this and subsequent poems from rare sources.)

謁二程夫子祠

萬古聞知統
東山誰嗣音
大儒南北宋
私淑弟兄心
座上春風滿
林邊理趣深
　（理趣林距祠里許）
讀書曾此地
千尺柏森森

Paying a Visit to the Shrine of the Two Masters, the Cheng Brothers

For thousands of ages, the line of learning was heard:
Who continued those sounds in the eastern mountains?
Great scholars of the Song, the northern and southern both!
I greatly admire their fraternal hearts!
This shrine is filled with springtime breezes;
Along the wood, deep the "Essence of Principle!"
　(*Poet's note:* "Essence of Principle Wood" is only
　one *li* or so from the shrine.)
This is a place where once I studied books:
A thousand feet tall, the cedars stand arrayed.

The brothers, of course, did not live into the Southern Song period. Line three merely means they were giants of the entire Song dynasty. Particularly interesting is the reference to a wood named Essence of

暴梅壑與思翁論畫日簡日發宋以上雪梅壑賦元四氣

惟倪黃淳此壽萬曹雲西徐幼文間有合作明名石田思尚而外

不少概兄世特論此也 方壺先生天真特畫家婁渭陳梅墾

母寬此畫既正雅初年筆而天真出淡神韻生氣達之云山由

宗流早得教私別傳耳 辰年坤此道出其正處眼藏宜

甚念于澤而世寶之也 癸巳秋惠庵張辰跋

甲辰夏初晤家滌崖兄於都下出示此用蓋梅壑早年

筆以請正於 方壺先生者梅壑以書畫擅名而畫高於

書知音在前尤不辜示政如管公明初見單子春談文蒸

範流不愧名士固當為識者所賞況先友遺跡乎予素不

Colophon and calligraphy dated 1713 by Wang Hongdu for an album of paintings by Zha Shibiao (1615–1698), courtesy of the Sydney L. Moss Gallery, London. Chinese text and translation are given at right.

曩梅壑與愚兄弟論畫，"曰簡曰冷：宋以前都不解此。元四家 惟
倪黃得此意義；曹雲西，徐幼文 間有合作。明爲石田，思白而外
不少概。" 兄其持論如此。方至先生，文章，詩，畫，家學潤深；梅
壑 因寫此就正。雖初年筆，而天眞幽淡，神韻生動遂已至此，由
其 宗派，早得教以別傳耳。胥原叔，此道中具正法眼，藏宜 其
念手澤而世寶之也。癸巳中秋息廬洪度跋。

*In the past, "Plum Valley" [Zha Shibiao] was discoursing on painting with
myself and my brother: "We speak of 'simplicity,' we speak of 'chill austerity.'
During the Song dynasty and earlier periods, no one comprehended this
style. Of the Four Masters of the Yuan dynasty, only Ni [Zan] and Huang
[Gongwang] mastered the meaning of it; and Cao Yunxi [Zhibo] and Xu
Youwen* [Ben; actually late Yuan – early Ming] *occasionally did works in
accordance with it. In the Ming, it was Shitian* [Shen Zhou] *and Sibai*
[Dong Qichang], *while anyone else failed to get even the least part of it."
Thus did my "brother" hold forth.*

Now Mr. Fangzhih [Wang Nanming, Diya 汪南鳴，滌崖，known
primarily as an ink-maker] *in prose, poetry and painting is deeply imbued
with the rich family tradition. Plum Valley therefore painted this album and
presented it to him for correction. Although it represents his early work, it
has clearly already achieved a high degree of heavenly naturalness, profound
understatement, spirit-resonance and lively movement. This is because, on
account of his family tradition, he early received instruction to facilitate his
individual transmission.*

*My uncle, Xuyuan, possesses the true Dharma Eye in this art. In holding
this work in his collection, may he keep in mind that it is a precious relic
of the artist, and may his family treasure it down through the generations.
Mid-autumn of the year* guisi [1713], *colophon added by Hongdu of the
Hut-for-Rest.*

Principle, "Principle," or Li, being the single most important concept in Cheng-Zhu thought, from which derives its very name, the School of Principle. The shrine as described by Zha could well have been a Buddhist or Daoist temple, as these are routinely surrounded in poetic description, and in actual reality, by superb scenes: in this case, a stand of noble cedars. But this is in fact a shrine to two Neo-Confucian thinkers, a salutary reminder that *Confucian* structures of importance too had a numinous charisma about them for their visitors. It is not the Dao or the Dharma, but Li, Principle, which invests this spot with its spiritual feeling. Endless attempts to distinguish Li from the "Ideas" of Plato have generally failed to make the case. The concept appears to be the same in essence: these are the archetypal ontological underpinnings of physical phenomena.

The scholars of the day were inspired by the presence of such institutions as academies and shrines in their midst, but they did not rest content with them. For them, it was essential to be able to find living exemplars in their own day of the perduring Confucian morals principles, such as *xiao*, "filial piety," and *zhong*, "loyalty." Probably the most important poet to dedicate a major portion of his work to this endeavor was Wu Jiaji (1618–1684).[22] Wu socialized extensively with Anhui scholars, poets and painters, very much including members of the Wang Hongdu circle, in particular, Wu Yuan (1638–1700), author of one of the prefaces to the collected poetry of Wang Hongdu, as well as one of the prefaces to *Huangshan lingyao lu*, and himself one of the finest poets of the circle. In one of a group of eloquent poems of friendship to Wu Jiaji, written on the occasion of Jiaji's departure after a visit to Anhui, *Reciprocating Wu Yeren* [Jiaji] *for His Gift of Louxuan ji* [the *Collected Works from the Lowly Studio*, Wu Jiaji's collected writings] *and Seeing Him Off as He Returns to Dongtao*,[23] Wu Yuan writes,

> Along the seacoast, years of real hunger:
> Your household now has almost no supplies.
> Son's crying mixes in with women's wailing:
> How can you read your books and poems at all?
> You sell your writings, change the cash for rice,
> Then bring it home back to your little hut.
> Your tiny sail now breasts the setting sunlight,
> Reeds and cattails shivering in the cold.
> Go home, my friend, and feel some consolation;
> For I remain—who'll live here with me now?

Wu Yuan and Wang Hongdu were undoubtedly inspired by Wu Jiaji's staunch refusal to "play the game" and enter officialdom under the Manchus. Instead, he lived in his homeland, the impoverished saltlands of coastal Jiangsu Province, meticulously collecting exemplary cases of filial or loyal behavior on the part of ordinary folks.

One singular fashion in which Wang Hongdu chose to follow in Wu Jiaji's footsteps was by compiling and publishing a remarkable work, *Evidence for a History of Women in Xin'an* (*Xin'an nüshi zheng*). A copy of this book, preface dated Kangxi *bingxu* (1706) is in the Shanghai Library Rare Book Reading Room. The author of the preface is one Wang Shuqi, courtesy name Yu'yi (1683–1760), a younger friend and apparently student of Wang Hongdu's in poetry.[24] The collection of prose writings and poems about women who engaged in heroic acts of filial piety and loyalty (private and public sides of the same coin), and chastity (*zhen* or *jie*) similar in style and purpose to Wu Jiaji's writings on these subjects, is introduced by Wang Shuqi with an emphasis on the *seriousness* of the project. He states that the *shi* (history) of the title is intended to conjure such classic texts as the *Shang shu* (*Book of Historical Documents*) or *Chunqiu* (*Spring and Autumn Annals*), the latter being the only classic actually attributed to the authorship of Confucius himself, and *regional* in focus (the Master's home state of Lu), like the current work. Wang Shuqi goes on to state that "the Yellow Mountains and White Peaks [another famed Anhui mountain range to the south] of our Province are wondrously rich in beauty, surging up to the sky, and the fine fish of the Lian and Jian Rivers [Lian Shui, Jian Jiang, the latter famously adopted as a nom-de-plume by the painter Hongren] are not hidden from notice." (To this day, Anhui natives pride themselves on certain local fish not obtainable elsewhere.) But, Wang Shuqi laments, the extraordinary acts of the women here recorded, "sufficient to startle Heaven and shake Earth," have not been adequately recognized or even written down. Wang Hongdu has thus provided evidence that although "the customs of the world have been deteriorating to an extreme degree," these women have been able to "act in such ways even as they encountered the catastrophic changes of the times," a reference, needless to say, to the Manchu conquest. [25]

Wang Shuqi is as explicit as it is possible to be: the moral actions of these local women of southern Anhui deserve to be recorded alongside of the beauties of the region's mountains and its famous delicacies, not only for the sake of mere fame, but for the greater glory of the region.

Again, as in Zha Shibiao's poem on the shrine to the Cheng brothers, the numinousness of nature parallels or embodies *moral* as well as *ontological* principles associated with Confucian thought. The Yellow Mountains and the virtues of filial piety and loyalty *go together.*

Eleven years after the publication of *Evidence for a History of Women in Xin'an,* in the year Kangxi *dingyou* (1717), Wang Hongdu would participate in another, communal project in honor of Confucian virtue in southern Anhui. This time, he would contribute the opening preface and poem to a collection of writings in honor of a beloved local magistate, identified only as *She yihou Jiang gong,* or "Town Magistrate of She Prefecture Master Jiang." This individual has been identified by Zhao Hongwei of Weifang University as a certain Jiang Zhenxian who is stated in the 1937 *Gazetteer of She Prefecture* (*She xian zhi*) to have served in this position from 1716 to1726.[26]

The resulting volume, entitled *Public Eulogies of the Blue Lotus* (*Qinglian yusong*) is extremely rare today, and a copy held by the Provincial Museum of Anhui Province, Hefei, may be the only one in existence.

Combining Wang Hongdu's preface with other accounts in the book, one learns that Master Jiang arrived in the area to discover a devastating famine under way. He personally traveled to nearby regions, collecting as best he could surplus grain that he then distributed to his own population, and prayed for rain at the Temple of the Dragon King. The result of the latter activity was a great downpour, leading eventually to abundant harvests. As if this were not enough, we are told that on the occasion of Master Jiang visiting the Fragrant Waters Garden along the Ruan Stream of the Yellow Mountains, blue lotus flowers, or *qinglian,* miraculously sprung from the ground, a clear omen from Heaven of His Excellency's *qinglian,* "pure incorruptibility." It was this Confucian *miraculum* that persuaded people to compose poems in praise of this wonderful administrator, and to publish them as a book in his honor. Here is Wang Hongdu's opening preface and poem, again given in its entirety in Chinese because of the rarity of the book:[27]

青蓮輿頌, 詠青蓮花贈邑侯蔣公——有小序

丁酉春，我歙邑侯蔣公有請告之舉；諸 上憲體 上 嘉惠
元元至意，正已率屬，咸與維新；知公清德仁聲，方資撫
字，同心慰留，乃於六月朔復盟神聽政甘霖大沛，年穀順
成，而闒 [printed in error for 閤, an alternate form of 合] 邑

歡勝矣。偶過阮溪時，水香園忽放青蓮花數朵，公愛賞不
置；父老爭折送歸。一時聞風而慕傚者亦各折花一枝以獻
曰公之清廉有如此花也。
同人作詩以頌之屬。余叙其緣始並作穅秕之導云。

折取青蓮碧沼隈
乘涼侵曉入城來
皆言雨復從天下
何異花新自火開
黃海高峰分黛色
練江明月育珠胎
知公只飲新安水
特供清香露一杯

Public Eulogies of the Blue Lotus, Presented to Town Magistrate Master Jiang—with a Short Preface

In spring of the year *dingyou* [1717], the Town Magistrate of our She prefecture went through the process of requesting [to resign?]. All the provincial authorities petitioned His Majesty, that his benevolent grace might be fully satisfied [with this man's work] in all respects; and as he [the Magistrate] met the standards fully, they were unanimous in hoping that his tenure would be renewed. Upon learning that His Excellency was a man of pure virtue, with a reputation for humaneness, of staunch character and nurturing towards his people, His Majesty agreed to retain him in position. Thus, on the first day of sixth month of the year, His Excellency renewed his vows to the gods to preside as magistrate. Sweet rains fell plentifully, and the harvest proved to be bountiful; all within the district were delighted.

As he passed one day along the Juan Stream [of the Yellow Mountains], within the Fragrant Waters Garden there suddenly bloomed several blue lotus flowers: these His Excellency loved and enjoyed without interruption. The local elders vied with each other in plucking the blossoms to offer him as gifts on the occasion of his retirement. Those who learned of this craze wished to emulate it, so they too each plucked one flower to present to His Excellency, saying, "His Excellency's pure incorruptibility [*qinglian*, a homonym of the word for 'blue lotus'] is like this flower!" At the same time they wrote poems of the eulogy type for him. Here I have narrated the origins of these works, thus providing dregs as an introduction! [Wang's poem:]

> He plucked a blue lotus from the banks of an emerald pond,
> Enjoying the coolness, at the crack of dawn,
>> came into the town.
> All say that rain has fallen again,
>> coming from Heaven;
> What difference from these flowers
>> newly generated by "Fire?"
> The towering peaks of the Yellow Ocean
>> share their dark color;
> The bright moon of the Lian River
>> nurtures these pearls in the womb.
> Knowing, Sir, that you will only drink
>> Xin'an water,
> We offer to you this pure fragrance—
>> a cup of lotus dew.

The place where the blue lotus are said to have grown was in fact the ancestral residence of Wang Hongdu's friend and student, Wang Shuqi, author, as we have seen, of the preface to Hongdu's book on Xin'an women. Also, the garden estate functioned as a publication venue, issuing among other titles a supplement of illustrations to the important 1690 gazetteer of She prefecture edited by another influential scholar-official-poet and patron of the circle, Jin Zhijing (Magistrate of She during the 1680's). Although the 1690 gazetteer already had superb illustrations by an artist named Wu Yi,[28] the latter was also asked in 1692 to produce a volume entitled *Illustrations of the Mountains and Rivers of Ancient She Prefecture* (*Gu She shanchuan tu*), which was issued by Wang Shuqi's "Fragrant Waters Garden."

Here the Yellow Mountains function as an arena of what can only be called Confucian numinosity, providing the very soil in which Heaven plants the miraculous omen calling attention to Master Jiang's worthy administrative record, that is, to his moral character. The peaks themselves share their dark colors with the (dark) blue lotus flowers as well, just as they are nurtured by the waters of the local Lian River (not to be confused with the Lian Stream associated with Zhou Dunyi, written with a different character). In addition to earth and water, the element of fire plays a role in stimulating the growth of the plants. This is not the burning fire of a forest fire, but the elemental energy of nature. Wood is perhaps represented by the flowers themselves, while metal alone of the "five elements" (*wu xing*) seems not to be represented. The appearance of the flowers is a moral event, and a cosmological one as well, the "overflowing moral energy" (*haoran zhi qi*) of Heaven and Earth, described by Mencius, demonstrating its on-going vibrancy.

What, if anything, really happened? Could one of the many flowers native to the Yellow Mountains, and found nowhere else, have been mistaken for the "blue lotus?" The recently published comprehensive catalogue of "rare flora of the Yellow Mountains" published by the China Forest Publishing House in 2006[29] records no such flower. The many meticulously accurate paintings of Yellow Mountains flowers prepared by the monk-painter Xuezhuang (c. 1646–1719), largely apparently lost today, which inspired Suzhou magistrate, scholar and poet Sung Luo (1634–1713), also author of one of the prefaces to *Huangshan lingyao lu*, to write poems about twenty of them, and Wu Yuan and his friends to collaborate on a lengthy linked-verse poem inspired by them,[30] do not appear to have depicted such a flower. Or was the entire episode invented? For us, the telling thing is this: conceptually, Heaven's moral authority and nature's generative power are ultimately one in the cosmological worldview underpinning the thought of Wang Hongdu and his associates.

Precipice of Now-I-Believe-It Peak, photo by Wang Wusheng.

DAOISM, BUDDHISM, AND THE YELLOW MOUNTAINS

Everything about the legendary history of the Yellow Mountains is associated with that mode of Daoism that involves the attempt to refine the "elixir of immortality," or *dan*, and the quest—through this means as well as through the imbibing of various herbs—to become an immortal, or *xian*. The very name of the range derives from that of the Yellow Emperor, Huangdi, whose alchemists were supposed to have attempted the elixir here. But by the period we are concerned with, the late Ming to the early Qing, although isolated practitioners may have been continuing the age-old search for the elixir at the Yellow Mountains, there do not appear to have been any significant "official" Daoist foundations there. What is more, the literati almost from the beginning of what we may call Xian Daoism, after Herrlee Creel[31], have been divided into those who were interested, and those who questioned the legitimacy of the endeavor, with Bai Ju'yi (or Po Chü-I, 772–846), for example, putting his finger on the precise contradiction between the serene acceptance of death in Philosophical Daoism, versus the urgent attempt to conquer death in Xian Daoism:[32] "And then the Sagely Ancestor of the Primal Origin [Lao Zi], in his Five Thousand Words [i.e., the *Daode jing*] / Says nothing of herbs, / Says nothing of Immortals, /Says nothing of ascending in broad daylight to Heaven!"

The culmination of this trend in literature would occur in the hilarious satire included by Wu Jingzi (1701–1754) in his great satirical novel *Unofficial History of the Scholars* (*Rulin Waishi*), on quack alchemists and the outrageous scams they would pull off against gullible clients.[33] Hong Hanxian (Hong the Silly Immortal), Wu's swindler, is one of the great comic creations of Chinese fiction.

The association of the Yellow Mountains with the Yellow Emperor and his alchemical endeavors is nowhere more emphasized than in the fragmentary extant texts of the earliest compiled gazetteer of the mountains, *The Illustrated Classic of the Yellow Mountains* (*Huangshan tujing*). In a meticulous recent study,[34] Zhang Yong and Pan Zhongli date the original compilation of this book to the Jingyou period of the Northern Song dynasty, or 1034–1037, by the hand of an anonymous author. After many vicissitudes, the remaining fragments of the lost original were gathered and published in 1612, together with an *Investigation into the Illustrated Classic of the Yellow Mountains* (*Huangshan tujing kao*) by the scholar Pan Zhiheng (c. 1536–1621), in 1612, in his massive encyclopedia of materials related to the Yellow Emperor and the Yellow Mountains, *Huang hai* (a term referring to the displays of "cloud ocean" in the mountains). This work, itself quite rare, was reprinted in 1996 in the vast *Collectanea of Works Whose Titles Appeared Only in the Table of Contents of the Complete Books of the Four Treasuries* (*Siku quanshu cunmu congshu*),[35] in other words, books which were themselves deemed to be too dangerously anti-Manchu in some fashion to be included when the *Siku quanshu* was being edited during the Qianlong period. (This fact in itself helps demonstrate the link between Yellow Mountains literature and the Ming Resistance movement.)

Sampling the *Huangshan tujing*, one discovers that it presents a listing of the thirty-six major peaks (thirty-six being a magical number in Daoism), opening with the Lian dan feng, Peak for Refining the Elixir, undoutedly the early form of the place name Lian dan tai, Terrace for Refining the Elixir, which would be in use by the late Ming or earlier and is still used today. This is a central spot in the range, affording a magnificent view of the two tallest peaks, Lotus Blossom and Heavenly Capital, from directly across. According to the Northern Song text:[36]

> Master Fuqiu here, on this summit, refined the elixir. After eight cycles of sixty years [480 years], the elixir was completed. The Yellow Emperor, imbibing seven granules of it, without evening supporting himself on clouds and mist, in broad daylight ascended to the empyrean and wandered about in joy. On the peak is a Brazier for Refining the Elixir, and below is a Source for Refining the Elixir. At this source can be found a River for Refining the Elixir, a Stream for Washing Herbs, and a Rock for Pounding Herbs, whose stone mortar and pestle are still to be seen, exactly as they were.

Master Fuqiu is said to have been the Yellow Emperor's Alchemist-in-Chief, although other sources make the Yellow Emperor his own alchemist.

The other place descriptions in the *Huangshan tujing* are equally imbued with an essentially Xian Daoist approach to the Yellow Mountains. Wang Hongdu and most of his friends may not have believed in the efficacy of such practices, or may have felt varying degrees of skepticism about them (while some indeed may have continued the attempt with varying degrees of commitment), but that by no means implies that what might be called the Daoist charisma of the Yellow Mountains was lost to them. Wang himself, climbing Lotus Blossom Peak, right across from the Terrace for Refining the Elixir, could not help but be moved by the Daoist associations of the spot, particularly as he apparently met a certain Wang, Master of the Dao, while he was there. Hearing either this man or someone else playing a flute out of doors, he was moved to write a poem:[37]

蓮花峰頂聞簫贈王道士

玉簫吹徹在何峰
散作秋濤入萬松
我欲青天騎白鳳
高尋子晉躡仙蹤

At the Summit of Lotus Blossom Peak, Hearing Someone Playing a Flute, Sent to Wang, Master of the Dao

That flute of jade, penetrating the void—
    which peak is it coming from?
It ripples into autumn waves,
    roaring in ten thousand pines!
I wish to ride the White Phoenix,
    soaring to blue Heaven,
Seeking there Prince Wang Zi-jin,
    treading his immortal footsteps!

In Master Wang, Wang Hongdu encountered at least one Daoist practitioner, still active at the Yellow Mountains, and so he accords him the highest possible praise, suggesting he may achieve the same glorious results as his fellow member of the Wang clan, Prince Wang Zi-jin, a semi-legendary figure who is said to have succeeded in becoming an Immortal, "ascending in broad daylight."

Buddism at the Yellow Mountains is an entirely different matter. While the Yellow Mountains never joined the ranks of "official" sacred mountains of Buddhism, such as Mount Tiantai in Zhejiang, Five Terraces Mountain in Shanxi, or Mount Emei in Sichuan—just as they never were reckoned among the Five Sacred Peaks of Confucianism— nevertheless there was active Buddhist monasticism there, and Buddhist monks in fact played a key role in opening up the mountains, as described in considerable detail by Wang Hongdu throughout the pages of his *Huangshan lingyao lu.*

Buddhist practice at the Yellow Mountains was bound up with Ming loyalism in certain cases—that is, a number of members of those circles "left the world" and became monks, residing in the Yellow Mountains. In addition, several of the leading painters of the Anhui School, most notably Hongren and Xuezhuang, were themselves ordained monks as well as being highly sympathetic to the Ming loyalist cause. But established monasteries existed there as well. There existed, indeed, what may be described as a spectrum of monastic modes for monks at the Yellow Mountains, and the very fact that the locale was *not* under an overarching Buddhist administration may have left practitioners at greater liberty to engage in a variety of monastic practices as they chose. One is, in fact, strikingly reminded of the range of types of monastic practice in Christianity, Eastern Orthodox Christianity in particular. At Mount Athos, the ancient center of Orthodox monasticism, still flourishing today, we are told, "In addition to the eremitic, semi-eremitic and cenobitic monk on Athos, there is a further type—the idiorrhythmic monk."[38] That is to say, there are monks living in large monastic establishments—the cenobitic type; and then there are those who live in smaller communities, or spend part of their time in solitary practice, the semi-eremitic type, while there are individual hermits who either follow closely the supervision of their spiritual fathers (eremitic), and finally those who follow "their own rhythms," that is to say, they establish their own regimen, and these are called idiorrhythmic. One might easily adopt this terminology to the range of practices in Yellow Mountains Buddhism during the late Ming to early Qing.

Wang Hongdu in his *Huangshan lingyao lu* records a number of contributions to the opening of the Yellow Mountains by monks such as Pumen,[39] to whom he gives credit for being the first to climb to the very summit of Heavenly Capital Peak, as well as being the founder of what would later become Ciguang si, Compassionate Light Temple, and quite possibly the single individual most responsible for the opening of the Yellow Mountains in the mid-Ming period.

But an especially interesting monk, to whom Wang gives his attention and by whom he records a lengthy essay of his own on the Yellow Mountains, is known by his monastic name of Bo'an. This individual turns out to be a classic example of a Ming loyalist "leaving the world" for a Buddhist monastic vocation after the Manchu conquest. A native of Shexian originally named Xiong Kaiyuan, he was a sufficiently fine poet to be included by Zhu Yizun in his magisterial anthology *A Compilation of Ming Poetry* (*Ming shi zong*).[40] Zhu informs us that Xiong obtained his *jinshi* degree in 1625, and embarked upon a typical scholar-official's career under the Ming. After he memorialized against a favorite of the last Ming Emperor, he received the bastinado and was sent into exile. Becoming a monk with the Manchu conquest, he maintained close relations with a number of the Yellow Mountains poets, as well as other important figures of the time. He settled at a monastery in Suzhou, but left word that he wished to be buried in the Yellow Mountains. Quite possibly the greatest single poet of the Qing dynasty, Wu Weiye (1609–1671) has a pair of poems inspired by a portrait of Bo'an, with a lengthy, informative preface.[41]

Not surprisingly, at the Yellow Mountains as elsewhere, literati would visit Buddhist monks for spiritual advice, even though they were not necessarily lay practitioners themselves. Perhaps the most detailed account of such a conversation is found in a poem by Cao Zhenji (1634-1698), known for his *ci* or "lyric" poems,[42] but praised, for example, by Suzhou magistrate, scholar and poet Sung Luo for his suite of what we now know to be no less than thirty-seven "poems on travels to the Yellow Mountains" (*Huangshan jiyou shi*). It is the major Qianlong period anthologist, Shen Deqian (1673–1769) who reports in his important *A Separate [or Special] Anthology of Qing dynasty Poetry* (*Qing shi biecai ji*)[43] that Song was saddened by the lack of good poems about the Yellow Mountains, noting that everyone praised major poet and cultural arbiter Qian Qian'yi (1582–1664),[44] for his; but now, "Qian has been crushed by Shi'an [Cao Zhenji]!" And yet Shen laments that in his day, only *one* of Cao's Yellow Mountains poems survives! As it turns out, Cao's complete set of thirty-seven has today been recovered, and printed in *Siku quanshu congmu congshu* along with other recovered poetry by Cao.[45] One of these is translated here:

Staying Overnight at Mañjuśrī Cloister and Having a Nighttime Discussion with the Monk, Master Fu of Zhongzhou

I find myself above a thousand turnings,
The luminosity still fresher, sterner.
The gemstone dipper hangs above the railing;
The crescent moon shines mystically, alone.
In coldness, flowers are formed by the Snow Maiden;
At night, back to their valleys float white clouds.
Amidst the vastness of the misty "ocean,"
This is the one place where I now would stay.
The Master is imbued with wondrous feeling:
His yak-tail whisk emits a whispering sound.
The old monk speaks about what is Unborn:
Cross-legged he sits, as if a withered tree.
And yet his tongue produces blue-green lotus,
Words flowing freely just like pearls or jade.
Severely warning this dust-dwelling scholar,
"You just don't see the crisis that you're in!"
Such marvelous teaching!—I hear all Three Carts,
Noble discourse, breaking Five-Deer's horns.
How could I expect, beside this Fire-Ox,
To receive the blessing of Half-a-Taro?
All night long, the winds sound out from heaven,
Their fierce force rattling the wooden building.
I pull the cotton blanket way over my head,
And on my comfortable bed, suddenly fall fast asleep.

Here we have an unprecedented degree of substance from the poet's conversation with the Buddhist Master, who clearly confronted him in a kind of spiritual intercession in his life. The poem bristles as well with Buddhist allusions: Yak-tail whisks were held as emblems by Buddhist teachers. Three Carts, in a well-known parable told by Buddha in the Lotus Sutra, were given by a father to persuade his children, unaware of the danger, to emerge from a burning house; the carts, pulled by a goat, a deer, and an ox, represent three different modes of Buddhist teaching used by Buddha to awaken man to his spiritual crisis. Five-Deer, or Wulu, was actually the double surname of a Han dynasty scholar, Wulu Chongzong, described as arrogantly self-assured about his knowledge of the *Yijing*, or *Book of Changes*. A superior scholar, Zhu Yun, whose biography in the official history of the Han dynasty, the *Hanshu*, relates this incident, defeated Wulu in debate, and was thus said to have "broken his horns!" From this time forth, "breaking Five-Deer's horns" has meant to engage in superior rhetoric. Master Fu is described as a Fire-Ox, in Chinese astrology, a person born on a year of the Ox when in conjunction with the element of fire. Such persons are thought to be natural teachers of wisdom, but with stern personalities. Whether Master Fu actually was born in such a year is impossible to say. Half a taro was given to the young scholar, Li Mi (722–789), by a poor monk named Lancan (Lazy Remnant) when Li had to stop for the night at a remote temple. Seeing Li was hungry, Lancan cut his taro in half, and offered half to Li, telling him that he would become a high minister. Li went on to become precisely that, serving in the courts of no less than four successive emperors.

There is no mistaking the seriousness of Master Fu, nor of the poet, who is clearly serious about seeking advice. One is again reminded of Mount Athos, where monks are today routinely sought out by men from the cities of Greece who travel to the holy mountain for spiritual advice.

That Cao Zhenji and Wang Hongdu knew each other there can be no doubt at all. Their fellow poet, Wu Qi (1619–1693), a man of She prefecture, has a prosepoem on a little pavilion which the Wang brothers built at a place of hermitage (possibly prior to moving to Start-to-Believe Peak), called *Xinghua chun yu lou*, or Pavilion Tower of Spring Rain in the Apricot Blossoms.[46] In the prose introduction, he states that "Yuding and Wenye [Wang Hongdu and his younger brother, Yangdu (b. 1647)], the two Wangs, were living deep among the apricot trees at Songming Mountain near She prefecture. Mr. Cao Shi'an, the Hanlin Scholar [i.e., Cao Zhenji] adopted the line by a Song dynasty[47] poet, *Xing hua chun yu Jiangnan* ["Spring rain in the apricot blossoms South-of-the-River"] as a basis for writing the name plaque, dubbing it Pavilion Tower of Spring Rain in the Apricot Blossoms." Wu goes on to relate how on a visit to the spot, he fell in love with the new pavilion, and so wrote his prosepoem about it.

The final word on the interrelationships among Confucianism, Daoism, Buddhism, and Ming loyalism at the Yellow Mountains may well be spoken, or sung, by one of the premier poets of the day, Wu Jiaji

(1618–1684). A friend of both Wang brothers (Wang Hongdu and his younger brother Wang Yangdu), Wu sent them a group of three poems for "inscription on their thatched hut at Start-to-Believe Peak," a location which they may have selected in part because of its connection with one of the most revered of Ming loyalists, the redoubtable hero Jiang Tianyi (1602–1645).[48] The third of these poems is a virtual manifesto of the meaning of the location for sympathizers with the Ming cause:[49]

> The true monk, riding transformation, is gone;
> Only the ruins of his hermitage remain.
> And in what era did that man tread upon the void,
> Residing here with gourd and bamboo hat?
> His stone stove, cold, no smoke arises;
> Only the bright moon ascends beside the stove.
> Abruptly towering high, coming here to sit alone:
> I've also heard of this man, Martyr Jiang!
> A pure breeze, twirling clouds among the peaks,
> A winging crane, resting among the waterfalls!
> But suddenly, encountering crisis for lord and father,
> He gathered up his robes, took his leave of mulberry fields.
> His hair stood up as he passed Triple Mountain;
> His head lopped off, cast to the Nine Avenues of death!
> Who needs the blueness of lotus blossoms?
> What good the purple of magic fungus?
> This martyr is a Buddha, an Immortal!
> Ah, how I admire him, Master of the Cold Stream!

This powerful poem is as eloquent an expression as one could hope for of the passionate admiration stimulated in men like Wu Jiaji or Wang Hongdu by such a man as Jiang Tianyi. Jiang indeed led resistance forces to fight against the advancing Manchu armies, dying in the attempt. The poet adds three detailed prose notes, interlineated with lines 2, 3, and 8 of the poem, to put in perspective his view of the hero: "The monk, Yi'cheng built his Hermitage for Stabilizing in Void on the top of this peak." (Wang Hongdu will later have more to say about this Buddhist hermit.) "The [man referred to in line 3] is the Daoist Niao'ke [Bird Nest]." And finally, "On the stone cliff face are inscribed the five words *Han jiang zi du zuo* ['Master Cold Stream (Jiang Tianyi) Sits Alone'], written in the calligraphy of Jiang Wenshi [Jiang Tianyi] himself."

Wu's astonishing idea is that the quest for transcendence need not wait upon Buddhist or Daoist alchemical practice. (The use of the lotus to characterize Buddhism is commonplace, of course, but it should be recalled that no less a Neo-Confucian master than Zhou Dunyi wrote a famous essay in praise of the flower, "A Discourse on Cherishing the Lotus," [*Ai lian shuo*], hence its appearance in the previously dicussed poem by Wang Hongdu as a *Confucian* omen). Two famed exponents of those schools have been here, and have now disappeared. But a Confucian martyr has shown himself at least their equal, in achieving the glory of self-sacrifice. Thus the maxim "The Three Teachings are One" (*Sanjiao wei yi*) is indeed true at this spot, Start-to-Believe Peak; it is a sacred spot, sanctified now by the death of Jiang Tianyi.

As it happens, rock inscriptions in the mountains do not necessarily last forever; Jiang's has long since disappeared, and it is not impossible that it was purposely effaced. But in 1957, a commemorative calligraphic plaque in attractive bluestone was inlaid into the rock at what is believed to have been the location of Jiang's calligraphy.[50] The calligrapher is Li Yimang (or Yimeng; 1903–1990), well known as a political figure as well as literary scholar. Li begins with the five characters described by Wu Jiaji

Detail of commemorative plaque to Master Cold Stream, the revered Ming loyalist Jiang Tianyi (1602–1645), at Start-to-Believe Peak.

in his poem "Master Cold Stream Sits Alone," and then goes on to give a straightforward biography of the hero.

Master Cold Stream Sits Alone

The late Ming anti-Qing martyr Jiang Tian'yi once inscribed the above five words at the Start-to-Believe Peak; some claim he inscribed them on the bramble gate of his hut, while some claim he did so directly on the cliff face. But his inscription today has disappeared. On his behalf, I wish to provide this to take its place. For this martyr, in the first year of the Hongguang period [1645] followed his teacher, Jin Sheng [1589–1645] in raising a militia. He took up his defensive position at Jixi [in Anhui], but his troops were defeated, and he was captured. Yet he would not submit. On the eighth day of the tenth month he went unto his righteous death at Nanjing. His younger brother, Tianbiao, gathered his remains and had him buried at Twinbranch Embankment. The martyr's courtesy name was Wenshi, although one source makes it Hanhao. In addition, he later changed his courtesy name to Chunchu ["True to Origins"]. He was a man of River Village in She prefecture. As for me, in addition to wandering about to enjoy the scenery here, I was delighted to discover that there could have existed so heroic a martyr as Jiang Tian'yi in the struggles of our people! Recorded by Li Yimang in the summer of 1957.

With this stone-cut text, Li Yimang assimilates the Confucian glory of Jiang Tian'yi and its relationship with the Yellow Mountains and southern Anhui Province with a thoroughly modern nationalism, if not jingoism, characteristic of communist parties everywhere, ironically and uneasily co-existing with the ostensible *inter*nationalist ideologies of those parties. But for Wang Hongdu, Wu Jiaji and their friends, Confucian, Daoist, and Buddhist elements cohered synergistically, all founded ultimately opon a shared cosmological vision of reality.

Perhaps because this vision is so shared among the Three Teachings of China, the common practice of eclectically synthesizing elements from any two or all three of them runs through the history of Chinese religion. On the literati level, an actual movement self-designated The Three Teachings are One existed at least as early as the Ming dynasty (1368–1644).[51] By the same token, on the popular level, anyone visiting a shrine or temple in Hong Kong or Taiwan, where there has been relatively little or no ideologically driven government interference with religious practice, or increasingly now once again in China itself, and observing everyday activity there, or with particular good fortune, the celebration of a special festival, will wonder if there is not a *fourth* teaching, unnamed officially, which might simply be summarized as *Minjian zongjiao*, or Folk Religion.[52] And that this too was interwoven with the life of the Yellow Mountains is indicated by Wang Hongdu's remarkable attention to various folk religious practices associated with the site. To take just one especially telling, unique example, in the section on the *Tiexian tan* or Iron String Pool, Wang, as usual to indicate that what he records is based on accounts transmitted to him and not the result of personal observation, gives a detailed description of how, in the case of inadequate rainfall or outright drought (one is reminded of the appearance of the "blue lotus," drought clearly having been one of the major problems in the region during this period), residents of nearby villages would attempt to awaken the hibernating rain-dragon of the pool while purloining a vaseful of pool water. The time-release mechanism they fabricate employs a stick of incense with a weight at the end; one brave individual is lowered by rope close to the surface of the rock-pent pool, inserts the ignited incense into a crevice while dipping a vase into the water, and then is lifted back up again. The entire party now runs away as quickly as they can; the incense burns down, the weight falls, and the splash awakens the dragon. Immediately, thunderclouds appear and there is a great rainfall, while the water in the vase itself is thereby "activated" so that wherever it is carried, rainfall will follow! The people even provide themselves with armed guards to ward off robbers who are likely to attempt to rob them of the water-filled vase (see p. 145). The *long*, conventionally translated "dragon," is of course associated with the element of water. There are various dragon-kings connected to the "court" of the divine Minister of Water (*Shui guan*), sometimes depicted in paintings of the *Three Ministers* (of Heaven, Earth, and Water),[53] exercising universal authority. But what Wang is here describing is a truly *local* cult, one of several in fact, dedicated to the *particular* dragon-deity of this particular pool. Again, the numinosity of the Yellow Mountains make them a perfect venue for such gods, appealing in this case not so much to the literati, as to the peasantry and common folk.

One might think that here, at the Yellow Mountains, there thus existed two separate levels of religiosity, Confucianism-Daoism-Buddhism, appealing to the literati class, and folk religious practices such as the "awakening of the dragon" at Iron String Pool, to the local peasants. But in fact, as already seen, both levels ultimately share the same cosmology. And what is more, Wang Hongdu was not at all alone in his interest in such practices. Examples in contemporary literature are legion,[54] but we may note one extraordinary example not merely of literati interest, but of literati participation in what would otherwise be dubbed folk beliefs. This is found in the writings of Shi Runzhang, again, one of the most influenctial literati of the circles we are concerned with. Under the heading "An Account of Defiling the Image of a Deity" (*Wu shen xiang ji*), Shi relates the following astonishing episode experienced by a man from Shi's hometown of Xuancheng:[55]

> Mr. Wang Guanyu of my town is a man of brilliant talent. As a youth, he stayed at a Buddhist temple, using it as his study. One day, he noticed beneath one of the elevated corridor walkways a wooden [Buddhist] image lying on the ground, rotting away. In jest, he urinated on its head! That night, he dreamed that the deity angrily spoke to him: "You will never get beyond the level of a local magistrate with a *juren* degree. How dare you be so discourteous!"

A *juren,* literally "man recommended for advancement," is the second-lowest level in the examination system, and sure enough, Wang Guanyu discovers that he cannot get beyond that level in his career: "He ended an impoverished old man; nor did it matter how remorseful he felt. He would frequently cite his experience as a cautionary lesson to the youth of the day. My friend, Huang Yigong personally heard him hold forth to this effect."

In this episode, the extensive overlap between literati and folk beliefs is made evident. Particularly significant is the way in which dreams function as *predictors* of success or failure in the examination system that played such a crucial role in the lives of the scholar-officials, as well as the active involvement in their official careers of supernatural elements, whether friendly or, as here, hostile. Many such cases are reported by Miyazaki Ichisada in his classic study *China's Examination Hell.*[56]

The evidence of such examples is bolstered by the case of the Yellow Mountains. There too, literati and folk experiences tended to demonstrate the truth of Maurice Freedman's excellent formulation:[57] "The Confucians [i.e., the scholar-officials] ... shared with the rest of the population a basic system of religious belief ... [There was a] steady interflow of religious ideas between the Confucians and the general population ... Elite and peasant religion rest upon a common base."

Double Scissors, Stone Bed, and Stone Figure Peaks,
photo by Wang Wusheng taken at Fairy Peach Peak.

WANG HONGDU AS POET

The author of *Huangshan lingyao lu* has remained an obscure figure, only recently coming to light as a painter, especially with the publication of a work executed in what was probably his last year of life, "Reading the *Yijing* on a Snowy Night" (*Xue'ye du yi tu*) in the Paul Moss Collection, London.[58] In his inscription to this work, Wang informs us that "there was a great snowstorm" on a spring night in the year 1721. Someone sent a gift of wine, "and I set my brush moving to thank him." At the age of seventy-six by Chinese count, and soon to pass away, Wang added this poem, which conveys beautifully the feelings of his entire circle of recluse-scholars:

> The night grown late, I hear the dog bark:
> Someone is knocking at the bramble gate, bringing a gift of wine!
> The season already past Yellow Chrysanthemums [the ninth month],
> And still I'm amazed at a friend in a "white robe"!
> I've just become aware of wind in bamboo,
> Helping the snowflakes now starting to fall.
> Out for a walk, turning back when clog-teeth lose the way,
> Running into mud, good time to clomp on home!
> Twisting, turning, red blanket way too thin,
> The night so long, impossible to sleep!
> And so I rely on my three-volume *Book of Changes*,
> A single lamp to keep me company.
> The wine takes me towards spring stream warmth,
> The cold invades my inkstone, freezes it up.
> And yet I don't refuse to blow on my frozen brush,
> To write this in thanks on Shan-stream paper!

We find Wang, depicted in the painting and described in the poem, reading his *Book of Changes* (*Yijing*), the Confucian classic of divination, and enjoying the gift of wine sent to him by a friend like the iconic

Wang Hongdu, "Reading the *Yijing* on a Snowy Night" *(Xue'ye du yi tu)*, 1721, hanging scroll, courtesy Sydney L. Moss Gallery, London.

"white-robed" friend in the poetry of Tao Qian (365–427), whose memory is also conjured up by the chrysanthemums he famously loved. The friend, identified only by his courtesy name as Zhicun, is almost certainly an Anhui man, the native of Xuancheng, Shi Li, the grandson of Shi Runzhang, known as a poet who emulated the style of his far more famous grandfather.[59] Wang is probably shown in his retreat in the Yellow Mountains.

That Wang Hongdu was greatly admired in his day we can glean from the way in which his mentor and patron, Wang Shizhen, speaks of him in his writings. In one passage, after recording in full the texts of two poems by Wang Hongdu, he writes, "The above two poems are eloquent in their expressiveness, therefore I have recorded them in full. Yuding [Wang Hongdu] is a man of She prefecture in Xin'an. He is my disciple. His collection, *Xilu shi*, [*Poems from the Resting Hut*, named after the retreat at Start-to-Believe Peak in the Yellow Mountains shared by Wang and his younger brother, Yangdu], was edited by myself."[60]

It was, of course, a tremendous honor to have one's own poetry anthologized, edited, and published by such a figure as Wang Shizhen. What is unclear is whether the book was immediately printed and circulated, or had to await the year *renchen* of the Qianlong period (1772), sixty-one years after Wang Shizhen's death, and some fifty years after Wang Hongdu's, to see the light of day. This is the date borne by the copy of this rare work I was able to inspect in the collection of the Anhui Provincial Museum, Hefei. On the cover occur the words *Wushi dushuyuan cangban*, which might be rendered, "From woodblocks preserved in the Garden Where Five Generations Have Read Books." This was apparently the name of a garden estate known to the brothers Wang Hongdu and Wang Yangdu, if it was not in fact one of their own family estates, because according to Paul Moss, the connoisseur Rong Geng (1894–1983) records having seen a handscroll of an estate by this name, with a painting of it by Hongdu, and a prose account by Yangdu, now apparently lost.[61]

In any case, this, apparently the only surviving anthology of Wang Hongdu's poetry, is a key source for our understanding of the man and his circle. There are two important prefaces, the first, as expected, by the editor, Wang Shizhen:[62]

> Wang Yuding of the Jiangdong region, as well as his younger brother Wenye [Wang Yangdu], as a youth was thoroughly conversant with the classics. Both of them later associated with men of the world. But afterwards, weary of that life, they relinquished it and withdrew to Start-to-Believe Peak in the Yellow Mountains. There, in the company of a very few old hermits and aged Buddhist monks, they investigated the essence of Heavenly and personal nature and fate. In this, they were very happy. But they could not keep to themselves the brilliant wonder of their spirits, which from time to time would issue forth in poems, written to amuse themselves. Their elder brother, the Hanlin scholar Zhouci [1636–1699][63], from time to time would speak to me about them. In the spring of this year, I obtained from the coffers of the Hanlin scholar Lengxiang [Wu Yuan] a scroll of poetry by him [Hongdu]. It was refreshingly true and powerful, manfully profound, elegant and strong. In these poems, he was clear that he is not imbroiled in the fashions—the likings and dislikings—of the day. His very nature has been informed and transformed to a great extent by the various mountains and streams. For among the valleys and wooded foothills, clouds and mists, the sun and moon, all emerge and disappear again, their magical transformations entwined with blue-green and woven with purple. Those in the mountains, seeing these things every single morning and evening, they can often become a kind of chronic obsession, being entrusted for

expression to conversation and poetry, being chanted or whistled, without one even realizing it! And how much truer is this when it is the Yellow Mountains that are involved, their jutting pinnacles and precipitous cliffs being the most spectacular in the whole world! Should an untrammelled scholar of extraordinary gifts sleep and dine in the midst of such scenes, he will go off into a vast distance, entirely cut off from the folks of this world! Thus, when it comes to Yuding's poetry, how can it possibly be gauged by the same standards as apply to his contemporaries, as they manipulate sheets of paper and moisten their writing brushes?

At this time, throughout the world, the depredations of military combat have ceased, and the mood of the people as a whole is peaceful and content. Those scholars who reside among the cliffs and drink water from mountain springs are being selected to enter the dormitories of government, there to lend their assistance to the civilized administration. Would Yuding, I wonder, now be willing to relinquish his mountains and forests, and wander down the corridors of power? There he might view the treasures collected in the libraries of Heaven, uncover secret wonders hidden in the Orchid Terrace [Imperial archives]; the vast resources of magnificent literature there are such as one cannot encounter in the barren soil of the mountains! And should he do so, perhaps he could write eulogies of this great dynasty's virtuous achievements, engraving them in bronze and stone, for transmission to the Music Bureau: and I myself would then be pleased to listen to people singing the lingering tones of his works in the pure halls of the dynasty, sighing three times in admiration with each phrase!

Wang Hongdu must have been delighted by such praise from Wang Shizhen, but one can only speculate as to how he may have felt about the somewhat unexpected call to serve the current dynasty in the final passage. After all, this was a man whose deepest sympathies had been, or still were, with the Ming loyalists. But perhaps we must keep in mind that once it was clear that the Qing dynasty was firmly established, it was entirely possible for nostalgic respect for the lost Ming cause to co-exist with commited service to the current regime. One need only think of the official, playwright, and descendant of Confucius himself, Kong Shangren (1648–1718), the author of one of China's greatest dramas,

The Peach Blossom Fan (*Taohua shanji*). In this masterpiece dating from 1699, Kong implied strong sympathy with the loyalty (*zhong*) of the Ming loyalists, while functioning in his own life as Chief Officiator at the Confucian Shrine in his ancestor Confucius's hometown of Qufu. For Confucians, respect for moral principle ultimately can trump dynastic "partisanship."

The second of the two prefaces to Wang Hongdu's collected poetry is by his friend, Wu Yuan, already mentioned above:

> In the past, Lu Lize [the great Southern Song poet Lu You, 1125–1210] in his "Colophon to a Calligraphy by Huang Shangu [the major Northern Song poet and calligrapher Huang Tingjian, 1045–1105] in the Possession of Cheng Zhengbo [a little-known scholar, Cheng Gai; Lu's visit to him, during which he viewed the calligraphy, is known to have taken place in 1186],"[64] said, "[This calligraphy] ought not to be carried into an inn in the [capital city of] Chang'an, nor should it be viewed amongst the mats and caps of men of high status, or amongst the gold-bridled horses, the shouting out of commands as officials enter their official precincts. No, only when one is residing amongst pure mountain springs and the blue-green shade of forests should one bring out this handscroll to read together with men living in the mountains; only this will suit the case."[65] But I say, not so! Of course Chang'an is a place where men of letters assemble. For sheer size, this is where books and archives are collected, like those "hidden in the eastern wall" [the classics of antiquity, hidden away to evade the "burning of the books" under Qin Shi Huangdi]; as for scope, this is where brilliant literary talents from all five directions gather together, where scholars in full array, men of comprehensive knowledge who weigh and consider everything they encounter; how can one possibly claim that here there would be no compatible souls?

> My friend, Master Wang Yuding, and his younger brother, Wenye, have a reputation comparable to that of Ji and Yun [an apt comparison to the great literary brothers Lu Ji (261–303) and Lu Yun (262–303), who were also separated by only one year and the elder brother far more accomplished]. The Great College Rector, Master Wang Ruanting [Shizhen] of Xincheng upon obtaining the recent poems of Yuding, exclaimed in astonishment, "These are

the lingering tones of the ancient music of the "Elegentiae" [the two books of the *Shijing,* or *Book of Songs,* known as the *Da ya* and *Xiao ya*]!" Beating out the rhythm [as he chanted them], he showered them with praise. Yuding had been living in reclusion in one of the great mountains [the Yellow Mountains], but now in a single day, his name resonated throughout the capital! Of those who are leaders at the altar of poesy, puffers of literary reputation of today, there is not a single one who does not regard Xincheng [Wang Shizhen] as his mentor. For such a man in particular thus to eulogize our Yuding's poems, means that all mouths beneath Heaven will be chanting them in alternation!

Does not Changli [the great Confucian thinker and writer Han Yu, 768–824] say, "When one is [mired in poverty and low station] unknown to the world, it is only upon having the good fortune of meeting with a sage that one can achieve higher status."[66] Mr. Wang Taihan of our prefecture [Wang Hongdu's great grand-uncle and well-known playwright Wang Daokun, 1525–1593], together with Yanzhou [Wang Shizhen, 1526–1590] was a leader of the literary altar of the day. Yanzhou is on record as saying of the writings of Yulin [one of the latter group of the so-called Former Seven and Latter Seven (Orthodox) Masters of Ming literature, Li Panlong, 1514–1570] that they had "unfathomable transformation, like the [military formations] of the Eight Gates and Five Blossoms. But I also feel that Boyu [Wang Daokun] has [in his work] a feeling of war horses whinnying forlornly, and war banners flapping in the distance." Thus with a single dictum, Yanzhou established the relative standing of the two writers, Li and Wang [apparently implying to Wu that Wang Shizhen preferred Wang Daokun's style as being, perhaps, more powerful or atmospheric]. Today, Yuding is of course Taihan's great grand-nephew in the fourth generation. Taihan won the admiration of Yanzhou while now Yuding has earned the recognition of Xincheng: These soulmates in literary judgment, past and present, share the same expertise! [The two Wang Shizhens, of Ming and Qing, have both selected members of the Wang clan as literary exemplars.] Who would say that stallion or mare, black or brindle, would not be delighted to obtain the approval of a Sun Yang! [The legendary expert on horseflesh, also known as Bo'le.] I myself once praised Yuding, saying that his extraordinary talent and prodigious scholarship are not unworthy of achieving great fame in the world. Should there be anyone in the world wishing to criticize Gongsun Hong[67] or are willing to settle for "merely knowing of Guan and Yan,"[68] let him take up the matter with Xincheng: from him he will get a definitive judgment!

Wu Yuan appears to be particularly anxious to establish Wang Hongdu as a world talent, not merely a favorite son of the southern Anhui region. And, like Wang Shizhen in his preface, he would seem to be appealing, although more subtly, to Wang Hongdu to leave, at last, his long reclusion, and enter the world of service to the by now well-established Qing dynasty.

Wu Yuan's worries about Wang Hongdu's reputation appear to have been well-founded, in that Wang would never be seen as a major poet of the era, although individual poems of his would occasionally meet with anthologization, right up to the present day. But both he and Wang Shizhen are right on the substantive value of Wang Hongdu's verse: although we do not possess a large number of his poems, on the basis of what survives in *Xilu shi* alone, plus other isolated poems found inscribed on paintings and calligraphies or cited in other books, we can say that Wang Hongdu is indeed a serious poet. And given the eloquence of the descriptive prose in his *Huangshan lingyao lu*, he may take his place as one of the relatively few writers in Chinese literature to excel both in poetry and prose.

Like several of his friends and contemporaries, and not at all surprisingly, Wang Hongdu devoted some of his poems to the Yellow Mountains, although unlike Can Zhenji and Wu Yuan,[69] he does not seem to have compiled these into a separate collection. We have already considered one quatrain, about hearing a flute at the summit of Lotus Blossom Peak (see p. 27), but Wang's most ambitious work of this type must be one that he composed for the greatest of Anhui-Yellow Mountains painting master, Hongren.[70] Wang Hongdu is on record as holding forth thus about the development of painting in Anhui: "The painting of our region came to fruition early in the current dynasty, starting with Songyuan Laoren [close friend of Qian Qian'yi, the painter and poet Cheng Chia-sui, 1565–1643], followed by the monk Jianjiang [Hongren], Ch'eng Gouqu [Cheng Sui, 1605–1691], Zha Meihe [Zha Shibiao, see above], Zhu Zhuangyou [Zhu Chang, *jinshi* degree 1649] who were skilled in landscape ..."[71] This is, of course, a virtual who's who of Anhui painting. That the two men, Wang Hongdu and Hongren, actually knew each other is indicated by the fact that Hongren actually sent to Wang a painting of a scene in the Yellow Mountains, to which Wang replied with a letter: "Living away, I was suffering from the heat, and yearning intently for my hometown. All of a sudden, I received— unworthily!—your Yellow Mountains painting, sent to me from a thousand *li* away! After having unrolled it and examined it, the blue-green mistiness and freshness of Lotus Blossom, Heavenly Capital, and all the other peaks have moved me almost unbearably."[72] And Wang was inspired as well, by this painting or by another, or by Hongren's work in general, to compose the following.

> *Song of the Pine Trees Painted by the*
> *Yellow Mountain Monk, Master Chien*

To the gate of Master Jian [Hongren]
    few visitors ever come,
When he awakens at the northern window,
    his feet remain quite bare.
On a hundred feet of silk that glistens
    like chilly Wu-Song River,
Brush dipped in ink, he paints these pines,
    austere and bold in spirit.
The wealth of forms on which long since
    he's dined unto repletion
In just one morning all emerge
    from in-between his fingers!
Frost-bitten bark, ebony colors
    sprayed by flying falls,
Down-sweeping branches, skinny trunks
    hanging from crumbling rock!
Upper boughs, pitch black, will block
    the roc-bird's journeying wings;
Lower boughs—dark shade—press caves
    where dragons hibernate.
Pulsing, striving, as if they'd fly
    by grasping thunderbolts;
Ice and hail harshly attack
    these hairs that grow from stone.

Clearly as he loosens his robe
    pure inspiration shows:
From where, oh Master, blow the winds
    your fingers now waft forth?
The painting hangs high in the hall,
    the pine-winds sound, SAA, SAA …
The height of summer, and one feels
    like donning a padded coat!
The Yellow Mountains must have been
    your homeland, native soil,
And every winter you've been glad
    to make friends with these pines!
Roiling Dragon clutches high
    Embankment of Scattered Blossoms;
Welcoming Hand seems flung far from
    the Brazier for Elixir!
And then there is the Broke-Through-Rock,
    fantastical formation!
[*Poet's note*: Roiling Dragon, Welcoming Hand,
and Broke-Through-Rock are all the names of pine trees.]
It twists and clutches as it were
    half-snapped off by the lightning;
Who would have thought some deity
    would stand in guard of it,
So now again, from withered limbs
    fresh sprouts are seen to grow?
My hut as well was once there where
    the deepest clouds will form;
The pines reflected on my face,
    both stayed quite green all year!
Whenever guests stopped by to visit,
    they'd gather up pine cones,
And when alone I breasted clouds,
    I passed between pine needles…
But now my wandering steps again
    have landed me in mud,
From autumn pillow far, so far,
    my dreaming soul returns!

Opening this painting now,
    seeing the old mountains again,
My hempen sandals yearn to tread
    the moonlight in those pines!

It goes without saying that the pine trees of the Yellow Mountains were one of the most appreciated images of the place—so much so that they were given special names, as noted by the poet—along with the fantastically shaped rocks, and the cloud formations. All of these were age-old emblems of nature's transformational power in Chinese civilization, as is well-known, although Stephen McDowall shows how for the men of Qian Qian'yi's generation, they took on renewed significance.[73] (As a salutary caution against too much emphasis on "cultural determinism," let it be noted that the actual pine trees of the Yellow Mountains are indeed, as it happens, so *botanically* unique that they have been secondarily designated *Pinus hwangshanensis* Hsia, the primary designation being *Pinus taiwanensis* Hayata.)[74]

It is certainly the case that Wang Hongdu was not alone in devoting a poem specifically to the pine trees, and indeed a painting of pine trees, of the Yellow Mountains. Shi Runzhang, for example, has a poem on weirdly shaped pine trees there, and another on paintings of pine trees of the Yellow Mountains for another great master of the school, Mei Qing (1623–1697)—who like Hongren, was especially noted for his depictions of this subject.[75] But Wang triumphs with the sheer verve he brings to the task, culminating in the synaesthetic issuing of the sound of wind blowing through the pine trees, from the painting. Because Wang is now apparently away from his native place, the pine in the painting comes to represent at two removes his homeland, and his yearning for his homeland. Zhang Changhong has recently argued that nostalgic homesickness was a key motivator of the wealthy Anhui salt merchants who routinely patronized the artists; as they traveled about on their itineraries, the paintings would serve as emblems of their beloved homeland.[76] Merchants, needless to say, have no monopoly on homesickness.

When Wang Hongdu and his younger brother Yangdu eventually took up residence in the Yellow Mountains, a withdrawal from the world that would last some ten years, they selected Start-to-Believe Peak, associated, as we have seen, with the Ming loyalist martyr, Jiang Tianyi. Characteristically, Wang's friends and Wang himself chose to celebrate the occasion in poetry. Wu Yuan sent the following poem.

For Inscription on the Thatched Hut of Wang Yuding and Wenye at Start-to-Believe Peak[77]

Wandering clouds hang from Heaven's edge,
Sink their roots upon this mountain slope.
Remarkable scholars, who thought to save the world,
Task not yet done, took refuge from distress.
The Rear Ocean commands fantastic beauty,
This single peak, especially precipitous.
Elder and younger brothers came here to build a hut,
Guarded and protected by beings divine.
Single pine trees serve as rafters,
Old gibbons sometimes stop by to visit.
The eaves touch all celestial bodies,
Sun and moon adorn the courtyard steps.
For eating, they have ice and snow,
For clothing they have leaves and vines.
Spring breezes come to visit in due season,
Blowing the Purple Rod flowers into blossom.
Then this realm reverts to the Golden Age of Yu and Xia,
And hermits Nest Father and Xu You have more than enough.

In his accompanying letter, Wu Yuan asked Wang Hongdu, how to get to his place of reclusion? To which Wang responded as below.[78]

Wu Luyuan [Wu Yuan] *has Asked of Me the Route to Start-to-Believe Peak; with this Poem, I Answer Him*

This is my place for living in reclusion:
Now you approach with your short hiking stick.
Where a cut-off cliff overhangs an inaccessible gully,
Halfway up the face, grasp on to the solitary pine.
In rainfall, by bejewelled grottoes,
In rosy morning mists, past lotiform peaks…
The tawny gibbons will know how to guide you:
The path is hidden—simply follow them.

Poems such as this perfectly fuse the ancient tradition of nature poetry with the specific exigencies of personal experience. A tone of understated wit helps to humanize the situation: Do you want to know how to get here? It is so remote, only the pine trees and gibbons will be able to guide you! One is reminded of eccentric Chan-Buddhist poet, Han Shan, or Cold Mountain (? early ninth century), and his cautionary notes about the difficulty of reaching his place of seclusion, which also functions in his case as a metaphor for Buddhist enlightenment.

Wang's masterpiece in poetry must be considered to be the sequence of twelve regulated verse poems (five characters per line) composed in 1674, before his long-term period of reclusion in the Yellow Mountains, thus earlier than the above poem, and recounting how Wang and his family on one occasion withdrew into the mountains to evade a "rebel uprising."[79] This turns out to have been the anti-Manchu rebellion of Geng Jingzhong (1644–1682). Geng, a member of the "Chinese Plain Yellow Banner," joined forces with the famous Wu Sangui (1612–1678) as two prongs of a three-pronged rebellion;[80] this was no longer a Ming loyalist enterprise, of course, but could be seen as in some measure a recrudescence of the feelings aroused by the Manchu conquest. In any case, the rebels themselves wreaked havoc in southern Anhui, and then, when the government forces moved in to suppress them, they were if anything even crueler in their oppression of the local population, indiscriminately assuming that all locals might have sympathized with the rebels, or even harbored them in their homes. Squeezed between these two opposing forces, ordinary people suffered a good deal. We are told of Wang Hongdu's good friend Wu Yuan, who was as we have seen to become the author of one of the prefaces to his poetry collection (and of one to his *Huangshan lingyao lu* as well), that "at the time of the uprising of rebels from Min [Fujian, i.e., Geng and his troops] in the year *jiayin* [1674], the area was devastated by military action, and he [Wu Yuan] experienced the complete ruin of his household."[81] Wang Hongdu may have been marginally more fortunate:

Written in My Mountain Retreat on an Autumn Day—Evading the chaos of the rebel uprising, in the year *jiayin* [1674]

1

Snatching the opportunity, they put on Yellow Turbans:
Rowdy youths from a neighboring province assembled!
We've dragged along donkeys—no need for horses—
Transporting family treasures, not carrying any of us!
Beacon torches at night illuminate the trees;

Banner poles in daylight, darkened by dust.
As we enter the mountains, I shout to wife and children:
"Our neighbors are tiger caves now!"

2

Blocked by thorns, overgrown with brushwood, this road,
Mist-drenched mornings, evenings of driving rain...
Overhung cliffs scare us as they split the ground;
Sheer rock-faces thwart us as they obscure the sky.
I cover my son's mouth—to stop him from crying;
Glance backwards, where the rebels' fires approach!
Who has time to notice, among the maple leaves,
A vapor spreading, turning ten thousand hills all red!

3

There is a road, but now a bridge is out;
There is no boat, but now we tread through water!
Grasping them for support, we trouble the tender willows;
Collapsing on the ground, regret the damage to fragrant plants!
The trees are changing their pre-autumnal colors;
The stream grows louder with new, post-rainfall sounds.
Ah, mandarin ducks, how I envy you,
Quacking as you fly freely, ducklings close beside!

4

Unawares, my eyes transform their view:
Here among clouds, a separate universe!
Hedges are sparse, surrounding pumelo trees;
A pestle pounds, mingling with the brook's rush.
I would like to live here in this Peach Blossom Spring:
But how could I afford to rent a thatched hut for sleep?
The chickens occupy every sliver of territory:
I wonder how much they charge by the day?

5

Perhaps you'll say, here, among blue-green mountains,
Pine tree blockades are sealed forever by clouds?
But the bad guys know the road that leads here:
Joining their forces, they'll come with swords in hand.

In pale moonlight, they'll penetrate thick woods;
In the middle of the night, hide out in the bush!
How secure after all are these cliffside caves?
—The crickets have plenty to lament about.

6

At midnight, government forces arrive:
On a thousand peaks, war horses whinny!
In the roaring of the wind, who can discern the crane?
In the light of dawn, we cannot hear the rooster.
The rebels have lost their stomach for fighting:
In hasty retreat, they stumble all over themselves.
And the looted pearls and jades they carried up with them
Lie scattered now in mud beside the road.

7

So now the war torches have settled down;
The villages are half burned down to ash.
New geese are comfortable beside a lake,
But dogs are uncertain which is their old home.
In the mountains, cut off are the banners of war,
And the winds are purified of the sadness of war-trumpets.
But now they announce that 100,000 bowmen
Are approaching us over the ridge!

8

We hear that the military is imposing its might,
Searching everywhere for rebels, leaving not one behind.
But they can't distinguish rebels from citizens:
Bone and flesh while still alive now part!
White-haired heads hang from sword-tips,
While red-cheeked youth escapes on horseback.
Within a radius of ten miles around,
Human life is a thread about to break.

9

From around the encampment, the siege has been lifted,
The order comes down: remove your uniforms!
So they form ranks, pour libations of wine,

And camp by camp, offer swords in sacrifice.
The wolf-tooth pennants flutter in the wind;
Battalion-like cloud formations hover over pines.
Now their horses are put to pasture outside the town walls:
Next year, time to build trenches against the rebels!

10

Village houses have burgeoned into a city,
Mountains surrounding, river an additional barrier.
The walls have had their undersides all strengthened,
And soldiers and horses all feel right at home.
And their provisions? "Contributed" by each hearthside;
Their firewood? Gates and beams all chopped right down!
But citizens are not mere hares or pheasants:
How can you confiscate all their good things?

11

At this time, the "Mongols" occupied Huizhou
Great war flags now, each tree blown by the wind!
The deep mountains turned into a battlefield!
With the fifth watch, the frost first whitens;
In the tenth month, the plants all yellowing.
When frontier geese encounter such a nightfall,
Barbarian lads yearn for their old homes.
But still they've not gone back through the Jade Pass...
Two streams of tears form lines right down my cheeks.

12

A black moon sinks beside the mountain;
Yellow thatch burns on from house to house.
Our souls are startled, cannot settle down:
The weeping of ghosts again seems to invite us!
Clearly, clearly, we hear it for a thousand miles,
Wailing, wailing, and all through the night...
The Heavenly River finally drips down some rainfall:
But who will wash away the armor and the swords?

Du Fu (712–770), often regarded as the greatest of Chinese poets, is
frequently called a "poet-historian" *(shishi)* because of the clarity and

poignancy with which he records and conveys suffering in times of hardship, that of ordinary people, and that of himself and his family. Perhaps his greatest work in this mode, and one of the undoubted masterpieces of Chinese literature, is his lengthy narrative poem "Five Hundred Words Singing of My Feelings, While Traveling from the Capital to Fengxian County" (*Zi jing fu Fengxianxian younghuai wubai zi*).[82] Recently, Lawrence C.H. Yim has entitled his superb study of Qian Qian'yi's poetry, *The Poet Historian Qian Qianyi*, adapting this cognomen to a late Ming-early Qing figure. Yim is precisely on target when he says of Qian, that his *shishi* ("poetic histories") "should not be reduced to a game of literary and historical allusions. His preoccupation was, on the one hand, to remember and preserve, and, on the other, to praise and blame."[83] The same must be said of Wang Hongdu's poems on his own experience of history, and indeed, the insight should be exanded to his writings on the Yellow Mountains as well: despite the use of allusion, in the minds of Wang Hongdu, Qian Qian'yi and their contemporaries (or for that matter Du Fu), they were responding realistically to actual realities. To skewer their experience into merely subjective constructs is to fail to grasp the nature of epistemology itself. Of course we bring cultural preconceptions to our experience, but noting the fact begs the far greater question, as to whether those "preconceptions" might not in fact themselves be based on truth. This is why Li Zhengchun is able to write in 2011 that "Du Fu's autobiographical poem-sequences even more completely [than earlier such writings] fuse together personal experience and contemporary events, thus possessing the value of 'poetry-histories.'"[84]

In his cycle of twelve poems Wang Hongdu is fully in the poet-historian tradition of Du Fu and Qian Qian'yi. As compared with Du, he purposely narrows his focus almost entirely to the personal level. Thus in poem 1, we are immediately thrust *in media res*, as Wang and his family barely make their escape by night. The rebels are referred to as Yellow Turbans, alluding back to the famed rebels of the late Han period, but rather than abstracting from current reality, the allusion gives greater depth and meaning to the very real events of the moment. With poem 2, the tension mounts even further; Wang must cover his son's mouth to prevent him from crying, and attracting the attention of the ever-approaching rebel forces. Poem 3 is nearly cinematic in presenting a montage of dangerous moments as they proceed on their perilous journey, unnoticed by the happy mandarin ducks, who can fly about *en famille*.

Ordinarily, the lovely scenes they encounter as they enter the mountains in poem 5 might conjure up thoughts of the lost paradise Peach Blossom Spring, which after all was itself a refuge for refugees fleeing from bad times. But reality beckons Wang back: *money* is required if they are to find a place to reside. Finally, in poem 6, the government troops appear on the scene, and they drive the rebels off; for a while, it appears as if things will now calm down. But in poem 7, this looks like a calm before a storm, as the government forces are now pressing down upon them (suspecting they might be rebel sympathizers). The crackdown reaches a climax in poem 8; no distinction is made between ordinary citizens and true sympathizers with the enemy, and so all suffer together. With poem 9, the pogrom is at an end, but instead of leaving, the government army bivouacs itself on the local community, against the possibility of a resurgence of the rebellion. Poem 10 has the troops engaged in full confiscation of the villagers' provisions, and even their homes, which are dismantled to provide wood for the soldiers' dwellings. The confiscation turns into a full-fledged occupation in poem 11, as the government forces are now referred to, dangerously one would think—as "Mongols." (Could this be why the book was not able to be printed for so long?) The incident is now seen as a replay of the ancient occupation of Chinese territory by the Mongol invaders and occupiers of the Yuan dynasty (1279–1368). The final poem 12 concludes on a note of profound uneasiness. Under a "black" moon, fires have broken out, souls are restless, even the ghosts of the dead are weeping. Even the appearance of the Heavenly River—the Milky Way—cannot salvage the villagers' serenity; there is no telling how this will all end.

It might at first be thought strange that Wang, whose sympathies for decades had lain with the Ming loyalists, would not be happier about an uprising against the Manchus. But by now he evidently realizes it is too late; such an uprising can only result in chaos and hardship and cannot hope to succeed in overthrowing the dynasty. What is more, the motives of these rebels appear to be self-interest, rather than the selfless sacrifice for a greater cause of the Ming loyalists. No, here Wang's attitude is "a plague on both your houses."

Indeed, one needs to repair to the works of Du Fu for so powerful and compelling a dramatization in poetry of the vicissitudes of the day.

Wang, again like Du Fu, or like Bai Ju'yi in his two magnificent series of ten protest poems, "Songs from the Qin Region" (*Qinzhong yin*) and his fifty "Neo-Music Bureau Poems" (*Xin yuefu*),[85] is also a master of presenting the sufferings of his fellow human beings. Following in the recent footsteps of his friend and fellow poet, Wu Jiaji,[86] Wang collects specific cases drawn from the lives of ordinary people, and deploys them in straightforward, powerful narrative poems. One of these, "An Old Man Treads on Ice," with brief prose preface,[87] was selected by Shen Deqian for his important anthology of Qing poetry, one of eight poems by Wang in this book, a relatively high number.

An Old Man Treads on Ice

An old man, carrying his infant grandson with him, trod on ice, and when he reached midstream, the ice cracked. He and the boy fell to their deaths.

In the eastern mansion, the grains are red,
In the western mansion, the rice is white.
But he returns empty-handed from a trip to borrow food,
Ashamed to appear before the River God!
But shame before the River God is something bearable:
"The whole family waits on my return
    to light the cooking fires!"
Now the river water forms icy bones, obstructing any ferry:
Clutching the boy, walking hunch-backed, hard to move ahead!
Who knew that the ice out in the middle
    was unfirm, breaking up?
The foxes there on the other shore
    watch as he falls through!
From withered mulberries, sighing, sighing
    a bitter wind now blows:
Prowling back and forth, wishing to cross,
    the foxes fear wetting their tails.

This sobering vignette of poverty, leading to the two accidental deaths of a grandfather and his grandson, inspired Shen Deqian to exclaim, "The extreme grief here expressed is such that one can hardly bear to read it." Shen, not only a fine anthologist but one of the more acute literary critics of the eighteenth century, gives voice here to to the powerful effect Wang's presentation must have on a sensitive reader. He also explicates for us the otherwise strange image of the foxes: "If the foxes feared wetting their tails, how could the old man and the little grandson be able to tread out there?" Aside from the contrast drawn with the lives of the wealthy, living in mansions and eating their fill of various crops, the poet wisely refrains from any comment. None is needed.

This poem has become the one "anthology piece" by Wang Hongdu, if one can use such a term here, as not only Shen Deqian in the eighteenth century, but the modern scholars, Wang Yuqi and Wen Guoxin have anthologized it as well, the only example by Wang included, in their *Anthology of Narrative Poems Down Through the Ages* [88] They expand upon Shen's interpretation of the image of the foxes, pointing out that the phrase "prowling back and forth" (*suisui*) derives from poem 63, *You hu* ("There is a fox…") in the classic *Shijing*, or *Book of Songs*. In the poem in question, the fox, warm in his natural fur, is contrasted with the husband of the woman who speaks; she is worried that as he fights at the frontier, he will go unprotected from the cold. Thus Wang is positioning his poem in the great Confucian tradition of protesting against inhumane conditions through the use of *Shijing* poetry and imagery.

The theme of separation between man and wife implied by the allusion to a *Shijing* poem, one which plays an important role throughout the history of Chinese poetry,[89] is explicitly addressed in another poem selected for anthologization by Shen Deqian, "Calendar Pearls," with a longer prose preface laying out the circumstances:[90]

Calendar Pearls

Mr. Wu X of Shexian, when he had been married but a single month, went off to engage in trade. His wife did embroidery to exchange for food, saving what was left over to obtain a pearl each year. These she would sew together with colored threads, calling them "calendar pearls." When the husband finally returned, the wife had been dead for three years. Opening her sewing kit, he found the pearls: there were over twenty of them sewn together.

> Mandarin ducks, waterbirds,
>   swimming around in pairs,
> While her fingers—soft reeds—grow used to sewing
>   birds in red and green.
> How many times has she moved the needle,
>   back turned to folks, in tears?
> And all the tears she'd weep in a year
>   congealed into a pearl!

But do not envy the many pearls—
    her eyes will dry, all parched;
Yet when she was young, she embroidered then
    a "blanket of mutual joy."
The threads may be broken, but the fate that joins them
    is tied tight, never undone.
Pearls pile up—
From heaven's edge, does he return, or not?

Shen Deqian, once again deeply moved, compares this poem to one of the true masterpieces on this theme, Du Fu's magnificent "Parting Newly Wed" (*Xin hun bie*),[91] in which the husband has no choice but to be pressed into service at the frontier. "But in the current case," notes Shen, "they are parting because of the pursuit of trade! Perhaps it might be entitled, 'Parting because of Prizing Profit and Looking Lightly on Separation!' The deep feelings here neeedn't be spoken—elegantly wistful and mournful in tone." It is hard to conceive of higher praise than this!

Students of Chinese fiction will immediately sense a connection with one of the finest masterpieces of Chinese storyteller fiction, "The Pearl-Sewn Shirt," published and probably written by Feng Menglong (1574–1646). In both cases the shirt stands as a symbol of the betrayed marriage.[92] On the other hand, Wang's example is local, coming from Shexian, just as Wu Jiaji's exemplars of moral behavior are all local to the region of his hometown in eastern Jiangsu, and the wife's actions here are diametrically opposed to those of the wife in the Feng Menglong story. She remains faithful for twenty years, whereas Feng's character eventually gives in to the temptation of another affair.

The image of the pearl is particularly poignant when one takes into consideration the fact, noted by Edward Schafer, that "[To the Chinese,] pearls were solidified lunar essence—and female essence. It was thought that they waxed and waned in fetal form within the oyster in harmony with the menstrual cycle of human females."[93]

Shen Deqian was followed in anthologizing this poem by the late-Qing scholar, Zhang Yingchang (1790–1874) in his extraordinary anthology of social protest poems, *The Tocsin Bell of Qing Poetry* (*Qingshi duo*), published in 1869,[94] where he presents it as the second work in the section on poems about marital relations. This fact alone demonstrates that the poem was indeed interpreted in Qing times as quietly protesting the mistreatment of the woman by her husband, while eulogizing the woman for her steadfastness of character.

The situations described in the previous two poems could, unfortunately, have happened at any time, given the vulnerability of human beings to the vicissitudes of fate and human cruelty. But as we have already seen, in the cycle of poems dealing with his experience of the Geng Jingzhong rebellion, Wang was very much alive to the specific vulnerabilities of himself, his family, and others to the concrete events of the historical moment in which he lived. Several other of his poems present unforgettable accounts of the plight of his fellow humans during a particularly tension-ridden period. The following two, like the previous two, also take the form of Neo-Music Bureau poems, in the tradition of Bai Ju'yi or Wu Jiaji. To begin with, there is the question of poverty, already broached in "An Old Man Treads on Ice," but more specifically linked to the newly emerged problem of refugees from the ongoing fighting, as well as from flooding and other natural disasters which exacerbated the crisis. "The Flower Drums" shows us with stark realism the lives of women reduced by their refugee status to begging, singing in the streets for food; the poem is preceded by a brief prose preface:[95]

The Flower Drums

Refugees from the flooding have spread out in all four directions. Women, playing flower drums, and going from door to door, sing songs to beg for food.

> Market officials, so aloof!
> Now not holding court.
> But daily sound—boom, boom!—
> Flower drums gathering along the streets,
> Throats dry with hunger trying to sing,
> > but lacking any force.
> Daytime exposed all day to sun,
> Nighttime asleep on dew-soaked earth.
> And they dare not try for space in homes,
> The household census
> > being taken for taxes.

The presentation here definitely implicates officials in the hardships undergone by the women: they are simply ignoring the situation, not opening their doors to hear from the people what is going on. But even worse, they continue to impose taxation on local households, based upon residency per household. Hence, no one is prepared to take the women in even temporarily, because they would be counted as residents and add to the tax burden!

The beggars of this poem may be undergoing tough times, but even more desperate is the plight of a woman who has been compelled to abandon her child, in "The Baby Beneath the Flowers," again with prose preface:[96]

The Baby Beneath the Flowers

A traveler, passing by a field of flowers, heard the crying of a newborn infant. He sought out the child, and found inserted in its clothes a piece of paper with a note stating that the child was born on such-and-such a day of the month, and the parents, realizing theirs was an impoverished household and could not afford to raise another child, placed it among the flowers in the hope that a passerby might see it and adopt it.

> A child was born—"No need to grieve
>   our household is so poor:
> Fate might provide a chance to meet
>   a second mom and dad!"
> Bone torn from bone, flesh cut from flesh,
>   on earth beneath the flowers:
> About to part, the mom returns,
>   to breastfeed one more time!
> Then she looks back as sounds of crying
>   fade into the distance...
> The plants grow wild along the plains,
>   now lower, now much higher...
> Until a patch of deepest green
>   conceals the child's body.

The poet writes the entire poem from the point of view of the mother who is deserting the child. We never learn whether the baby was found, just as she herself probably never did. The odd number of lines—seven—gives a sense of lack of resolution, paralleling her uncertainty. The unresolved ending, while familiar in modern literature everywhere, is almost unheard of in traditional Chinese fiction or drama, and is disturbingly bold in this particular context.

Yet another woman became a local heroine by demonstrating the strength of her commitment to two key Confucian virtues, "chastity" (*zhen* or *jie*) being perhaps the more obvious, while her action of resolutely taking the place of her mother-in-law in this horrible situation illustrates the virtue of personal *sacrifice*, or *dai* (literally "substitution"), that is, actually offering to undergo a hardship to save another from having to suffer it, even to the point of death. (Wang uses this very verb, *dai*, translated below as "sacrifices [herself]".) Such is the motivation of the heroine of one of the most important Yuan dynasty dramas, *Injustice Done to Dou E* (*Dou E yuan*), by one of China's leading playwrights, Guan Hanqing (c.1240–c.1320),[97] who goes to her death in place of her foster mother; it is also illustrated pointedly in several of Wu Jiaji's social poems.[98] Wang Hongdu's poem is "The Pine-Embracing Woman," again with a preface.[99]

The Pine-Embracing Woman

The fiancée of a certain degree-holder in Xuancheng, of a certain maiden name, before she had been invested with the hairpin of a married woman [before the marriage had taken place], together with her mother-in-law fled from marauding troops, hiding in a grove of pine trees. The mother-in-law being wounded, the young woman, to distract attention from her, sacrificed herself by emerging from the grove. The troops, pleased by her beauty, tried to compel her to go off with them, but refusing, she held tight to a pine tree, weeping and cursing the troops. Angry, they killed her on the spot. For three days, her corpse continued to clutch the pine tree, without falling down.

> The pine is tall,
> The woman, fine:
> She turns into a vine that clings
>   to dragon-twisting branches.
> The woman, fine,
> The pine is tall:
> "How could I do their will? I'd rather have the purity
>   of your frozen bark!"

> This woman's blood, unwilling to curdle in death,
> Prefers to mingle with pine tree resin,
> > and petrify to stone!
> Stone strikes sparks
> That rise to heaven,
> Swords to kill the bad,
> To drive them from the world!

Rather than subtlety, here Wang has recourse to rhetorical intensity, and succeeds, because of the very sincerity that is so apparent in his moral indignation, and his sense of inspiration by the woman's heroic self-sacrifice. But the fact that the tree was a *pine tree* of course gives added symbolic and imagistic resonance to the locale of her death. As we know, pines were one of the most highly prized treasures of natural beauty in the Yellow Mountains—that natural beauty is only enhanced by the ancient Confucian use of the pine tree and other evergreens to represent staunchness, incorruptibility, and loyalty. The woman dies *embracing* the pine, and she refuses to let go, ready to take on the indestructible agelessness of the tree, which eventually will even petrify.

The action of this woman came to the attention, *inter alia*,[100] of Wang Shizhen, who relates the episode in his influential *biji* ("brush notes," a collection of miscellaneous comments, anecdotes, etc.), *Chibei outan*,[101] as well as that of Shi Runzhang, who was also moved to poetry, including his version of "The Pine-Embracing Woman" in a specifcially designated "Music Bureau" section of poems.[102] Shi's preface is nearly identical with Wang's, except that, like Wang Shizhen, he identifies the woman as a lady née Sun, married to the Xuancheng degree-holder Lo Kai, and he specifies that the woman held on to the pine tree for *three days* after her death without falling to the ground. For his short poetic treatment, Shi chooses to use the metre of the ancient poem "Encountering Sorrow" (*Li sao*) attributed to Qu Yuan (339–278 BC) and the *locus classicus* for expressing resentment at not having one's moral worth recognized:

> The evergreen of the pine tree, ah!
> > the gracefulness of the lady!
> The sad soughing of the pine tree, ah!
> > the pure chastity of the lady!
> The pine tree might be cut down, ah!
> > the lady will never turn from her purpose!

Right down to the root of the pine tree, ah!
　　her blood congeals to emerald,
As thousands of years pass by, ah!
　　with the pine it petrifies to stone.

The pine, together with its resin mingled with the woman's blood, petrified to "emerald," joins the blue lotus that magically appeared during the administration of Master Jiang as a perfect image of natural beauty and moral beauty, conjoined into a perfect unity.

One might think that with "The Pine-Embracing Woman" one had reached the limit of moral revulsion at human suffering. But Wang Hongdu takes us still further with "The Human Food Market."[103] Here the prose preface is actually lengthier than the poem itself, laying out the actual events in question, and leaving to the poem the heroine's final words, followed by the transformation in imagery of her eyes into stars, in keeping with the Confucian idea that through moral action, man can form a trinity with Heaven and Earth. This seemingly incredible tale of self-sacrifice is based on the premise that a man should if possible die and be buried in his homeland. The arrangement by which the couple in this poem had to take up residence with the wife's family in a different province, rather than with the husband's in his home province according to custom, was seen as a shameful one.

The Human Food Market

When there is a great famine, people will sell flesh cut from their own limbs in the marketplace; this is called "human food." There was a man from another district temporarily residing with his in-laws of such-and-such a family in our district. One day, his wife, suddenly produced 3,000 cash and gave it to her husband, urging that once they had enough money, they might quickly leave and return to his own home. Then, holding back her tears, she withdrew. The husband, angry, said nothing, but had someone follow his wife, to find out where she was getting the money. This man reported that she had already had her arms cut off and hung out for sale in the market. The money she had brought in was partial payment in advance for her body, and was intended as a contribution to traveling expenses on the way back home.

"My limbs can be cut off;
My head can be lopped off;
But for my husband to die in a strange land?—
      how could I let that be?"
So wielding the knifeblade, strips of flesh fly off
Until from down in the underworld,
      her eyes flash brilliant beams,
Competing with the stars and moon
      to light his way back home!

The kind of direct emotional vitality in these depictions of the sufferings of others is applied by Wang Hongdu to his personal pain as well. On the loss of a daughter who was only two or three years old, Wang composed a poem of great poignancy in regulated verse of seven characters per line.[104] The theme was not unprecedented in Chinese poetry; this greatest of tragedies, the loss of one's child, was treated by other poets in the past, perhaps most notably by Mei Yaochen.[105] But Wang Hongdu in this work shows his deepest humanity:

哭幼女瑞

出門猶記繞衣牽
嬌小音容倏下泉
抱汝如兒能幾日
知余爲父僅三年
蒿萊塚上增新土
風雨燈前盡舊緣
阿母桃花勤靧面
朝來都漬淚痕邊

Lamenting the Death of My Young Daughter, Rui

I still recall when I left each day,
      you'd come running, tugging at my robe…
And now—in a flash!—your sweet voice and face
      have sunk to the Springs below.
How many days was I able to hold you,
      loving you like a son?
And you, knowing me as your loving father
      only for three years.

> Where crab-grass is growing on your grave,
>   we've added some new soil;
> In wind-swept rain, before the lamp—
>   old karma, all run out.
> Your mother moistens her face each evening,
>   diligently, with peach blossoms:
> In the morning, I see them, clinging,
>   beside the marks of tears.

Wang Hongdu's evident empathy for ordinary people was no means confined to cases of high tragedy. Wang was entirely capable of a lighter note, and shared with contemporaries of his such as Wu Jiaji, Qu Dajun, and others,[106] an interest in folksong, or folksong-related poetic forms, such as the "Bamboo Branch Songs" (*Zhuzhi ci*), which poets had been emulating since the Tang dynasty and earlier. These were quatrains of five characters per line throughout, or (more commonly) seven characters per line throughout, expressive of romantic feelings—usually from the woman's point of view, and often in a tone of petulent frustration with the man—or descriptive of local customs. Wang brilliantly combines the two modes in his set of three "Bamboo Branch Songs of Yangzhou" (*Yangzhou zhuzhi ci*),[107] which assimilates popular proverbs about the city of Yangzhou and an anecdote about Yangzhou flowers with romantic situations, even providing a note after each poem to ensure the reader's awareness of the background. Yangzhou, of course, was a city of great importance for the circles of writers and artists we are considering, not merely because of its geographical proximity, but because it was the hometown and central headquarters of the wealthy salt merchants who were their primary patrons.

1

> The bright moon shines three parts in all,
>   just like you, my lad!
> Two parts shine upon me alone,
>   as it emerges from high clouds.
> I lift my head: whenever will
>   I see it shining full?
> And I wonder—who's the other girl
>   attracting a third part of the light?

[Poet's note:] A proverb says, "Of the three parts of the moon shining on the world, two parts are reserved for Yangzhou town alone."

2

The Golden Sash Wraps you round,
    but why boast about that?
I only wish your love for me
    was like this bejeweled flower!
Just let it be transplanted to the Forbidden Gardens,
    and it will have no love in its heart—
Only when it's back in Yangzhou
    will it love its original home!

[Poet's note:] The Golden Sash Wrap is the name of a famous variety of peony from Guangling [Yangzhou]. This "bejeweled" flower twice was transplanted to the Forbidden Gardens [of the two capital cities, of the Northern and Southern Song], during the Qingli and Chunxi periods of the Song dynasty [1041–48; 1174–89] respectively; in both cases, within just one year they drooped and wilted. But when they were returned and replanted back in Yangzhou, they came back to life and flourished as before.

3

My lad, please say, are your feelings for me
    really deep? Or shallow?
Remember how you swore by the clarity of the waters
    that we shared the same heart!
From ancient times, one only has faith
    in rivers flowing east;
Who would have thought you'd "flow to the west,"
    right to the present day?

[Poet's note:] A proverb says, "Only in old Yangzhou does the East-Flowing River flow *west*."

The question of authenticity of Chinese "folk poetry" has been debated at length; there would in fact appear to exist a spectrum of degrees of authenticity, from actual folk examples, orally transmitted and in some cases transcribed accurately by literati scholars, to works of the the sort represented by Wang's "Bamboo Branch Songs," openly declaring that they are literati productions "in the manner of" folk songs.[108] Authentic folk material gathered in the field by pioneering Chinese folklorists, such as Gu Jiegang (1893–1980) readily confirm that such songs are characterized indeed by the tart wit and mocking humor deployed by Wang in these three poems.

It is a shame that more of Wang Hongdu's poetry does not survive. But what we do have confirms his place in the poetic history of the Qing dynasty, and adds further depth to his achievements as painter and prose essayist.

As we have seen, Wang deploys all of the Three Perfections of poetry, painting, and calligraphy in his work "Reading the *Yijing* On a Snowy Night." He ends his inscribed poem with these lines: "And yet I don't refuse to blow on my frozen brush, / To write this in thanks on Shan-stream paper!"

Wang writes on what he calls Shan-stream paper, Shan Stream in Zhejiang, south and slightly east of Shaoxing, being famed in antiquity for its fine, hand-made papers. In Wang Hongdu's day, his own region of southern Anhui was especially noted for its superb papers, which are being made there to this day by patient craftsmen.[109] But Shan Stream was also associated with the sage-recluses of the Six Dynasties period, especially Wang Huizhi (d. 388), son of the great calligrapher Wang Xizhi (309–c. 365). Wang Huizhi is said to have thought of his friend, Dai Kui (d. 396), one snowy evening, and traveling by boat to Dai's residence at Shan Stream, he disembarked, walked up to Dai's front door—then, without even knocking, turned around and traveled home again. Asked why by a puzzled friend, he responded, "I went there on the inspiration of the moment; as soon as the inspiration died out, I returned. What need was there actually to see Dai?"[110]

Wang's multileveled allusion links the proud local craft of papermaking with the high tradition of "pure discussion" (*qingtan*), the transcendent, Dao-oriented discourse of the so-called Seven Sages of the Bamboo Grove and their friends during the Six Dynasties period (220–589). Just as he brings together the Three Perfections in this work, he shows us again the ultimate compatibility between Confucian (*Book of Changes*) and Daoist worldviews for those inspired by the Yellow Mountains.

Disciples of Buddha, photo by Wang Wusheng.

COMPREHENDING THE ESSENTIALS OF THE YELLOW MOUNTAINS

A Complete Translation of the *Huangshan lingyao lu*

Completed in 1696, Wang Hongdu's book on the Yellow Mountains falls into the category of mountain gazetteers, arranged in accordance with the famous sites and features of the mountain range. These include the actual peaks, streams, valleys, and in the case of the Yellow Mountains in particular, individual rock formations and pine trees, with their own traditional names. Also characteristic of the Yellow Mountains are the cloud formations that appear as if by magic, and these too are addressed specifically. Within these sections, far from limiting himself to mere description of the sites, Wang relates the experience of passing through the landscape in the manner of "travel essays," or *youji*. Thus his book is best seen as belonging to the travel essay genre.

A scholar like Wang Hongdu would approach friends and ask them to contribute prefaces (*xu*) to his work. Here there are three such prefaces, by three of the most important figures in contemporary cultural affairs, all of whom were friends of Wang Hongdu, and all of whom have figured in the discussion above: Wang Shizhen, Song Luo, and Wu Yuan. A colophon (*ba*) was added in 1775 by Wang's great-great grandnephew, Wang He'de, on the occasion of the first printing of the book.

Wang Hongdu also appends texts by other writers to certain sections of the book, also part of the tradition of such compilations.

Preface to *Huangshan lingyao lu* by Wang Shizhen

"Gazetteers" are a type of history. They record mountains and bodies of water, while histories transmit the biographies of men. Although each of these genres has its own proper form, mountains-and-waters and human figures all have forms, and all have souls of their own. One wishing to depict them to the life must encapsulate the form and capture the soul. Once this is done, there will be no essential difference between the two.

Thus, if one writes in a worn out, conventional style, the work will be stale and flavorless, whereas if one writes in an overly heroic style, it will be dense and lacking in freedom. Only if one writes in a lively, vibrant style will the contents burst forth from all sides, leaping and surging from the page, leaving nothing hidden, but allowing the spiritual essence to emerge.

When it comes to historians possessing a lively style, throughout all of antiquity the bays have been given to one man alone: Zizhang [Sima Qian, China's great historian]. Now, an argument has been made that if in some later period, there had indeed been a Zizhang, in the absence of the men and events recorded in the *Records of the Historian* [*Shiji*, by Sima Qian], although this later Zizhang had a good writing style, he would still have lacked the material to which to apply it, such that it could be transmitted. Zhenchuan [Gui Youguang, 1506–71, a major prose writer of the Ming dynasty] is also on record as having stated that he regretted that in his lifetime, he never encountered men as remarkable, scholars as outstanding, or events as rich and majestic as those of Zizhang's time to write about. And he did have a point.

Still, I say, not so! Although we may no longer have such men or events as those recorded in the *Shiji*, how can we deny that in the cosmos there exist wonders sufficient to compare with them, in fact so fully comparable to them, that even if the attempt were made to transmit them, it would turn out to be impossible to do so in full? With this realization, let us take our material from the clouds and streams, rely upon the pine trees and rocks: why should their souls not be transmitted complete with "these things?" [i.e., eyes, from anecdote of legendary painter, Gu Kaizhi, in which he states that "these things" are that which truly transmit the soul of the subject in a portrait.]

This is precisely why my disciple, Yuding [Wang Hongdu], has written his book, *Huangshan lingyao lu*. For the as yet unrecorded wonders of the Yellow Mountains have been awaiting some gifted historian who has not fulfilled his dreams, so as through him to reveal to some small extent their unexpressed essence.

Yuding in his recording of the Yellow Mountains has put forth an entirely new mode of weaving the tapestry, with his own grasp of the mountains and gullies, at once sweeping away the conventional vulgarisms of gazetteer writers. He moves rapidly and freely, allowing his brush to go where it will, bringing the true inner principles to life: and this is quite simply because his is a "lively" style.

What is more, through merely presenting the primary essences, the true appearance of the complete mountain range comes clearly into view, just as Zizhang in transmitting the life of a man captures the key point of his biography in just one or two phrases, and yet nothing of the man is left unexpressed. This is indeed to master the subtly wondrous technique of transmitting the essence.

Ah, Yuding's masterful brush is fully deployed in recording mountains-and-waters, sufficiently to show him as lacking precedent and without later equals. This being the case, men should only worry about lacking a style. Although we may suffer the absence of "men as remarkable, scholars as outstanding, or events as rich and majestic as those of Zizhang's time to write about," if we desire wondrous subjects as fine, why should there no longer be any worthy of expression?

> —composed by Wang Shizhen of Jinan, Lecturer of the Classics
> Colloquium, Secretary of the Bureau of Punishments, former
> Chancellor of the Censorate and Left Censor in Chief,
> on the day of the summer solstice of the year *gengchen* [1700].

Preface to *Huangshan lingyao lu* by Song Luo

When it comes to famous mountains of the world, aside from the Five Sacred Peaks, the Yellow Mountains are supreme. The Monograph on Commanderies and Kingdoms [*Jun'guo zhi*] declares that Heavenly Eye Mountain is 18,000 fathoms high and yet merely reaches to the foothills of the "Dark Mountains" [*Yishan*, an old name for the Yellow Mountains], and that the Dark Mountains are especially tall. These Dark Mountains are in fact the Yellow Mountains. The *Water Classic with Annotations* [*Shui jing zhu*, an early geographical text], refers to them as the Dark Mountains; the change of the name to Yellow occurred in the sixth year of the Tianbao period [747].

The mountains are not only particularly tall and unusual, but the clustered peaks towering above each other, the dawn vapors and evening mists taking on thousands upon thousands of different aspects, the mountains cannot be limited to a single realm, nor do its realms limit themselves to a single season. Even though thousands upon thousands of people travel there, each of them will individually experience what he himself sees, and no two experiences will be the same.

Mr. Wang Yuding of Xin' an is enamored of antiquity, and is a talented writer. He established a residence in the Yellow Mountains, and, finding it suited his nature, he forgot to return.

And in his leisure moments taken off from studying, he has clambered over cliffs and penetrated sources, entering deep woods, sitting upon fantastic rocks, winding amongst the greens and twisting in and out of the whites, not failing to reach any portion, however remote! Only after these explorations did he grasp the essences of the place, and record them. He produced over fifty entries, editing them in two volumes, and further compiled a diagram of the mountains to present before the text [*sic;* unclear if this ever appeared], carefully selecting the accounts of his travels and placing these after. With this, the wonders of the thirty-six peaks, eight cliffs, twelve caves and twenty-four streams of the Yellow Mountains appear with crystal clarity in this work. Even if a man has never packed up provisions and developed calouses on his feet hiking through the Yellow Mountains, they still are piled high right there upon his desk!

Now, in the world, famous mountains and streams are extremely many in number, innumerable in fact. Unless a man is possessed of heroic stamina, how can he possibly wander throughout all of them at the eight ends of the earth, completing a circuit of ten thousand miles? When Xiang Ziping [together with Yan below, one of two legendary sages] wished to marry, he ended up traveling to all Five Sacred Peaks. And in Yan Junping's day, there were Nine Provinces: he considered that to travel to the other eight of them would be a hardship. Should we consider these two sages to be men who failed to "grasp the essences" of places? And as for men who have "grasped the essence," consider Zong Haowen [Zong Bing (375–443)] who painted mountains on his walls, and played his *qin* zither and sang, wishing for the myriad peaks to echo in response: thus he "traveled reclining" in his single house, and considered this sufficient.

But I have said that in reading books, or composing writings, there is always some "essence" involved. And this must simply be experienced by each for himself.

This gentleman's ancestor, Vice Prefect [Wang] Boyu [the playwright and scholar Wang Daokun (1525–1593), who was a great grand-uncle of Wang Hongdu], had some ten thousand cases of books in his house. When a guest peered at them for a long time, he said to him, "Do not be overwhelmed by their numerousness! What a scholar needs to do is merely to read thoroughly several important works." And we may add that Lu Shiheng [Lu Ju (261–303)], in his *Prosepoem on Literature* [*Wen fu*] writes, "Establish terse diction while residing in the essence." This is certainly the key phrase in the entire work.

Thus in this world, it must take a man who is enamored of antiquity and a talented writer, such as Yuding, indeed to be able to "capture the essences of Yellow Mountain" and record them.

—composed by Song Luo of Shangqiu

Preface to *Huangshan lingyao lu* by Wu Yuan

Within one's inch-wide heart, if there is no aspiring, overflowing spirit, wishing to expand but with nowhere to go—then there would be no point in writing a record such as this. Or perhaps roof-tiles press overhead, so that your horizons are limited, and city walls enclose you round about, so that your soul is hemmed in, and you are quite willing to be like a louse residing in a pair of pants, with no intention of shaking your robe and ascending thousands of feet—then you can well do without reading a record such as this.

If oceans of cloud float from your breast, and rocky streams wash your ears, and with equipages of cranes and roc birds you embark from the azure blue expanse in the morning, reaching the realm of vast forests of paulownia trees by sunset—then you might well burn up a record such as this.

But if it is not thus, then given these mountains, how can you go a single day without this record?

"Comprehending the Essentials" means grasping the mountains' spiritual wonders, epitomizing their customary appearance, like the Grand Historian Sima Qian transmitting biographies of men such that reading them a thousand years later one feels as if one is seeing them face to face. Their true nature is preserved therein.

In the year *bingzi* [1696], I accompanied my friend Yuding on an excursion to the Yellow Mountains. Upon returning, he stayed at my Blue Magic Mushroom Studio, and we wielded our brushes in lamplight. Wang completed this record without even hesitating to punctuate. Marvelously spiritual and free-wheeling, the work, completed before mine could be, captured my heart, and I decided to write no further. If happily on some future occasion I and my friend are able to fulfill our desire to reside up in the mountains, clouds and mist our associates, gods and immortals our companions, I could still not bear to burn it up! I would leave it behind so that if, a thousand miles away or thousands of years later, there should be someone else whose intention it is to shake his robe and ascend thousands of feet, it might provide him with a quick read!

—composed by Wu Yuan of the same hometown

Colophon by Wang He'de

The wondrous beauties of the Yellow Mountains are preeminent in the world. Books and gazetteers recounting them do not number less than several tens of titles. But there have been distinctions among these between those whose itineraries were more or less detailed, whose authors were more or less insightful, whose records were more or less skillfully done—as none have ever sought to "grasp the essences." Thus, readers of such works have found themselves confused and befuddled, and often it has proved difficult for them to rely on these writings as guides to these mountains, such that at a single glance they might feel as if face to face with old acquaintances.

The late Yuding built his hut at the top of Start-to-Believe Peak, and studied there for ten years. He epitomized the great essentials from all accounts transmitted past and present of the wonders of peaks, pine trees and rocks, and composed this *Huangshan lingyao lu*. The one work he divided into two volumes, corresponding to the Front and Rear Cloud Oceans, passing in clear sequence through the sequential formations of the mountains, the essential beauties of the various texts being brought together as a complete whole.

The two gentlemen from Xincheng and Shangqiu [Wang Shizhen, and Song Luo] of that time loved this work, and wrote prefaces for it.

And yet regrettably to this day there have been no plans carried out to have it printed. I, He'de, carefully copied the text from the MS into book form, and with dispatch handed it over to the printers. May those who share the author's love for undertaking sightseeing excursions take it along with them in their satchels as they traverse the mountains and cross the gullies, which will now identify themselves as clearly as if one were pointing at one's own palm. The wondrous beauties of the thirty-six peaks are all complete in this record. Thus it can be said that here the great panorama of the Yellow Cloud Oceans are presented to the full, and there is no need for any regret.

    — respectfully noted by great-great-grandnephew He'de in the fourth month of the year *yiwei* of the Qianlong period [1775]

Stone Bamboo Shoot Peak, [Two] Immortals Playing Chess,
taken at Now-I-Believe-It Peak, photo by Wang Wusheng.

黄山
Huangshan, The Yellow Mountains

With Appended Comparative Appreciation of Mounts Huang and Hua
by Zhu Lu of Changzhou [Suzhou]

The Yellow Mountains encompass hundreds and thousands of fantastic peaks, clutching the earth and rubbing the sky. Within an area of several hundreds of square *li*, on all four sides there is no point at which there is the least break. The range properly faces towards the southeast, glitteringly deploying its awe-inspiring beauty, supreme in the human realm. And yet in antiquity, this name, "Yellow Mountains," did not exist. Later on, Li Daoyuan [469–527] in his *Water Classic with Annotations*, wrote, "Going still further north in Zhejiang, one passes through the Dark Mountains [*Yu* 黝; sometimes substituted for *Yi*]; the county seat is located on the southern side of the mountains, therefore the county folk take their surnames from this term." Luo Yuan of the [Liu-]Song dynasty [420–478] in his *Gazetteer of Xin'an* wrote, "The Yellow Mountains, named the Dark Mountains, are 128 *li* to the northwest of the county seat; they reach a height of 1180 *ren*. To the southeast is She County, to the southwest is Xiuning County, and the northwest is covered by Taiping County of the Ningguo Prefecture."

It is transmitted that the Yellow Emperor once, together with Masters Rongcheng and Fuqiu, concocted the elixir in this spot. Later on, there were also such immortals as Cao and Ruan there, and so among the peaks are ones called Rongcheng and Fuqiu, and among the streams are found such names as Cao Stream and Ruan Stream.

In the sixth month of the sixth year of the Tianbao period [747], a proclamation decreed that the name be changed to Yellow Mountains.

We note that in the Jiangnan [South-of-the-Yangzi] region, among the great mountains are such as Heavenly Eye [Tianmu] Mountain and Heavenly Terrace [Tiantai] Mountain. The *Monograph on Commanderies and Kingdoms* states that Heavenly Eye Mountain is 18,000 fathoms high and yet merely reaches to the foothills of the Dark Mountains, and that the Dark Mountains are especially tall. But then the various mountains in neighboring districts must be branches from these [Yellow] mountains.

The mountains consist of thirty-six peaks, as well as thirty-six springs, twenty-four streams, eight cliffs, and innumerable numinous sites. The waters all flow downward, eventually merging into the Yangzi River, and becoming the source of the Zhejiang River.

I take the liberty of noting that the *Gazetteer of the Entire Realm* [*Huanyu zhi*] also refers to these mountains as The Northern Dark Mountains [*Bei yi shan*]. *You* 黝 is the same as this *yi*. When a color is slightly bluish-black, it is called *you*. When it is deep black and moist it is called *yi*. The "skin" of these mountains has been completely peeled off, leaving only the rocks. The congealed effect of their pure dark color produces a darkish look from far off. What is more, the sinew-patterns are fine and rich, with a fructifying moisture of fresh appearance, so that the practice of naming the mountains *yi*, "Dark-moist," would seem to be ineluctable. But starting with the Tang dynasty, those fond of Daoist theories fabricated a forged text called *Records of Strange Matters from the Book of the Zhou Dynasty* [*Zhoushu yiji*], which cited the Yellow Emperor as grounds for changing the name to The Yellow Mountains. And subsequent generations followed this practice.

In the Ming dynasty, Zhao Fang [1319–1369; an Anhui man][111] declared that the Yellow Mountains had declined in their central reaches and faded away in their four extremities, being overtaken by a *kun* [weakened, feminine] spirit. Thus, he felt, the name should be purified from the vulgarity of the designation derived from *Records of Strange Matters*.

Upon consulting the *Water Classic with Annotations*, we find that it records that a certain Ch'en Yeh-chih of Shang-yü towards the end of the Han dynasty engaged in austerities to purify his person, hiding his traces in the "Dark [*yi*] Mountains." The Classic Records of Guiji [*Guiji dianlu*] by Yu Yu [c.285—340)], also states that he retired to the *Yi'she*, and that his character was as pure as frost and snow, his upright nature being equivalent to that of [the great hermit of antiquity] Liuxia [Hui]. Alas! Such is the very reason that those who gave prominence to famous mountains in the past only praised and recorded men of this calibre. May those who now enter these mountains also pay careful attention to the way in which they conduct themselves.

Vol. I [上/2a–3a]
Comparative Appreciation of Mounts Huang and Hua
by Zhu Lu[112] of Changzhou [Suzhou]

Both the Huang and Hua ranges show strange bones. Hua is heroic, Huang is lovely. Hua is vast, Huang is widely deployed. If one takes the "heroic, vast" one, and journeys to its apex, one's vision will be elevated and one's breast will expand; with a single gaze one will be replete. But if one selects the "lovely, widely deployed" one, travels wherever one should reach, one's heart will be touched with love and one's soul will be intoxicated, every sequential view enticing one to proceed.

The Great Hua range is like a powerful hero, his grandeur overwhelming all who are ordinary; what is lacking is hidden charm. The Yellow Mountains are like a cultivated scholar, his scintillating brilliance outward flowing in all four directions, so that one comes to sense his many postures. Great Hua is a great Deva General: one sight of him, and the myriad demons are obliterated. The Yellow Mountains are like thousands of heavenly nymphs, wondrous in their solemnly awesome attributes, such that as they are approached by the worldly, those of decadent sensuality all feel ashamed.

The Great Hua is like the Four Great Devarajas keeping guard in all four directions from the apex of Mount Sumeru, on patrol there day and night, above and below. The Yellow Mountains are like a gathering of Immortals joining together for a banquet at Jasper Pond, the Gardens of Immortality, with all Three Isles and Ten Islets of the Immortals arrayed before them. As for attempting to use pegs so as to get past tough places like Lang-tang Pass, of a difficulty such that even gibbons and monkeys find them difficult, so as to discover the most remarkable sights—Great Hua is that. But the Yellow Mountains, no. As for the fourth and fifth months displaying jewel-like flowers and gem-like plants, filling the peaks and valleys, so that even at the height of summer it seems like spring, and the mountains grow in beauty because of this—the Yellow Mountains are like that. But Great Hua, no.

The Great Hua has three peaks, all stony but with few crevices, so that one trembles at the thought of ascending. The peaks of the Yellow Mountains are finely furrowed and cleverly carved, so that all of them can be ascended by winding and twisting. At Great Hua, should a single rock shift, it can block a whole *mu* in area [over 600 sq. meters]; if several shift, it is as if one is being entirely covered over. At the Yellow Mountains, the rocks are not entirely hidden from view: they stand bolt upright or slant in a crouch, all with fantastic shapes to them. At Great Hua, the pine trees display only about six or seven "twisted dragons," braving the frost from ancient times. At Yellow Mountains, a thousand pines display a thousand different shapes, all of them classified and presented to us in epitomized form by Mr. Wang Shiduan [unidentified]. But all considered, I would not presume to attempt a ranking of these two fantastically towering mountain ranges.

Vol. 1 [上/3a–5b]

雲門峯
Yunmen feng, Cloud Gate Peaks

With Appended Account of the Cloud Oceans

Upon entering the Xin'an area and reaching She Bank, you see two peaks towering beside each other. The tips of both peaks are extremely pointy, as if they were attempting to slice the blue empyrean above. These are popularly dubbed The Scissor Peaks of the Yellow Mountain. But when we consult the *Mountain Gazetteer*, we find them called Cloud Gate. It is said that those who have resided for long periods of time in the mountains have noted that the clouds perched above these peaks never disperse, morning or evening. What is more, when clouds emerge or return, the root of their movement will always be this spot, hence the name. If you gaze at the mountains from 100 *li* away to the southeast, and then proceed forward, you will find that all other peaks sometimes disappear, sometimes reappear—while these two alone are always visible from every position. Once you reach Fragrant Village, and then pass it to approach Hot Springs Mouth from left or right, then you yourself enter among the clouds, and the "Gate" no longer is visible.

These peaks are in fact the westernmost point of the range. Mr. Hong Zong, Gu'yi,[113] states that rocks are the "roots" of clouds, and the western reaches of the Yellow Mountains, where earth begins to turn to rock, start at Cloud Gate. Below these peaks is Floating Stream, from which branches off Fengle Creek, and this in turn flows into the Xin'an River.

Vol. I [上/3b–5b]
An Account of the Cloud Oceans

There are no clouds that are not an "ocean," but none are more remarkable than those at the Yellow Mountains. And that is why only those at the Yellow Mountains are actually called oceans. For clouds are produced by mountains and streams through their exhalations forming rain. Once they are formed, they may travel relatively close to their point of origin—tens or hundreds of feet—or as far as many tens or hundreds of miles, even reaching distances of thousands of miles away before they come to rest.

As for the full vastness of Heaven, no one knows how many thousands or tens of thousands of miles it encompasses. How could clouds reach to every single place? Thus when one gazes at clouds from behind, and looks down from those places themselves unreached by the clouds, what one sees are oceans. But if there are no people present, or if one is standing at the uppermost point of the clouds themselves, then of course there is no way for this phenomenon to be seen.

Nothing is more precipitous than mountains. And of such mountains, none are more so than the Yellow Mountains. If one takes one's position at the very top of the Yellow Mounains, the clouds will be *down below.* The clouds are deployed below in one white swath reaching an area of ten thousand acres, and they are in constant, pulsating motion: if one does not call this an ocean, what else would one call it? Some claim that Mount T'ai's clouds touch off from the rocks and then merge together a mere skin's-width or one inch from the surface; it isn't that the mountain isn't tall, nor is it that one isn't standing at the uppermost point of the cloud formation. And yet one has never heard of the "Mount T'ai Ocean." I would say this: the basic form of Mount T'ai is straight upright, and all clustered together. The Yellow Mountains' structure, however, is rich and scattered abroad. To be upright and clustered is to rise nobly in solitary splendor. Although the clouds there are expansive, there are no individual peaks amongst which they might amass their peculiarities. They can make formations, but they cannot make oceans. Moreover, Mount T'ai has its own ocean-like bodies of water, and does not need to rely on clouds to form oceans.

But to be "rich and scattered abroad" means that the Yellow Mountains display peaks carved out for hundreds and thousands of feet, towering above two entire districts, She and Xuan. When clouds arise there, the clouds from peaks near and far spread vastly and then, with prodigious plenitude, join all together in one great circuit around the myriad peaks, then gradually dissipate. The only peaks where they never dissipate are the three: Heavenly Capital, Lotus Blossom, and Refining Elixir. The clouds at these peaks at times tremble so violently that people fear they cannot survive. But the clouds lack the power to rise to the very tops of these peaks, so in emerging or returning they habituate the midpoints of the peaks, leaving the tips of the peaks to protrude *above* the clouds, where the clouds no longer attempt to compete with them.

With this, the clouds go along with the winds, sweeping and burgeoning above and below, until there is a great divide formed, with Heaven's vault above all, a perfect blue, while below, in the midst of the cottony forms, beams of sunlight flicker and penetrate, and the forms of the peaks, following these, sometimes peek out and sometimes are again swallowed up, while purple-bluish-greenish forms produce thousands and thousands of aureoles, and thousands and thousands of types of scintillating light. And that is why everything beyond the mountains is one vast panorama of voidness, as even as the surface of a mirror, while within the mountains it is as if thousands of skeins of silk are twisting and turning, floating and dangling amongst the crevices of all the peaks. Above all is zig-zagged; below all is perfectly level. It is like the Isle-Mountains of Paradise jutting upwards towards Heaven, while in the windswept ocean waves the towers and pavilions of the mountains of the Immortals glitter clearly one after the other, unobstructed. Or it is like tens of thousands of lotus blossoms growing together, or scintillating wavelets of lake-light shaking and swaying in the breeze, and never settling down.

What is more, wherever the clouds go, they take the wind along with them. The pine trees on these mountains number in the hundreds of thousands. As the wind passes, altogether the pine needles on ten thousand mountains angrily cry out in chorus in the midst of the clouds, and the roaring symphony grows wilder and wilder. And at times when the white moon hangs high above, and mists and vapors float in the void, the snowy billows and silvery waves ripple and flow endlessly. This too can be called a "moonbeam ocean."

I have heard from those who have grown old living in these mountains that the clouds actually have *homes*. They come from a particular mountain, and will inevitably return to that same mountain! On hot summer days, in wind-swept rain, the dragon-clouds arise and fade; at such times it is difficult to keep track of them in the haze. And there would seem to be no way to determine if the clouds of all the near and far mountains are in fact facilitated by Yellow Mountains clouds, but in fact they are. Their emergence and their return are entirely controlled by the force of the clouds of the Yellow Mountains. And these clouds in the Yellow Mountains make the rocks their home. Now the rocks of the Yellow Mountains are austerely pure and nobly stern: amongst them heavy fogs cannot last long. Therefore ten thousand layers of vast waves will suddenly strike heaven and earth, and then immediately dissipate, like ducks swimming off or rabbits fleeing away. Now the peaks' bluish colors and the pines' greenery will appear in precise detail, and the vapors of moments ago have disappeared one doesn't know where.

I have further heard that once in the past there was a visitor here who was seated at his mountain window, grinding his ink, and painstakingly working at poetry, when a cloud suddenly flew in through the window, approached his desk, totally absorbed the liquid ink, and then departed, leaving his inkstone as dry as if it had been rubbed clean!

My friend Min Linsi [1628–1704][114] says that at times there is a distinction of moist and dry among the clouds of the Yellow Mountains. When the clouds are moist, then one's clothes will become soaking wet, and books and scrolls will seem to have passed through frost or dew. When dry, the opposite is the case. Thus truly one cannot speak of the clouds of other mountains in the same breath as these!

Vol. I [上/5b–6b]

浮溪
Fuxi, Floating Stream

The interior portion of the mountains is empty, with springs filling the cavities. The springs of all the peaks come together and form the Twenty-four Streams. These are found starting from Taiping proceeding to Jing County. When one reaches Wu Lake, they enter the Yangzi River, but Floating Stream alone emerges from Cloud Gate Peaks and becomes the source of Fengle Creek. This then flows southeast into She. Twenty *li* from Cloud Gate there is a "Floating Stream Bridge." The gazetteer states that above Floating Stream in the past there were ten thousand ancient plum blossom trees twining about the rocky crevices. At the time of fruition, the pathway along the stream would be extremely narrow and difficult, so that people were not able to glean from these completely. Thus the fruit was left for gibbons and rodents, and even these were unable to devour them all. Thus they were left to drop to the ground, the fruit giving birth to further trees, until they thickened into an entire forest. The time of flowering for them is at the juncture of spring and summer: their fresh green borders the sky, encaging the clouds and enmeshing the snow. The mountains ordinarily do not experience complete nightfall: the cliffs at dawn and the escarpments at evening appear and disappear in the interstices between the blossoms. Swarming bees pursue them, and thunder like the rumbling of carriage wheels mingles with the sound of the stream. The pure line of the stream's flow is partially visible twining in and out amongst the petals. If you walk ten *li* through these blossoms, you still will not come to the end of them.

It is said that the Altar of the Immortal Fuqiu [Floating Hill] was somewhere among the blossoms. There was once a man who reached it, and he saw towers, terraces and a white lotus pond spread out on all sides, as well as piles of such provisions as salt and rice. He later led an expedition to the spot to gather the latter, but became confused and lost his way.

Vol. I [上/6b– 8a]

祥符寺
Xiangfu si, Temple of the Auspicious Token

The Temple of the Auspicious Token was founded in the eighteenth year of the Kaiyuan period [730] by Chan Master Zhiman. Today's Lotus Blossom Hermitage stands on its original location. In the fifth year of the Dazhong period [851], the Inspector Li Jingfang, inspired by the visionary appearance of a white dragon, first moved it to the west of the Hot Spring. In the second year of the Tianyou period [905], the Inspector Tao Ya refounded it as the Hot Springs Cloister. In the second year of the Baoda period of the Southern Tang dynasty [944], the name was changed to Cloister of the Divine Spring, and in the first year of Dazhong xiangfu ["Great Centricity Auspicious Token," 1008] it was designated a "temple," and denominated Auspicious Token. People kept calling it Hot Springs Temple though, because of its proximity to the hot springs.

The temple building is constructed in an ancient and simple manner, with openness and interconnecting corridors but with the buildings tightly bunched together. Inscribed on the walls are two poems:

> Woods of purplish blue-green—suited for barefoot walking;
> From the Pond of the White Dragon
>   one may view the green mountains.
> Where do you suppose are the herb-brazier
>   and the well of cinnabar?—
> The misty moon shines cold
>   above the Thirty-Six Peaks.

And again,

> What year was it when in broad daylight
>   one rode on phoenix-back
> To tread and tatter misty clouds
>   on Heavenly Capital Peak?
> I wish to resurrect the Yellow Emperor,
>   ask, "Where are the Nine Tripods?"
> And in Daoist robes serve once again
>   the Lord of Jade Voidness!

The signature reads "The Banished Clerk of the Southern Palace and Woodcutter of the Cloudy Valleys inscribed this." The calligraphy is superbly magnificent and free wheeling; indeed, it is the work of Luo Wengong [Hongxian, 1504–1564] of the Ming. In the past, this was located at the entrance to the temple. Early in the Kangxi period, the entire wall was moved and inlaid into the existing wall beneath the tower. To the left it has a pavilion facing Purple Rock Peak, inscribed by Wine Libationer Feng Mengzhen as follows: "Purple Jade" [*Zi yu*]. Behind this in turn is a tower: Heavenly Capital, Purple Rock, and Green Phoenix Peaks—their chilly radiance and moist blue-greenness pour upside down through its windows, invading one's hairs and bones! Herein the Yellow Emperor is worshipped, as well as their two excellencies Fouqiu and Rongcheng [two famed immortals]. Wine Libationer Wu Yuan[115] has inscribed this place as follows: "Source of the Immortals" [*Xian yuan*].

Before and behind the temple are sheer walls of precipitous cliff. When those who enter the mountains from the southeast reach this spot, they can see that the rocky surface is gradually increasing while the earth is gradually decreasing. A stream from Hot Springs Ridge breaks through the chaotic rocks here, gurgling without stop, and then continuing on to White Dragon and below, where the rocks get larger and larger, the size of rooms in buildings or gigantic wheels. And the water increases in fury, waves dashing up like clouds leaking, while the sound increases in loudness, the pools where shallow producing tones like drums and gongs, and where deep, like cannon exploding.

Outside the gates of the temple, ancient trees and towering bamboo intersperse their leaves across the banks of this stream, so that looking upwards one cannot see the sun, while looking downwards, one sees the reflection of the sun! Wind and wave jostle each other, the reflection never resting an instant. If anyone stands right before one, he is invisible; and if words are exchanged, one can barely hear the other.

To the right of the temple, halfway up the mountain, there is a grotto. If a man sits in this grotto and gazes out at the stream, his heart will naturally open brilliantly; the sun setting over the mountains, its beams will deflect and radiate inside, transforming purple and green in color instantaneously. Outside this grotto, there are two other smaller caves, which are particularly flooded by the setting sunlight. These are called the Caves Which Dine on Mist. Further to the left of these, there is a rock shaped like a horse's hoof, the Horse's Hoof Rock. Alongside is a square, long rock which naturally forms the shape of a stele. It is called The Stele of the Yellow Emperor.

To the right of the caves, of old there was a Hermitage of Master Hsia, but this has long been abandoned.

Many are the songbirds at this temple whose chirping seems like antiphonal singing, faster and slower in tempo in alternation. These are called "mountain music birds." Once down the mountain, one cannot find any of them. They are referred to in an essay by one Wang Wenjie, Zemin of the Yuan dynasty [1279–1368].

Now, as it happens, these mountain music birds are not all of the same genus. I and Pipeng Xuegong [i.e., the painter-monk, Xuezhuang[116]] have together investigated this, and found that there are three types whose songs are most clear and transcendent:

i) A type which is slighter larger than a mynah bird. Whenever they gather, there will inevitably be several dozen. Their feathers are light reddish-yellow in color; when they fly and sing, they expose their under-feathers, and then one notices that their abdomens are covered with patterns like tattered embroidery in brilliant bits, as if performers were dancing for one, showing the patterned beauty of their inner shirts. When travelers are about to arrive, these birds will always gather before their actual arrival and, flying in formation and chirping in rhythm, they will suddenly produce what sounds like human speech: *Ke dao, ke dao* ["Guests come, Guests come!"]. Yes, they are actually playing music to escort in one's visitors!

ii) A type somewhat like the "hundred-tongue" [blackbird]. These too form flocks of several dozen. Their songs shift constantly; at one moment they sound like a stringed instrument being plucked, but then they'll switch to a sound like silk being torn. Sometimes they are raucous, like a carriage wheel rumbling through a marketplace, but then they'll turn to delicate, sensuous sounds like the lingering notes of a flute, fading but never ending.

iii) A type very small and light, never flying more than a few yards. It has a sound like that of the faintest bells and chimes. They will flock up to the hundreds and scatter among the copses and reeds. The sounds are tiny, delightful to listen to—but suddenly they float off with the wind, scattering in all four directions and disappearing.

Vol. I [上/8b–9b]

朱砂泉
Zhusha quan, Cinnabar Spring

The warmth of hot springs usually derives from the flourescence of the sulphur content. But there are three springs in the world whose warmth does not depend on sulphur: Mount Li Spring, which uses *arsenic*, Anning Spring, which uses *verdant jade*, and that of the Yellow Mountains, which uses *vermilion sand* [i.e., cinnabar].

Cinnabar Spring lies above Fragrant Spring Stream, issuing from a stone basin naturally formed, some ten feet or so long and half as much wide. In depth it is no more than three feet, and is crystal clear so that one can see the bottom. To the side is a leaning rock of greenish color on which one can lie. Above rise steamy vapors as if from a cauldron on the boil, and below are spread tiny sandlike particles, amongst which can be seen bubbling froth like crabs' eyes or fishes' eyes. These ascend and as they do so gradually change to the size of pearls, then disperse and shoot off in all directions. Down where the bubbling occurs, the particles are so hot they cannot be touched. Any fish or shrimp that mistakenly enter this basin will die immediately. And yet there is a moss-like plant in the water that has never changed its green color from ancient times until the present. In springtime, these plants turn slightly reddish; in summer and autumn, when the water boils even more scaldingly, separate streamlets of cold water emerge from crevices in the rock, and then flow into the basin, causing the balance of warm and cold to be precisely maintained. With winter, the separate streams dry up, and the water increases in warmth again.

On the left bank are small holes in the rock, and when the waters overflow they drain through these holes, taking with them any dirt or slime, rushing quickly without ceasing all day long. Thus, even when people bathe here, no dirt accumulates.

In the old days, there used to be a slab of rock covering about half of the basin, this being, again, a naturally formed source-point. But at some unknown time, somebody had carved out a stone-tile pavilion like a bridge spanning the basin, which visitors have deplored to this day.

In the Dali period [766–804], Inspector Xue Yong established here a hut equipped with basins and tubs for ill people to use for bathing. There were many cures. In the Dazhong period [or Taizhong, 860–874], Inspector Li Jingfang, who had suffered for many years from a neurological disorder, entered the waters only twice, upon which the White Dragon was moved to put in an appearance, and the illness was cured. In the first month of third year of the Yuanfu period [1098–1101], three citizens of Xiuning and Taiping came to bathe. At the crack of dawn, they saw the waters turn a reddish color, as the earth quaked, and the waves of bubbling water made a sound as of thunder. They rushed to announce these events at a nearby temple, and the monks there told them that this was a manifestation of the cinnabar. When the people living below the mountains heard of this, they hurried to the spot to draw and drink of the waters. In the Chenghua period [1465–1487], the source turned red for three days, without anyone realizing it. But a local monk bathed in it, and subsequently lived to an age of over one hundred. In the year *imao* of the Wanli period [1615], the cinnabar particles were seen to spread until the entire stream was red in color; there was a fragrance that could be smelled for several *li*. In the Tianqi period [1621–1627], Mr. Shao Shusheng,[117] while bathing in the hot springs, saw a rat over a foot long and pure red in color, come leaping up out of the earth. This is known as the Cinnabar Rat.

According to the gazetteer, the mountains have two hot springs, of which this is the "upper basin." The stream flows on for several tens of paces, then forms the "lower basin." The latter further divides in two, a small one rather narrow, and a larger one about twice its width—but these have no covering stones. The sand particles are covered in shallow water, and small stones appear among them in formations that look like pomegranate seeds. The mountain monks have often planned to excavate these basins for the use of possible visitors; meanwhile, they have barred this spot to all but special guests.

Above the basins are protruding precipices a thousand feet high, thick with bamboo, forming a canopy all around; the moss below is thick like carpeting. Cliffside flowers adorn the stone walls. Engraved here is the name of Mr. Zheng Yu of the Yuan dynasty, and on the facing bank of the basin is inscribed "Mr. Shi [i.e., Zheng Yü] Once Fished Here" [*Shi Xiansheng chang chui diao qi shang*]. People call this Master Zheng's Fishing Rock.

Vol. I [上/10a–11a]

桃花源
Taohua yuan, Peach Blossom Spring

Old folks report that below Peach Blossom Peak, along the stream, in ancient times there were several tens of thousands of peach blossom trees. When they blossomed, their splendid loveliness covered the mountain— all in red. The place was then called Peach Blossom Stream; when the blossoms fell and were swept along in the stream, this was known as Waves of Peach Blossoms. Where they entered the hot springs, the latter would be called Peach Blossom Hot Springs. A townsman, Shao Shusheng [see previous entry], erected a retreat in the valley just above this stream. (Of old, this was known as Herb Valley.) This he called, Peach Blossom Source.

Those who seek this Source take a turn to the left from The Temple of the Auspicious Token, entering into a forest of stones. Here will be found the pathway that was opened up by Shao Shusheng. As the path parts further from the temple, it approaches a group of huge rocks piled high, the size of houses. If one twists and turns through the spaces between these, one comes to the spot; the sound of the water is in one's ears, the shadow of the peak is before one's eyes, the way is lined with large rocks and towering trees, forming zigzag patterns and setting each other off. The rocks are all draped with ancient vines in marvelous patterns, and ornamented by the strange trees. After a further half *li* or so, there is a single huge boulder shaped like a toad gazing downwards. Another two feet beyond this is another boulder lying on its side, as if receiving the toad's gaze. Once past this, one climbs straight up clinging to the cliff. Below again there is a small creek cutting across, but the path is connected to the other side by a plank bridge. One crosses this bridge and climbs further up the stone-cut steps, turning to the right. Here there is a boulder shaped like a bun, flat both top and bottom and perhaps three feet or more in thickness, forming a ring of 30 feet. There are two further boulders supporting it, one of which is shaped like a nose pointed upward to support the ring, the point of contact being less than two or three inches across. On top of this formation, there are open views in all four directions—one can spread a mat there to sit on. Below it, there is a cave entrance large enough for a man to enter.

If one then makes a further turn, there is a stone cliff face slanting several tens of feet across, with rocks on the side clustered together to form a small embankment. From this point on one is distanced from the sound of water which starts to diminish. There are four ancient plum blossom trees which, when in bloom, entirely overcast the upper portion of this embankment. (Of old, this was called Plum Blossom Mound.)

With a second turning, and then a climb, one finally sees the path to the retreat. To reach this spot, one has covered just over one *li*, and yet there have been forty-two turnings, and thirty-six separate points of ascent, and with each turning and each ascent, the scenes change in marvelousness.

Within the actual stream, there are also many boulders; the larger ones the size of elephants, the smaller ones, of sheep. There is a separate pathway linking the larger boulders, and this too was made by Shao Shusheng. There is a pavilion directly facing the so-called White Dragon

Pool, and flying waterfalls from ten thousand peaks all rush together into one common flow.

To the side this spot faces Luohan Escarpment, with the "Luohans" fully exposed and arranged as if along a spine. In the midst of this formation there is one gigantic boulder jutting up. After a rainfall, the rainwater flowing off the "spine" upon reaching this boulder crashes against it forming chaotic waves which, thwarted from flowing in a straight current, angrily go splashing off to the sides, and then continue down after dancing about in the air. The woods here are chilly, the stream majestic, its momentum such that in its rush it actually produces a wind.

The leaves of the trees on the mountains on all four sides never wither away in autumn or winter. As the wind blows past, the leaves sing, competing with the various flows of water in producing echoing sounds. If you sleep in the pavilion here, all night long from your pillow you can hear a rushing, gurgling sound, suspecting that a wind-driven rainstorm is suddenly unleashing its attack, or it may be likened to a distant traveler's hearing the roaring of waves in his dreams of rivers and lakes. Thus the name given to the west-facing balcony is Intimate with the Waves. The waterfalls from Heavenly Capital, Bluegreen Roc Bird, and Begging Bowl Peaks come crashing down directly before this pavilion.

And the Brilliant Flowering Pavilion carries an inscription by Chen Jiru[118] of the words "Flying White" [*Fei bai*]. If one exits this from the rear and climbs the steps, one comes to another pavilion surging above the pool carrying an inscription by Cao Fen[119] of Fengjun of the words "Sounding Snow" [*Xiang xue*].

Vol. I [上/11a–b]

白龍潭
Bailong tan, White Dragon Pool

Inspector Li Jingfang of the Tang dynasty (see above) once saw a white dragon in a pool of Hot Springs Stream, and therefore built a hall to the west of the hot springs, engraving its name on the rock. The name White Dragon Pool started with this. Some claim that when the rain falls here, a wind arises and the waterfalls from the mountains in all four directions dip their heads and wag their tails, looking from afar as if they were rushing dragons, hence the name of the pool.

The pool is a hundred or so square feet in overall size. There are numerous large rocks piled up around it, thus forming the pool. Indeed, it has the appearance of a construction that has been planned. The pool's waters receive all the surrounding streams and waterfalls plunging down through the void from several tens of feet of height.

There is one central rock, concave and upward facing, which receives the waters like a mortar receiving the pestle. The sound is thundering, and the waters descend so rapidly that the "mortar" cannot absorb them all at once, and so they dash back up again, spraying out in all directions, and then dripping back down into the pool. These waters obtain their initial force from the piled-high layers from which they fall, but when they are diverted off to the sides of the central rock, they naturally lose some of their impetus.

When rainfall is intense, the streams become as if angry, and impatient of following their accustomed routes, they soar through the air sideways, overpassing the pool, and then flying down again, carrying thousands of thunders with them. At times of calmness, though, the pool is crystal clear and transparent, having the appearance of thin glass, and to the gaze almost seems to be nonexistent. When flower petals fall into the pool, and a slight breeze raises ripples, then and only then can one discern that this is a watery surface.

On all four sides are tall vines and ancient trees, as if a canopy were spread about, or as if there were layers of flags and pennants. At certain times, groups of gibbons linking arms drop down to drink.[120]

It should be noted that White Dragon Pool is the gateway of all the waters of the entire mountain range. When it is about to rain, sometimes there can be seen a white strip of cloud arising from the pool which spreads in an instant throughout all the mountains and valleys, upon which the rain falls profusely.

Vol. I [上/11a–12a]

蓮花菴
Lianhua an, Lotus Blossom Retreat

If one takes one's position in a tower upon the town walls, to the northwest one will see a mountain towering above the lesser peaks below, which are lined up on either side, piercing the skies above, like attendants to the main peak. If one enters amongst these mountains, as one goes further in, they all gradually disappear from view. This is because of the main peak being so tall while the others all join together into a single cliff face. What is required to see the complete view again is a spot facing it from close by, but nearly equally high—could it be that Lotus Blossom Retreat occupies precisely such a spot?

The Retreat is built upon the ruins of the old Hot Springs Hall; the Hall was later moved to the west of the hot springs, while the ruins of the first hall were still preserved up in the mountains. The mountain in that area is pure rock, slanting dangerously down, and with very little water available. But this one spot happens to have plenty of soil, and is several acres wide, with Peach Blossom Stream winding below it. A citizen of the town, one Bao Yuanze [121] purchased the land and built a retreat, a cleft on the left-hand side being occupied by a "Residence of the Pure Woods," with behind this an "*Avataṁsa* [Skt.; Chin. *Huayan*; "Flower Garland"] Pavilion." In the Southern Ming [Ming resistance period in early Ch'ing, 1644–1647], a Mr. Yuan Huang [unidentified] gave the name Lotus Blossom to the retreat, because of its facing Lotus Blossom Peak, although it actually is not aligned precisely across from Lotus Blossom.

When a traveler lodges at Lotus Blossom Retreat, upon rising at dawn he sees all the various peaks emerging from the foggy vapors, as if bathing in them. Heavenly Capital Peak is dead center, like the Lord of Heaven seated, back to a screen and with crown jewels hanging. Bluegreen Roc Bird surges up to the left of this peak: what one can see is just its flowery "crest"—supported by cinnabar sands and purplish rocks—as if the bird were spreading its wings, but with its tail foreshortened.

Lotus Blossom Peak juts up to the right of Heavenly Capital, like buds of lotus not yet fully blossomed, and thus, as if it had a pair of peach blossoms in bloom protecting it from both sides, the central peak is a Jade Folding Screen occupying the space between them, forming a cliff face. Lion Forest and the Bridge of the Immortals are seen in the midst of the darkly swirling haze, acting as buttresses to the scene. For the Retreat acts like a mirror, with all the peaks reflected therein, like a beautiful woman glancing at her reflection and taking pleasure in it.

The Retreat of old had three natural "furnishings:" (1) A lizard-shaped "bench," raising its head, with protruding eyes, all four feet touching on the ground, and its claws angrily spread out, looking as if it were running quickly, with four extensions emerging like scales, such that a man could sit cross-legged on top with four other men around him; (2) A "bell and drum hanging frame"[122] as if beautifully ornamented with elaborate carvings, and bent "iron hooks" comparable in pattern and size to a set of ten thousand saw-toothed hooks—and indeed one might use them to hang real bells or drums; (3) an "altar table," with something like the head of a Persian barbarian, horns jutting upwards, carrying a stone upon his head, positioned in front [as if offering tribute?], and square *gui*-type vessels,[123] to the left with lotus blossoms, to the right with lotus stamens, as if one could separately present the various sacrificial offerings—and yet a viewer at first would fail to realize that the whole consists of ancient tree roots! After rubbing it carefully for a long time, the monks will say that it is sandalwood, or that it is hibiscus wood, or that it is bramble-wood.

The Reteat possesses a bell engraved with a date in the fourth year of the Jianwen period [1399–1403], when it was made. Emperor Chengzu [the Yongle Emperor, r. 1403–1425] got rid of all inscriptions in metal or stone, on stelae or even in the form of woodblocks for printing, and had them all replaced with new ones. That a bell from [just after] the Hongwu period [1368–1399] should have survived for three hundred years cannot be explained other than by the fact of the mountain's extreme remoteness.

Vol. I [上/13a–14b]

鳴絃泉
Mingxian quan, Singing String Waterfall

If one proceeds along Fragrant Stream for several *li*, one encounters limitless examples of what appear to be wondrous carvings displaying their skillfulness; but on close examination, they prove to be rocks. Along the stream itself, there is a tiger blocking one's way, rearing its head high up, exposing its fangs, and looking as if it is about to grab you and devour you. A rock in front of it props up its chin from beneath. Should one come upon this formation unexpectedly, one will be terrified. And so one crouches down, and crawls slowly beneath its belly. This is dubbed Tiger Head Cliff. One *li* or so up this cliff there is a monk on the bank of a brook, standing and vomiting; his hands are holding his back as he strains his neck forward, robe and sleeves fluttering like those of an immortal. It seems as if he couldn't hold his drink, and escaped to this spot to purge himself. This is called Drunken Rock.

Alongside this rock a sound is heard, TONG-TONG, descending from above the forest trees, and the source of this is called Singing String Waterfall. The mountain as a whole is concave in the center and bulging around the sides. In the concave part are rocks piled high, from which the waterfall plummets hundreds of feet to halfway down the mountain, where, obstructed by rocks, it splatters and splashes back upwards, scattering into several tens of streamlets, losing much of its force. Below this point, there is a horizontal rock thirty feet or so in length placed across the void at the base, like a zither [*qin*] placed on a table. This is hollow inside, and the waterfall's main stream passes through it. The splashing froth splatters on this rock, and it sounds as if the frozen strings are being tuned up, all five tones of the pentatonic scale complete! In spring and summer when the waterfall is at its height, the tonic tone is the Yellow Bell, and it sounds like ocean waves swept by winds from heaven, or it beats like a prelude of thunder—yet all these sounds are those of a zither! This is called Horizontal Zither Rock.

Beneath this in turn is a huddled rock which looks like an islet, an atoll, or an island. In color, it is whitish on the obverse and darkish on the bottom, like a pile of snow left over from high antiquity, still not yet melted away. This is called the Rock of Resting Snow.

If one further enters the valley for half a *li*, one comes upon a stream murmuring as it flows against rock, forming a series of three holes. Filling these holes, it further descends, strikes against rock again, and forms an additional five holes. This stream glitters with brilliant light, and is called the Waterfall of the Falling Star. Taking a turn, immediately one encounters on the path a rock leaning against the cliffside, full of cracks, called Sword Rock. Below it, all is stream water, and amongst the chaotic rocks strewn throughout the stream at this point is a well, with narrow mouth and shallow interior, the bottom rounded like a bowl. This will hold ten or so dippers of water. The bottom consists of multicolored pebbles; if these are removed, a new bottom will form, like the bottom of a bucket, just as before. It is impossible to determine how far down these pebbles go. My late father dubbed this Elixir Well.

Above the well is an object bristling with scales—if you happen to touch them, they will cut your hand. It is dragon-like, but lacks a head, horns or whiskers. This is called Scaly Rock.

In the midst of the stream at this spot there is a waterfall rushing along and striking against the rocks. The rocks are unable to stop it, so it sprays wildly into crazy waves and angry froth. This is one huge rock in the middle which blocks it, upon reaching which the flow bends and twists around, with a great display of spinning ripples and twirling whirlpools. Vice Censor-in-Chief Jiang Dong of the Ming dynasty named it Rock of the Swirling Waves.

Alongside the stream here, up on the cliff there is a rock shaped like a great ship just emerging from the Three Gorges. It seats over twenty men. If one sits in it and looks all around, the myriad peaks encircle one, like vines and creepers spreading everywhere, their reflections falling in the water below. All, above and below, is azure blue. My late father inscribed the rock at this spot: A Boat Hidden in the Gully.

Vol. I [上/14b–15b]

仙橋
Xian qiao, Bridge of the Immortals[124]

Mr. Pan Zhiheng[125] states that "according to the alchemist Shen Jingxu, he once went to the Bridge of the Immortals, climbing by means of cotton ropes. In the year *bingwu* of the Wanli period [1606], the monk Dayong constructed a shrine-niche just in front of the Terrace for Concocting the Elixir, and would routinely do meditation walks across this bridge at night. In the summer of the year *imao* [1615], the monk Focheng undertook an excursion to the mountains, and upon returning boasted to me that at the Bridge of the Immortals, in an instant's time appeared out of nowhere creatures like birds flying back and forth in the void, and looking around him, he saw that the peaks were all *scattering about and dashing off in all directions*, and it was as if someone was shouting at them and whipping them on like horses!"

Mr. Fang Gongqian[126] states that "as I descended Brilliant Light Crest, I gradually found myself parting from Heavenly Capital and Lotus Blossom Peaks, and crossing a ridge; I suspected I was already down off the mountains. But although I may have been further down than previously, I was still on the ten thousand foot-long Hibiscus Crest, following stone steps along a stream for two *li* or so. These steps eventually terminated at Separate Peak Retreat. Separate Peak does not connect with Heavenly Capital and Lotus Blossom Peaks; to the left and right are various sword-like peaks, jutting up like halberds. From here I found a pathway in the direction of The Bridge of the Immortals, but when I reached Lion Peak, the path had already run out." Fang ordered his servants to precede him, cutting a way through with sickles and hoes, so he was able to continue climbing, using his hands as if they were feet, and eventually passing Lion Peak with its four great boulders. Moving further down, he came to a grotto, and then ascending again, to another grotto, altogether covering five or six *li* proceeding like snakes slithering or gibbons leaping, experiencing the full range of dangers. The last grotto led finally to a stone platform named the Terrace of Fresh Coolness. Climbing this, he caught sight of Heavenly Capital and Lotus Blossom Peaks, as they burst upon his range of vision. And now he was able to perceive The Bridge of the Immortals like a vast rainbow overstretching a thousand precipices!

Mr. Yang Bu[127] states that "The Bridge extends over the 'Heavenly Ring' as the Tortoise supports Cold Spine Mountain, and not a single bird can manage to fly across it. Its three great boulders formed it together, but where a split appeared in the middle, a pointed rock came to be inserted, patching it up without the slightest flaw. Thus the boulders hold each other up in place in such a way that there is no danger of their falling."

To the side, the bridge overlooks the Abyss of Ten Thousand Feet. I might note that this Yellow Mountains Bridge of the Immortals was taken by many in the past to be a magical formation, sometimes appearing, and sometimes disappearing. It was only with "Mountain Chronicler" Pan [Zhiheng?] that it was first believed that one could actually ascend to it. Mssrs. Fang [Gongqian] and Yang [Bu] both came close to it, but still had the sense that it could only be viewed. The *Gazetteer* states that "if one sits above the Singing String Stream and gazes at the Bridge, it gives the impression of being at the very edge of heaven." It further states that "in front of the Hundred-Rung Cloud-Ladder as well it is possible to catch a glimpse of it." And again, "If one looks straight across at the Bridge from the Terrace for Refining Elixir, it displays five openings, which now hide and now appear, as if they had no fixed position." Still again, it states that "There was a man gathering herbs in the mountains who camped for the night under the Bridge. It was a moonlit night, and he heard, up on the Bridge, the sound of singing and mouth organs playing. At the crack of dawn, when he looked up to see the Bridge, it had disappeared."

And yet, even if the Bridge is *not* phantasmagorical, how could it tolerate to carry the frequent comings and goings of mere creatures like ourselves, with decaying bodies?

The Cypress Tree of the Bridge of the Immortals grows at the base of the stone steps leading to the Bridge. Less than a foot from the tip of the tree, its leaves are as thick as carpeting. Thus it is possible to do a meditation walk *across* the treetop, or to sit there cross-legged, or to lie there to sleep.

Vol. I [上/15b–16b]

老人峯

Laoren feng, Old Man Peak

In front of Compassionate Light Temple, if one gazes at the various peaks, Heavenly Capital surges up, while to the left and right, others seemingly act as props or supports to it. Old Man Peak imposingly stands alone, bowing as if taking the position of guest to the host. If one goes to the left of the temple, turn and proceeds upwards amongst the deep cliffs and ancient trees, when the cliffs come to an end, one will connect with a stream, with marvelous flowers and strange plants growing in clusters everywhere and emitting their rich fragrance. If the traveler sits on a rock here and listens to the stream, he will no longer feel as if he is somewhere in the mountains.

Something more than one *li* further on, there are three or four rock-fingers, shaped like the hand of Buddha, and this is named Buddha's Palm Cliff. Another *li* or so, there is a precipitous cliff to the left, leisurely hanging its escarpments halfway to heaven, like barricades or like walls. There is a gate and a hall, with towers and pavilions and pillared rooms perfectly formed in the midst of all this. This is called the Temple of Empty Signs, consisting entirely of stone cliff faces projecting shadows; it can be gazed upon, but cannot be reached by climbing.

Another three *li* or so is the so-called Guanyin Cliff. Below this cliff is a space which seats several tens of people. Another cliff face juts up to the left of this; in the midst of it there glows a reddish light, and this spot is known as Cinnabar Sand Cave. This cliff face is pocked with holes above but below has spout-like formations; gazing at it, it would appear to be on the brink of collapsing. Some claim that every five hundred years the cave splits open and cinnabar particles spurt forth: those who encounter this phenomenon become Immortals.

Passing beyond this cliff, there are sparse woods and wide rocks along which one can proceed while getting good views. After another *li* or so, one comes to Herb-Gathering Spring. From the midst of this Spring emerge escarpments called Green Hat Slope, Twisting Dragon Valley, and Fragrant Valley. Another five or six *li*, and there are thicker woods with greenish rocks, in complex confusion nevertheless forming a path. The traveler feels as if his body has nearly turned to petrified gemstone; just as it gets darkest and seemingly impenetrable, one suddenly emerges on an open space—and here is Old Man Peak!

The peak is a standing stone looking like an ancient hunchbacked man proceeding to his grave. If one broadens one's gaze, one will see spreading out widely lotus blossom and lotus stamen-like formations all arrayed in martial order and branching off towards Heavenly Capital Peak. And to the east are Bluegreen Roc Bird, Cinnabar Sand, and Purple Rock all branching off. In the center of it all is this peak. Indeed, it dips five times and rises five times, providing formations for the placement of temples therein. Mr. □□□ [three missing characters] of Changshu[128] states that "Proceeding from Guanyin Cliff and upwards, ancient trees support the path, and aged vines cover the rocks. Green bamboo and verdant sedge are everywhere intertwined to adorn the scene. The sunlight will suddenly penetrate all this, and flying waterfalls will abruptly splash through. Then deep darkness will settle in until it is no longer a human realm at all!" The portion of the mountain before one reaches the summit is known as "Blue-Greenery:" could it be for this reason?

Upon ascending to the summit of Old Man Peak, the expanse of heaven is broad and vast, and the clouds spread out below. All thirty-six peaks in varying heights and patterns surge into visibility from time to time. One is dazed, as if one has crossed into a different world. It was only after I attained this spot that I *understood* the Yellow Mountains!

Vol. I [上/17a–20b]

天都峰
Tiandu feng, Heavenly Capital Peak

The peak which is positioned at the center of the Yellow Mountain range, and to which all the other peaks pay court, is Heavenly Capital Peak— None Higher.

Mr. Fang Ye [unidentified] states, "People say that Heavenly Capital is the highest, but there is no basis for this. When I gaze at Heavenly Capital from Lotus Blossom Peak, then it lies before me like a topknot. If

I then follow the shortcut up Heavenly Capital and gaze from it towards Lotus Blossom Peak, then the latter's summit preens itself upwards, and is inaccessible. From this I realize that Lotus Blossom stands supreme."

My friend, Wu Song[129] too at first strongly supported this thesis, but when he stayed overnight at Mañjuśri [Chin. Wenshu] Cloister, and witnessed the sunrise, he came to believe with certitude that it was not so. He states that when the sun first rises, a reddish light obscures the southeastern quadrant of the sky, and a swath as of red silk [as it descends] first covers Heavenly Capital's summit, and only after a while does it also veil the single peak to the southwest. (This must be the peak to which Yuzhang Peak is attached.) Only after another short while, does it veil Lotus Blossom Peak. Thus Wu Song came to realize that in the whole cosmos there is no mountain that surpasses Heavenly Capital Peak.

According to gazetteers, the summit of Heavenly Capital cannot be reached by climbing. But in the mid-Ming period, the monk Pumen[130] and several associates for the first time managed to gain access to it. After this, a monk named Kuo'an, together with a cohort of nine people, gained the summit and piled rocks into a pagoda there. He further erected two poles from which he flew banners and hung votive dishes. Mr. Liu Zhizhi [unidentified] declared that there were Three Wonders of Heavenly Capital Peak, and wrote an essay about them. But few have been those who have braved the climb, because the danger is such that they do not wish to risk their lives.

Recently, however, a certain monk from a nearby temple has made several successful hikes to the top. Should an adventurer smitten with a fascination for natural wonders consult with this man, he will happily shoulder a great rope, insert a sharp pick, and take the lead. Using this technique, there have been several who have made the journey.

First you emerge from the pine-gates of the temple, wind and twist your way to the mountain crevice, when, lo and behold, already the path has run out. From this crevice, one ascends by grabbing hold of creepers and vines. Above there stands a rock like a great Guanyin, solemn and secure, positioned right in the center. If one carefully examines to the left or right, far or near, there is no other rock like it. Pine trees grow from its "arms," looking like willow branches. Behind this rock, light clouds scud past, while green and purple creepers wrap it around. It is just like a painting by Wu Daozi [legendary Tang dynasty painter] on silk! This is named Guanyin Rock.

Once past this rock, everything is overgrown and rough. The head of the man behind touches the heels of the man ahead, as they ascend like a string of fish. In the most difficult spots, one must hang on by one's fingernails and grab hold with one's toes. After five or six *li* of this [i.e., nearly two miles] one finally arrives at a peak, at whose summit reposes a stone like a sleeping ox. This is called The Peak for Plowing the Clouds. Around the base of this peak lie vast rocks all around, flat and smooth, while weirdly shaped pines and ancient cypresses encircle all.

After a short rest, one proceeds towards the east, passing around to the southern flank of the peak. Here one proceeds slowly while facing the cliff face. This cliff has many ancient pines, and on the lower portions creepers like dragon's whiskers, intermingled with mosses. Grasping hold of the pines, and tramping upon the moss one reaches the head of a ridge, then doubles back behind the mountain, now heading north. As cliffs and gullies twist and turn, the way becomes treacherously difficult, full of obstacles. One simply moves forward, hugging the cliffside. In front of this section of cliff, a ridgeback of stone protrudes at an angle, like a suspended cauldron, suddenly rising, suddenly dipping, its sheer mass standing ten thousand fathoms in height. The leader here first climbs, then slides down the other side, landing on his feet beside a secure rock projection which he grabs with his two arms, until he can embrace it and then turn himself around to move forward. This is called Saddleback Rock. When one is embracing the rock, if one looks back over one's shoulder, it seems precisely as if one is hanging in the void, and it is impossible to tell how one has managed to get there!

Next one winds around to the "belly" of the ridge, cuts back towards the south, and suddenly there stands a cliff some twenty or so feet high right ahead. It is impossible to ascend this straight ahead, and so it becomes necessary to rely on a device contrived from two withered trees to reach the top, for the upper part of this cliff protrudes suddenly, while the bottom portion recedes in to a narrower circumference. The leader cuts down branches of the withered trees and interweaves them to make a kind of ladder, and this enables one to grab the upper shoulder and pull oneself up to the top. This is called Tortoise Head Rock.

As one proceeds to the south, one sees yet another sheer cliff face, several hundreds of feet high and broad. There are no crevices or fissures one can grasp hold of, nor are there any places where withered tree branches could be set. The leader informs one that this is the Cliff of the King of Hell, Yama! At the top lies a ridge known as Poison Dragon Back, which is even worse! But once past this latter, it becomes possible to reach the summit with no further difficulty. Once an announcement to this effect has been made, the climbers tentatively crawl crab-like up the cliff, until the halfway point, where there is a transverse crack barely a foot or so in width. Above it protrudes a rock which presses right against one's body, preventing one from standing here. If one crouches in the mouth of this crack, one can reach inside it and grab hold of some pine roots, and thus manage to advance several tens of feet. A gigantic pine tree next blocks one's way, lying nearly horizontal; were one to grasp the trunk around and pass under, one's way would still be obstructed, and ascent would be impossible. Now, at the very top of the cliff protrudes a knob of rock the size of a fist; if one crawls along to the tip of the pine tree, secures the rope to this knob at one end and wraps it around one's body, then swings one's entire body free, hanging in the void from the rope, one can pull oneself up by the rope as by a hanging thread. Upon reaching the top, one can hang the rope back down so the next climber can attach it to his waist, and thus also ascend to the top by leaping into the void!

The ridge now attained winds and twists for over a hundred feet, rearing its head high like a dragon's back or a fish's back. (Poison Dragon Back, also known as Bream Back.) The two flanks are sheer and steep, straight down, and there seems to be no bottom. One dares not straighten out one's body by standing, so one straddles the spine of the ridge and proceeds like a frog, knees following as one's palms take the lead, edging forward by inches. This continues for some fifty paces, when suddenly there is a complete break! The gap is some three or four feet in width. The leader orders the climbers to stand upright. Having gained a secure footing, one then swings one's arms and leaps forward, reaching a level way on the other side! This lasts for just five or six paces, upon which, after a brief rest in a seated position, one again pulls one's way up a twisting climb on natural stone steps. One then emerges from the dense forest, cuts to the east, and winding about clambers to a cypress-grown summit, as if these trees constituted a roadway. These cypresses are less than a foot in diameter, the largest just filling a man's grasp. The branches and trunks extend over several acres of ground, almost dripping with blue-green colors. Fantastic rocks clothed in ancient moss are scattered everywhere among the cypress needles.

Here one cuts south, reaching a cave. Inside of this is a natural stone "oven" and stone "bed." From the cave one emerges on the northern side of the mountain, where one comes upon another cave, over a hundred feet in depth. From east to west it is only a hundred paces in width, while it is wide open both in front and in back. Above it is covered by a stone several tens of feet in width. This is known as the Cave Where Clouds Take Rest. This is the stone grotto visible on Heavenly Capital Peak when viewed from Mañjuśri Cloister. The reason it is so named is that when it is about to rain, clouds are seen to emerge from the cave. When the sky clears, they are seen to return to the same cave. Alongside of this cave is another grotto in which has accumulated a pool fed by a sweet mountain spring, dripping as if with droplets of jade lotion. East of the cave are mountain peaks folding back in wondrous transformations, while south of it are marvelous pines with fish-like scales. All of these trees grow from the summit and form a complex display utterly unlike the pines seen on other peaks. Beneath the pines, green moss grows to a depth of over one foot; if one steps on them, one sinks halfway up one's shins. One then returns to the relatively level area, and following the pines, propped against the cliff face, cuts west. Above now rises a precipice where there is a huge rock, broad and flat like a vast whetstone. The leader now puts down his rope and pick, and shows where, on this rock, formerly were hung the banners and votive dishes. He says, "This is called Three Peaks Shaped Like the Word *Pin* [品], and it represents the ultimate summit of Heavenly Capital Peak! Among all the peaks here, none surpass this spot in height."

When my own party had first started to ascend Heavenly Capital Peak, I noted the stone cliffs and was amazed to hear the statements of the leader. My flesh tingled. But having reached relatively flat places, my manner would become calmer. I noted that each tree, each rock was remarkable, and I loved them all. When we finally reached the ultimate point, we looked at each other and breathed a great sigh of relief.

The leader pointed to the thread of the Yangtze River below, with the various cities of Wu and Yue beyond, including Jinling [Nanking], Chang'gan and their pagodas faintly visible in the vast mist, as if one could count them individually. And now my eyes first opened fully, and my heart and soul first felt completely peaceful.

Now, let it be noted that every square foot, every square inch of the structure of this peak in made of piled-up rocks, crystalline and complexly perforated. Thus the trunks and roots of the pines and cypresses are able to get a root-hold in the crevasses and crannies; looking all around, everywhere there are empty spots visible, with heaven's brilliance gleaming through. No, the form of this peak cannot be established on one uniform basis. From below Heavenly Gate in the east, where Prime Minister originates, and then from this point of origin, looking from Stone Tower, all one sees resembles the five fingers of a great spirit's hand, suddenly expanding, suddenly contracting, separating or clumping together. But if you then climb to Compassionate Light Temple and gaze up, all is like a crown, or level like a suit of armor, whereas again if from White Dragon Pool you gaze at the whole, it all seems centered like a folding screen with no side screens. And if you climb to Light-Bright Summit, then you are facing Lotus Blossom Peak as you stand. For facing forward, turning back, shifting direction with every step, shapes transforming as if in a magic mirror, reflections appearing criss-cross therein—all is so varied that unless you linger there for a very long time, gazing at everything above and below, you cannot get even a vague impression of this single peak. And when you consider the shifts between rainy and clear weather, cold and heat, cloudy and misty, or in clear sunlight or moonlight, everything changing every instant, with no fixed forms at all, so that each man sees his own way and no two views are the same—then even if I managed to present the whole to you in my writing, in the twinkle of an eye it would all have changed again!

For in antiquity, masters of transformational skill would simply render in dyed colors those mountains which men were accustomed to viewing. Even if someone of them could manage to capture in dyed colors these scenes, people would think them too bizarre and unlike actual mountains! And to make matters even more difficult, how could anyone capture such colors as these in a dye!

Vol. I [上/20b–21a]

小心坡
Xiaoxin po, Be Careful Slope

Those who enter these mountains automatically speak of how difficult and dangerous they are! But difficult and dangerous are actually not the same thing. "Difficult" refers to the precipitous cragginess and exhausting steepness, such that one's sinews are stretched to the limit, and one's strength is drained: one's body yearns to rest, and yet one cannot get a moment's secure foothold. But since one continually encounters the wonders circling one on all sides, one's heart and soul are swept away, and one simply forgets the hardship.

But "dangerous" refers to the fact that one's body is unattached to anything; when one glances downward, there is no boundary there! One's heartbeat trembles and one's feet tend to lose their grip. If one fails to heed even a single step, then the terror of the moment is beyond calculation. Although "wonders" may be "circling one on all sides," one has not even an instant to pay heed to them.

Now the mountain paths are more difficult than dangerous. And yet from of old, there have indeed been several spots that are dangerous. Of these, Be Careful Slope is the most extreme. If one ascends from the base of Heavenly Capital Peak to Mañjuśri Cloister, it is necessary to traverse it. On this Slope there are two pine trees jutting out sideways, their roots gripping crevices in the rock, and their branches and needles linked to each other, bowing down before the climber: these are called the Welcoming Pine Tree and Seeing Off Pine Tree. Also on the slope is a huge boulder emerging at a slant, like a tortoise whose back is narrower than its shoulders.

To the left and to the right are sheer cliffs thousands of feet in height. As one climbs this slope, one's spirit feels defeated in advance. One must briefly rest, and settle one's soul, before proceeding again, groping with one's toes and pulling in one's heels. When it seems as if one cannot possibly advance, one looks for a stable spot and plants one's walking staff there, takes a deep breath, and then moves forward again.

Recently some benefactors have widened the path, and at the most dangerous spots have chiselled the rock into steps capable of providing toeholds. And where the two cliff faces are most sheer, they have laid slabs of rock into something like balustrades. Thus even the timid can now bolster their courage, and move forward. Those peaks and ridges which previously no one had an instant's leisure to gaze at now spread before one like a belt, allowing one at leisure to examine their mysteries.

Vol. I [上/21a–23a]

臥龍松
Wolong song, Reclining Dragon Pine[131]

With Appended Discourse on the Pine Trees of the Yellow Mountains

If one passes by the Welcoming and Seeing Off pines, and takes the pathway that leads up stone steps seemingly into the void, going straight up, although there are balustrades protecting one, one's heart will palpitate with fear, and as one squeezes into a constricted rocky crevice, one's spirit feels even more threatened by the danger. But suddenly, one comes upon a large rock, something like a meditation cushion in shape, and if one clambers up on this rock and sits there cross-legged, one will see Heavenly Capital Peak majestically surging upward, as if planting a banner halfway to heaven. Here at last one's mood lifts a bit. And then as well one sees a single pine tree slanting out from the left-hand cliff-face, its branches stretching across to the right-hand cliff face, perhaps ten or more feet in length, attractively coiling and twisting, exactly like a dragon reclining! But though it is reclining, its head seems abruptly to rise, with its horns spiking upwards and its mane bristling, as if it is preparing to rise from its reclining posture. And it is just where this pine ends that one emerges from the crevice.

One who loves the wondrous will here feel transcendence of spirit, and he will leave his affections lingering there in the crevice, and feel as it he cannot bear to leave.

Vol. I [21b–23a]
A Discourse on the Pine Trees of the Yellow Mountains

The pine trees that grow in the Yellow Mountains are praised exclusively on account of their wondrous beauty. Such has been the fate encountered by these pines.

Now, can what a pine tree encounters be described as fortunate? To this I would say, there are both fortunate and unfortunate encounters. What, then, would be described as fortunate? The Yellow Mountains are preponderantly *rocky*, and have very little *soil*. Thus no trees of any other type are able to grow here. It is only pine trees that do grow here, and one could almost say that they entrust their lives to the *rock*, making of the rock their "mother."

For the rock of the Yellow Mountains is precipitous and sheer by nature, slender and straight in structure, unctuous and moist in substance, bizarre and weirdly transformational in posture. Thus the pine tree being conceived in the bowels of the rock is like a divine sage who, prior to birth, first receives instruction in his mother's womb; once born, lending substance to their life are the sun and moon, and providing bathing and fructifying are the clouds and mists. Nurturing and lending color are the tens of thousands of peaks, surrounding and thus providing them with protection. The filthy, corrupted vapors and besmirched dust of the human realm has no way to enter within the four frontiers of the world in which they exist. They are, however, encompassed as well by lightning striking them, frost eroding them, cliffs and grottoes incarcerating and shackling them—and yet their jade-like substance continues to develop, without the slightest moment's let-up. Thus, as they grow, they show the effects of these depredations in a great variety of ways. On the contrary, all of this enhances their wondrous beauty!

Yes, their upright natures under the pressure of these stern forces may bend to accomodate precitious steepness, may be constrained over the course of the years in various ways, often splitting the rock and clutching the peaks, reaching out from the cliffs and stretching towards the gullies, displaying in full the marvelous results of their oppression in a great competition of wonders. Certainly these are utterly unpredictable, nor could they be have been anticipated or planned for by means of any uniform regulations. This is what has been fortunate about the fate they have encountered.

But when we speak of unfortunate, what do we mean? We are referring to the *times* they have encountered. These mountains have been silently nurturing and accumulating spiritual powers for hundreds of thousands of years. But in the mid-Ming dynasty, the monk Pumen first opened the mountains, and pathways were first cut through. And this was the first contact that the pines had with the men of the times. From this time on, men honored them as being Emperors (the Pine of the Roiling Dragon), ranked them with Buddhas (the Pine which Helps One Across), compared them to dragons (the Reclining Dragon Pine), and grew intimate with them as if they were playthings immediately at hand (the Chessboard Pine, the Meditation Cushion Pine, the Welcoming Pine and Seeing Off Pine, the Pine of the Crane Riding in a Canopied Carriage). The names of these pine trees may not have had legs, but they traveled throughout the world in all four directions!

With the names of the pines becoming daily more prominent, was it possible to guard against people flocking to the mountain anxious to catch a glimpse of them? At the present time, even the most remote cliffs and hidden valleys have had their rocks cut out, and trees axed so that crowds could approach on each other's heels. And my fear is that the treasure can no longer be preserved. It has even gotten to the point that ignorant woodcutters cut the pines down for firewood or charcoal, seeking even the most infinitesimal profit in the villages and towns. Yes, the unfortunateness of the pines' fate has reached such a point! Would one not rather that before the mountains had been opened up, their light could have been sheathed in the primordial beginnings, before Chaos had been carved out, so that their Heavenly infinitude of spirit might have been preserved? It would have been worth it, even if the pines had never come to be known at all. Whether one's fate is fortunate or unfortunate depends solely on what one encounters. I take the liberty of lamenting the unique extremity of the fate encountered by those pines that have grown in the Yellow Mountains. I record it here as a warning to those scholars who have been cultivating themselves privily.

Vol. I [上/23a–23b]

一絃天

Yi xian tian, Single Thread From Heaven

At first, when the monk Pumen—Master An—cleared ground for Mañjuśri Cloister, according to his own statement, upon entering the Heavenly Gates and stretching his neck gazing upwards, he saw the myriad peaks brushing against heaven, and wondrous pine trees covering and revealing each other, brilliantly thrusting forward as if they wished to burst forth, he concluded that up above there must be marvels indeed. So he cut the rock into stone steps, forging a path along the cliff face, and the further it progressed, the more marvelous became the sights. He came upon the Reclining Dragon Pine emerging from a crevice in the rock, took a right turn and suddenly found himself blocked by a rocky cliff right in front of him; looking downwards, it was bottomless. He could think of no technique that would allow him to proceed, and in sheer exhaustion, he lay down to nap for a while. At this point, it seemed as if there was a deity on the facing mountain summoning him. He awoke, and constructed a wooden framework which he was able to suspend in such a way that it bridged the space, and indeed upon crossing he came upon scenes of still more wonderful beauty. Then he had pine trees cut down to make a cantilever plank pathway, and named it End of the Ordinary Realm. Once past this pathway, another cliff abruptly rose in front, as if carved into a flat plane. Alongside of it was a single boulder touching the void above, as if it were rising upwards and attempting to contest with the cliff which was higher. These two rock formations seemed about to merge with each other, as if at one time there was a sudden force from on high that split them apart, leaving in the split just enough room for one man to pass through, coming or going, but not without enough room for his two feet to move side by side. The only way through was to crawl along spider-like. And from both sides of the formation, water was pouring down, like flying rain drops even under perfectly clear skies. The pines here all had needles forming whiskers, and bones of iron, their shade intersecting, and their blue-greenery encaging the place. As gibbons and birds called back and forth to each other, their sounds echoed as if inside a huge jar. A beam came shooting down from above, like a dark, dangling thread, and so he named this spot, Single Thread From Heaven. (This needs to be distinguished from the Single Thread From Heaven at Dragon-Fish Grotto.)

Vol. I [上/23b-25b]

玉屏峯 / 文殊院

Yuping feng, Jade Screen Peak, formerly known as *Wenshu yuan*, Mañjuśri Cloister

In between the two peaks, Heavenly Capital and Lotus Blossom, thrusting upwards is a tall peak which looks as if it occupies precisely the middle ground between the two so as to command views of both—this is Jade Screen Peak, and yet men still call it Mañjuśri Cloister. When this latter name was first applied, it would appear that since there were no records of immortals or Buddhas connected with the spot, there was no real basis for naming it thus. So given the peak, they simply called it Xuanyuan [name of the Yellow Emperor], and as for the cloister, they simply called it Mañjuśri. And yet Mañjuśri in fact never came to the East, and therefore is even less canonical than the Yellow Emperor! And yet no one ever changed this name.

It was the monk Pumen, Master An, who officially mandated this name as the result of a single dream. According to his own statement, when he was at Taizhou, he once dreamed that he came to a certain mountain, and, amazed, found himself attending upon the throne of Mañjuśri. Later, when he traveled south, he proceeded from the White Mountains into the Yellow Mountains, searching for the place in his dream but unable to find it. But then in the autumn of the year *guizhou* [1613], from afar he saw Jade Screen Peak and suddenly was moved in his heart; he clambered up there, reaching Cross-Legged Rock. And now he was greatly amazed to recognize precisely the scene from his dream! Thus he built on this spot a cloister dedicated to Mañjuśri. He cut the stone into steps so as to facilitate access, and further named the vantage point Terrace of the Dream Image. The increasing opening up of the hidden mysteries of the Yellow Mountains actually begins from this particular peak.

The marvelous sights on this peak are beyond enumeration. Among the most significant are The Cliff of Light Leaking from Heaven, Lion-Shape Rock, Cross-Legged Rock, The Terrace Where Snow Begins, Immortal Peach Peak, The Pine of the Crane Riding in a Canopied Carriage, the Divine Crows, the Emerald Rooster, and the Heavenly Horse. Once a visitor has crossed over the bridge End of the Ordinary Realm, he ascends the steps and finds overhanging cliffs and covering rocks above, joining together so as to form a deep darkness like that of night. If he looks up towards the summit of the rocky formation, there suddenly leaks through a beam of light from heaven. Here there is a cave shaped something like a well, and inside this cave is placed a wooden ladder perhaps twenty or more feet in length. One crawls along this ladder and emerges from the cave at the other end like a vase that has been pulled out of a well and above its railing by the well-rope. Once emerged, heaven hangs high above and clouds lie below, mountains surging and gullies dipping, and it is as if one had been secreted behind curtains for a long time and was now newly liberated and allowed to come out. This is called The Cliff of Light Leaking from Heaven.

If one now takes a further turn, after perhaps a hundred or so paces, there are stone steps above which pass narrow cliff walls, after which the pathway turns and arrives at the Cloister. The ground in front of the Cloister is level and open, several acres worth. One boulder, backed against Jade Screen Peak, lifts its head as it crouches to the left. It looks like a scholar teaching. Another boulder bows towards the right, trailing a long trunk like an elephant. Two stands of pine trees imposingly display a kind of feathered canopy, facing a rock they surround, as if robing it in monks' cassocks. On this rocks seem to be the marks left by someone seated cross-legged, and indeed this is Cross-Legged Rock.

Peach Blossom Peak faces the foot of Cross-Legged Rock, and flowing from it is Peach Blossom Hot Springs. To the east is Heavenly Capital, and to the west, Lotus Blossom. To the south is a wide-open panorama. This peak commands a downward view of a myriad peaks, like a hovering raptor poised to swoop down and strike. If one proceeds to the right of Elephant Rock, there is a terrace called The Terrace Where Snow Begins, which commands a view of the Rear Ocean straight on. The various peaks of that area will suddenly emerge like awls displaying their pointed tips, with the clouds acting as sheaths. As the clouds gradually disperse, thousands and thousands of cliffs and ranges reveal themselves in sequence, and one would take it for the Three Divine Mountain-Islands floating on the Ocean of Paradise, with the various Immortals and True Ones flying back and forth, and one feels as if one might mount upon the wheels of winds and chariots of clouds, link arms with them and converse with them!

Alongside this Terrace is a rocky formation shaped like a peach, and known as Immortal Peach Peak. To the right are numerous pine trees, all jutting out from cracks in the rock. The leaning "peach" seems to be soaring or flying, overlooking a remote gully below the Terrace. If, from a crevice in this rock, one peers downwards towards the bottom of the gully, one perceives a rock like a crane spreading its wings, and standing on one leg with the other leg withdrawn, and there is a pine tree growing on top of a peak which seems to cover it from afar. This latter is The Pine of the Crane Riding in a Canopied Carriage.

The mountain also features a pair of Divine Crows, which come swooping down from the summit to alight on the arms of the monks. They come to be fed according to a regular schedule. If guests are about to arrive, they will inevitably caw in advance to herald their arrival. And when any guests journey to the mountains, these crows will fly ahead as if to guide them.

Also, on top of the mountain, with the first dawn and as the waterclock is about to run out [around 5 a.m.], there is a bird that cries out in harmony with the crowing of the cocks below the mountains; this the monks call the Emerald Rooster. In form it resembles a pheasant, with blue-green shoulder-feathers and emerald green breast-feathers, and its call is clear and sharp. Unscrupulous scholars have pretended that this is the Heavenly Rooster.

There is also a creature something like a horse, known as the Heavenly Horse. Its coat is brilliant gold in color, and its feet are embraced by the floating clouds. The peaks may be several tens of feet apart, or several *hundreds* of feet, and yet it is able to leap from one to the next and continue galloping. Many of the monks and many travelers as well have seen him just in front of the Cloister.

Vol. I [上/25b]

破石松
Poshi song, The Pine Which Broke Through Rock

If one takes a right turn from the base of the Elephant Rock of Jade Screen Peak, one comes to the so-called Ridge Crossed by Suspension. The mountain path here seems to open, then seems to close up again, while water comes flowing profusely down the cliff face. Upon reaching the edge of the cliff, there almost lacks the space to gain a toehold, and one crosses only by dint of holding on to the rocky surface itself. The flowing water strikes up moist pearl-drops that soak one's clothing. If one then takes another sharp turn, after less than a *li* or so, one suddenly finds oneself in an area between Lotus Blossom and Lotus Stamen Peaks. Starting from a barren, spine-like ridge and piling upwards as if into the void, is the so-called Lotus Blossom Ditch. It is called a ditch because it is filled with rip rap and scrabble scattered everywhere; there is no stream or waterfall pouring through. At the point where this ditch nearly comes to an end, there is a boulder twenty feet high and more than ten feet in circumference, with a pine tree twisting and turning right on the rock, its branches spiralling out in all four directions, providing shade over several acres of land. People can see the top of this tree, but not the trunk, as the trunk is hidden within the bowels of the boulder. After having hatched and grown inside for a very long time, the tree burst through the rock and emerged: the whole looks like a mother embracing its child!

Vol. I [上/26a–28a]

蓮華峯
Lianhua feng, Lotus Blossom Peak

From a hundred *li* away, a blue-green cluster of lotus bloom surges beautifully above the ten thousand peaks; with one's first glance, one realizes that this is Lotus Blossom Peak. As one gradually draws closer, the complete form of the blossom increasingly reveals itself, displaying its shape to all four directions. It is only to the west that there is a gap of one petal. And another peak—Lotus Stamen—juts up from a gully, forming a pendant to this one from a distance.

The dangerous cragginess of Lotus Blossom Peak is not less than that of Heavenly Capital Peak, except that of the path entering this mountain, nine-tenths is more or less climbable. One proceeds along the precipitous cliff west of Mañjuśrī Cloister, advancing horizontally by this for some three *li*, and then descending another three *li*. Here one passes Lotus Blossom Ditch, and moves step by step upwards towards heaven for six or seven *li*. This takes brings one halfway, and here the structures of Lotus Blossom Peak and Lotus Stamen Peak separate from each other. After penetrating this split and proceeding west, if one stops momentarily and gazes about in all four directions, it appears as if one could take a flying leap and pass over the peaks Four Greybeards, Stone Banner, Bridge of the Immortals and the Tortoise-Fish, or could cry out and be answered by echoes from any of them. And yet they are actually any number of tens of *li* away!

Continuing on while gazing about, one proceeds along the northwestern foothills [of Lotus Blossom Peak], following the stone steps upwards. Here one comes upon a boulder hanging downwards, shaped like the trunk of an elephant, for several hundreds of feet. One climbs along this trunk to the left, and on the cliff face above there is a circle-shaped hollow something like a full moon. In the midst is a tree shedding a long, blue-green shaded area, like a shadow cast by a *sāla* tree. (It is popularly known as The Śāla tree in the Moon.) [Between two of such trees the Buddha passed into nirvana.] Below this in turn is a boulder looking to the life like a rabbit, lifting its head and gazing far off, and this is called Rabbit Rock.

Proceeding beyond this point and upwards, the path appears to come to an end, but here the cliff suddenly splits open into an opening like a cave mouth. One must enter this sideways, shoulders and back pressing up against the rock, and moving upwards until one finally emerges again. And then one enters a series of such cave mouths in sequence! Each time one emerges from one of these, one must stretch out one's neck and peer ahead, and then suddenly Heavenly Capital Peak will surge up right in front. And then suddenly Cloud Gate and all the other peaks will bow down before it. Then equally suddenly, Lotus Stamen Peak is jutting up right there in front, as if one could reach down and pluck it out! Suddenly again, just beyond one cave mouth, if one gazes downwards, there is no visible bottom, but there is a boulder slanting across. If one grabs hold of this rock while looking down, one can avoid a feeling of terror. And there, vastly expanding, all the peaks beyond Cloud Boat can be taken in in one limitless view. On emerging from each cave mouth, one's heart and vision are transformed, and there are no less than nine of these in a row! Finally one comes to a stone grotto-like hut, and the cave mouths come to an end. This hut is on the western side of the peak, on a protuberant cliff, and was established by the monk Pumen in the year *jiayin* of the Wanli period [1614] when he was opening up the pathway to this mountain.

In front of the grotto is an ancient cypress gnarled and twisting as the wind has shaped it, and emitting a fragrance that wafts down the mountain; it can be smelled by all for a distance of ten *li*. Alongside of the grotto is a mountain spring whose accumulated waters of a single day and night are sufficient to provide three men for an entire year without running out! (No name has ever been given to this spot; today, only the deserted ruin is left.)

Now climbing to the right and upwards, one comes upon a large boulder like a bloated stomach, with several depressions cut out of it. One continues only by embracing this stomach and clutching the depressions, and creeping windingly forward. With another turn, the danger becomes even more pronounced; the path on rock comes to an end, and wood has been placed here to form a bridge. Crossing this bridge, one next turns slightly, only to come upon a sheer cliff, and again the path runs out. Here wooden pieces have been placed to form a ladder. This ladder requires a couple of attempts, before ascending crossbeams that only provide a mere toe-hold! Here one is, body suspended over a drop of thousands of feet, climbing with knees rubbing the rock! And now one finally reaches the summit!

Before one started entering the cave mouths, gazing from outside one would have thought that ahead lay only firm ground to walk upon, and that the upper portion of the mountain was one solid, iron-hard wall. But after penetrating through the mouths, one begins to realize that there are hundreds of thousands of individual rocks alongside each other, linked together to form pathways which are hidden within the bowels of the peak. And these twist and cut back on each other like lotus stems penetrating the bowels of the peak and only afterwards emerging; or it is as if one were climbing multiple layers of terraces on the actual lotus blossom itself.

Finally sitting upon the summit, one perceives that this peak truly is positioned at the very center of the Yellow Mountains, and the ten thousand other peaks are like the pleats of its robe. Only Heavenly Capital Peak stands equal, and no lower than it. When the weather is clear, one has a view of tens of thousands of *li*, and all the rivers, mountains, and lakes are seen laid out in perfect order. To the northwest, where the sky seems to end, there is a dark shadow something like the shape of a bow lying down, vast in form and covering an entire corner of the horizon, remaining unchanging for hours. On careful examination, it proves to be a mountain range, but no one seems to be clear as to its name.

Along the summit ridge lie three peaks, one of which is slightly lower than the other two by several tens of feet. There is a clear spring flowing forth from it, sweet yet astringent in taste. Some claim that if one uses the water from this spring to wash the eyes of a blind man, he will be able to see again! Also, in this spring are produced fine sand particles which on being taken in the hand put forth a remarkable fragrance which will not dissipate even over night.

The other two peaks are equal to each other in height, but because of a crevasse in the rock, only one of them is climbable. The point where they split apart is so dangerously precipitous that it is absolutely impossible to climb. My friend Wu Zhilu[132] [1644–1715] says that his uncle, the Hanlin Scholar [Wu] Tingjian, once was inspired to *leap across* the gap, upon which he piled up some rocks to form a terrace to commemorate the event! But then, when he looked back, he became terrified, and his feet could not move! His companions, after a hundred attempts, managed to drop him a rope from the other side, and only with this was he able to be extracted. Today, the piled stones can still be seen.

Some several tens of paces beyond the summit is the Tortoise Rock, which is narrow and precipitous, with pines and junipers clustered on top. Its four cliff faces are absolutely sheer, and no one can reach the top.

Vol. I [上/28a–29a]

喝石居

Heshi ju, Residence Where One Shouts at Rocks

Passing two *li* or so beyond Jade Screen Peak, there is a rustic house with just a few bays of space. Several large rocks are as if glued to the cliff face above, protruding straight out and seeming as if about to fall while never falling. The house appears to prop up the rocks, and the one who resides there is at peace with the situation. The mountain monks have transmitted this account: when rocks fall from the top of the peak, just as they are about to strike the residence they suddenly stop dead in their tracks, just as if someone had shouted at them, "Halt!" Hence the residence has been named Where One Shouts at Rocks.

The monk here says that he once saw, late in spring, a troop of gibbons, each holding a flower, no two flowers of precisely the same color. When the entire troop arrived, in sequence they each ascended Lotus Blossom Peak, each selecting a rock on which to sit. One instant after this was completed, the entire troop let out a wail, and then they all scattered and disappeared. The monk followed, tracking them, but could not find a trace of them. One day, on the spur of the moment, he scaled his way halfway up the peak, where he found, hidden away deep within the mountains, a rock hollowed out like a wine beaker, the liquid in it pale red in color. He scooped some out, drank it—and it was wine! Sweet and crisp, fragrantly perfumed, and he realized it had something of the fragrance of the flowers held by those gibbons, as if infused in it.

For the immortal gibbons of the mountains, two grey ones for every white one, do not flock together with the ordinary gibbons. When the climate is clear and lovely, they will freely emerge to observe the cloud-sea below, white ones crouched on the rocks looking like snow. The mountain monks call them Old Snow Gentlemen. If they raise their hands to wave at him, he will look up, yawn, and, gazing at them, respond with a gesture of his hand! As for the grey ones, their whiskers too are entirely white. Often they seem to serve the white ones, one on each flank, scratching their backs or massaging their bodies, as if they were servitors not daring to stand upright in their presence. Few are those who get to see this.

The other gibbons form troops and do not reside in any fixed location. When they pass through a gulley beneath the cliffs, they inevitably search out the most hidden, remote spots, eating all the flowers and fruits they can find there until these are exhausted. Only then do they head elsewhere. Throughout the mountain, these gibbons will form troops and then form themselves into a circle. If one goes out to observe them, upon numbering them it always turns out that each troop has precisely ninety-nine gibbons. Their fur is greenish-yellow—not limited to a single color. It is warm and thick, suited to resist the cold. But when everything freezes over, the troop will huddle all together, forming a huge ball, and then *roll* along the clifftops! Those gibbons on the inside of the ball will, after a long while, rotate to the outside, changing places with the gibbons there, who take their places within. And thus they continue rotating places without cease. The people of the mountain call this the Ball of Gibbons.

Vol. I [上/29a]

白步雲梯

Baibu yunti, The Hundred-Step Ladder through the Clouds

Upon passing the Rock of the Lotus Gatherer in [The Pond of?] the Immortal Goose, one finds that the path abruptly comes to an end. Careful examination reveals that there is a ladder in a crevice of the rock; following this ladder downwards, the stone cross-beams become extremely narrow, incapable of accomodating an entire foot. The guide will frequently reach back to take one's hand, coming to a full stop on each rung. It feels as if one is falling from the sky! One traverses something over seven hundred of these rungs, and yet it is only called Hundred-Step Ladder because they have reduced the number as a consolation to the timid. And the reason it is called Ladder through the Clouds is because it is claimed that in the past, whenever someone descended the ladder, clouds would obscure the view below on purpose so that the person would not see how treacherous it was, and thus would dare to proceed.

After the ladder comes to an end, one turns into a rocky gorge with fantastic pines and beautiful rocks, and here at last one is able to gaze about on an open view. Then, arriving at the mouth of Tortoise-Fish Grotto, one sits on a rock to rest for a while. The guide now points back up to the ladder-rungs of stone one has just traversed, hanging like an elephant trunk down into pure void, apparently unattached to anything. Here are shifting sands, flowing downwards no one knows how far.

Vol. I [上/29b]

鰲魚洞
Ao'yu dong, Tortoise-Fish Grotto[133]

Mr. Wu Zhantai[134] states that after one has traversed the Hundred-Step Ladder Through the Clouds one comes upon a fish-like formation bristling its dorsal fin and thrusting its head up into the void as it leaps upward. This is called Tortoise-Fish Peak. Its northern summit is entirely blocked; were it not for the work of the Five Heroes in breaking through a grotto-tunnel here, there would have been no way to gain access to it.

First entering the mouth, it is so dark that people cannot see each other. Linking arms like gibbons, the party must ascend by leading each other. Finally, some light seeps through a crack in the cave wall, and one begins to be able to distinguish one's companions. Emerging from the grotto at the other end, one finds oneself as if floatingly hovering above the white clouds. Looking back towards the path one has followed to get here, it can no longer be seen.

For this is the spot where the pathways to the Front and Rear Oceans [of clouds] branch off from each other. To the right of the peak is a stone precipice that looks as if it had been carved out. Its fertile area does not extend for even a few feet, and yet it is several hundreds of feet tall. This cliff juts up into empty space, with nothing to either side of it. It is called Pine Stone-Bridge. From here, gazing about in all four directions, one overlooks thousands and thousands of feet of rock without the least bit of soil. The twising pine branches emerge bursting from crevices in the rock, as if reaching out to one. It is possible to drag oneself up by these, and to sit upon the canopy of the trees.

Vol. I [上/29b–30b]

天門
Tianmen, Heavenly Gate

Heavenly Gate is located in the foothills of Heavenly Capital Peak. There are two rocks there which have a grotto-like opening between them, like a double gateway opening up. If one ascends from Old Man Peak, step by step along the toe-hold pathway towards Heavenly Capital, it feels like a wisp of smoke from a seal-calligraphy incense-burner, wafting amongst the cliffs. Along the entire route are fantastic pines, and split rocks, weirdly gesturing as if with claws, soaring in a dance right before one's face. If several men are climbing together, and one happens to stop for the slightest rest, he will be lost to the others, and he will hear the cries of those ahead as if faintly arising from the very edge of heaven. If he pursues these voices, he will see ahead what appear to be men leaning against pine trees and awaiting him far ahead, but when he finally reaches the spot, they turn out to be rocks!

For many of the rocks here have a human appearance, while others are shaped like other varieties of creatures, and as men have exercised their imaginations to name them, no name has been given which fails to match the actual appearance. But in fact, these are merely minor displays of the Creator's artistry, and the names given are not elegant and suitable. True connoisseurs will ignore them.

One the front slope, there existed of old a teahouse; it is said that Mr. Gu Zongbo (Xichou) [unidentified] of Chaozhou changed it into a mountain post-house. Then, in the seventh year of the Chongzhen period of the Ming dynasty [1633], a monk who was staying here dreamed one night that a god appeared to him and told him that at the crack of dawn, he should take a pathway away from this spot so that he could avoid a calamity about to occur, and that he should not be afraid. The monk on awaking followed this advice, and just when he had traveled a mere half-*li* down the mountain, at the summit there was a great crash of thunder and howling winds, and huge hailstones struck down on all four sides. Large boulders were hurled about everywhere, and the uproar shook slopes and vallies. Rocks burst into flame and were reduced to ashes, as lightning flashed, clouds flew wildly, streams bubbled up and entire peaks collapsed. In the midst of all this there appeared a reddish light surrounding a dragon, which then flew away. With this, the sounds quieted down, the dusty atmosphere cleared, and the mountains were perfectly quiet all around, just as before the storm.

When the monk returned, he found that the house had been moved several tens of feet away, but that there was not the slightest bit of damage to its beams and tiles! The mats were still perfectly in place, and even the flowers in the vases were not the least injured. A vast boulder, carried by flowing waters, had come crashing down in front of the house, with five pine trees growing on top of it, but despite the movement of the boulder, there was not the least damage to the barks, branches and needles of the pine trees. Instead, they seemed almost to have feeling as they nodded and tossed and provided a belt of beauty; Today the pines and rock remain, but the house has long since fallen into ruin.

Vol. I [上/30b–31a]

擲缽峯
Zhi bo feng, Tossed Begging Bowl Peak

The mountain taken in in a panoramic view is entirely craggy and precipitous. But there is a rock, as if tossed down from on high, several hundreds of feet tall and several hundreds wide, shaped like a begging bowl, and covering the craggy and precipitous peak. Whenever there is a fresh clearing of weather, wispy clouds emerge and fade, partially obscuring and partially setting off the sides of this rock. One would suspect that when it first fell down and covered the mountain, it must have plummetted a very great distance, and thus even after landing its residual momentum caused it to grope to the left while moving to the right, continuing to wobble without achieving stability.

In the past, this was called Begging Bowl Peak; it is positioned between the two springs, Peach Blossom Spring and Prime Minister Spring. Rector Tang Binyin[135] changed its name to Tossed Begging Bowl Peak. At one time in the past there was an artisan who climbed this peak; he cut down trees to form a suspension bridge to an opposite cliff, and then by means of cut-off sections of wood reached the peak. There, in a cliff face to the side was a stone niche, from a lattice-like opening in which there shone forth a reddish glow, formed of pulsing beams of light. Axe in hand, the artisan entered this opening, and saw a branch of petrified lotus blossom, rooted in the very heart of the rock. This he cut off with his axe, and made an offering of it at a Buddhist temple. It is said that its radiance continued to pulsate for several decades, and that it never lost its color.

Nine Dragon Peak, taken at the Heavenly Sea,
photo by Wang Wusheng.

Vol. II [下/1a–b]

九疊泉
Jiudie quan, Ninefold Spring

If one proceeds along Bitter Bamboo Stream for ten or more *li*, one comes to a spot where ancient trees form a deep copse, with intertwining branches casting thick shade. Stone steps now lead one straight upwards to where, as if in the blue sky itself, there hangs a pavilion called the Heavenly Girdle Pavilion. Sitting here, one's ears are filled with the roar of windblown waves, continuing without cease. This is the sound of a mountain spring in a mountain gorge right before one. Gazing up, one sees the series of places where the stream comes flying down, fall after fall; and the series of places where the stream forms pools, basin after basin. Then it continues flowing down, into still further falls. Counting the pools, there are nine in all.

When the gorge is calm, and the water flowing relatively slowly, the pools are limpid and clear in appearance, as if a string of green pearls had been scattered about in the gorge, inlaying it with gemstones. But after a great rainfall, the flow rushes along with angry waves, twirling and twisting, crashing against the rock, and one feels as if all the streams of the entire mountain had turned into waterfalls, and that these had all united to add to the power of the flow.

Before autumn has lasted very long, deep in the woods the trees are touched with frosted reds and yellows, and these intermingle their embroidered colors with the bluegreens of the mountain pines. Then this stream, like unfurled silk, half hidden, half revealed, goes winding its way through the clouds.

The gazetteers give as one name for this sequence, Nine Dragon Pools. If one turns upwards to the right of the pavilion, and then looks back down, the nine levels are suddenly below one, and the sound gradually diminishes in the distance. But few are those who have been able to penetrate to the source.

Vol. II [下/1b–2b]

雲谷禪院
Yungu Chanyuan, Cloud Valley Ch'an Meditation Cloister

Cloud Valley Ch'an Meditation Cloister, also named Spring of the Grand Councilor, is located below Alms Bowl Peak in a mountain ravine. If from the tip of this peak one proceeds another five *li* toward higher ground, one may rest at the Pavilion of the Heavenly Girdle. Another *li* or more, and there is a rock with a gaping cavity like a gateway. If one squeezes one's body into this, a path winds on past fantastic rocks crouch and hide beneath towering trunks of ancient trees. Twisting and turning one's way further along, it gets more and more hidden and mysterious. Sounds of birds and sounds of the mountain spring, sounds of wind through the trees—unless you linger, sitting there for a long time, you cannot possibly distinguish them all.

Upon proceeding for fifteen *li*, past several hundreds of bends, one suddenly comes upon vine-covered pines, cypress, and tamarisk trees growing in straight rows on either side as if this were an avenue. Penetrating the shade of these trees is a small bridge, and this leads to the gate of the Cloister.

The Cloister at first was the private estate of Mr. Wang of Yen-chen [unidentified]. However, in the year *jiyou* of the Wanli period [1609], the monk Yu'-an, Master Ji, came to the Yellow Mountains. Mr. Wang discussed the matter with him, and the Master was delighted, upon which Mr. Wang presented him with the entire property. In just a few years, halls and rooms were completed in front and behind, and refectory, bathhouse, and dormitories were completed suitably.

Master Ji when young attached himself to Master Hong, Yunqi[136] and was ordained by him in full with all the vows, cultivating the Pure Land School. And upon founding this temple, constructing halls for serving Buddha, he maintained lamps illuminated for all twenty-four hours, incense inscribing its seal calligraphy forms on the air, all in gratitude for Buddha's beneficence. In the dormitories he housed the monks, using water clock and singing bells to demarcate the night, while wooden clappers and Sanskrit chanting would sound out purely, startling men awake from their delusional errors.

The dormitories were also used to welcome guests, and generous or parsimonious hospitality was appropriately meted out to demonstrate the ultimate equality of all. In all matters of rules and regulations he followed the regimen of Yunqi. There would be sixty or seventy monks at any given time, yet the place was as silent as if it were deserted. While residing at this cloister and promoting the Dharma, he insisted as well on welcoming those of "ancient virtue" in the world [i.e., upright officials and Ming loyalists]. Those whom I alone got to see there were Master Bo'an,[137] who had come from the Lingyan Temple, and Master Tiefu,[138] who had come from the Tiantong Temple, both traveling one after the other to stay at the Cloister.

In front of the Cloister, there is a peak surging straight upwards, halfway to heaven. It directly faces the Cloister gate. If one takes one hundred paces outside the Cloister gate, there is a creek flowing purely, suddenly speeding up, suddenly slowing down, with a vast rock standing like a pillar right in its midst. It has a squarish, broad top of remarkable regularity, twenty feet by fifty feet in size. If one climbs to this rock, and gazes upwards, one sees that one is entirely surrounded on all sides by mountain peaks. In front of this rock, along the creek, are growing many peach trees with twisting branches and curving trunks, the blossoms being different in color from the ordinary variety. Within the creek itself there is a type of fish with long tail and *four legs*, with a young dragon's head and an older dragon's spine. It is spotted black as lacquer. This fish can *climb a tree and eat the birds there.* Some visitors have actually witnessed this. As for the monks, they claim this is simply the manifestation of a dragon.

If you descend one or so *li*, you come upon the pagoda of Master Bo'an. This monk's original name was Zhengzhih, and he was formerly the Supervising Censor, Xiong Kaiyuan. Towards the end of the Chongzhen period, he petitioned against Senior Grand Secretary, [Zhou] Yanru, and was punished with the bastinado as well as with military exile to the frontier. Later on he became a monk, residing in this spot in his later years. I had the opportunity of visiting him, and he described to me all his various complaints and causes of resentment, speaking at great length without ending. He next moved to Mount Hua, but before too long, he passed away, leaving a last will and testament stating he wished his bones to be returned for burial in the Yellow Mountains.

Vol. II [下/2b–6b]
Appended document by Chan Master Bo'an recording regrets about the Yellow Mountains

What "resentments" could there be about the Yellow Mountains? In any group of hundreds of thousands of people, not even one is likely to get to come visit, and there can be no regret greater than this! I myself was so fortunate as to be able to come, but I cannot use my words as a substitute for the *eyes* of those hundreds of thousands who *could not* come, and so the regret is not dispelled. Why is this? When it comes to human affairs, one can describe them with considerable skill. In speaking of something where Heavenly [i.e., natural] and man-made aspects are half and half, one can vaguely approximate the truth. But in speaking of what is entirely Heavenly [natural], then there is nothing adequate one can say. Many can string together analogies for things, but very few can develop them into inferences. Therefore, the mere names of things cannot be developed into full descriptions. Thus, having heard the Way, one can patch together a description which will suit oneself; but what is suitable to transmit to others will be limited to superficial matters of the world. The profoundest Dharma is different from this: would attempts to describe it not produce delusion? When it comes to composing works "summoning to travels," few are the available analogies. Now, I had been familiar with the name of the Yellow Mountains from youth, and I considered that travels to such a place could not possibly be lacking in written accounts of them. So I read all the relevant travel essays, and with this, my motivation to write about such travels was suddenly deflated. This was because those writers had comprehensively covered everything with skilfull beauty, fully encompassing all the elements they had painstakingly sought out. How could there possibly be anything left over to cover?

But when I finally undertook my own trips, climbing to high places for views, I only then realized that the recording of such excursions must each be suitable to the particular places, and thus there were a multitude of aspects remaining unexhausted in such writings. Not only had earlier writers not exhausted all the twistings and turning, but even when later writers made the attempt, they too had not exhausted them. And indeed, not only have I myself at the present day not exhausted these twistings and turnings, but I can envision that in future days as well I will never fully exhaust them!

And so, can one really say that there is nothing at all to add to the sacrifices offered in such places by the ancient monarchs, or to the grotto-residences carved out by the Immortals? Indeed, one cannot. One may gradually get tired out, but then suddenly, one will come back to life. Things may be flat and dull for a while, then abruptly become dangerous and invigorating. One may be slightly constrained, and then greatly expansive. Such is human nature! The vast cannot be comprehended all at once. The dangerous as well can go unrecognized. Because of these three factors, one has often regretted bitterly not being able to encompass at the same moment the totality of the principles of things. One may grasp mountains and bodies of water, but it is hard to put them together to form the Ten Islets and Three Islands in the ocean of Paradise. Stones and trees may be grasped, but it is hard to cause them to jut up and flourish amongst pines and catalpas on the Western Sacred Peak, Mount Hua, and the Eastern Sacred Peak, Mount Tai. Are these not cases of the vastness of true "grasping?"

Thus what one views with one's fleshly eyes is no more than tiny holes in mustard seeds. And yet expand this slightly and one gets to the vast expanse of being!

After having crept along a few pathways, you will have stored in your mind a mountain here and a tree there, hardly worth the effort you have put forth. How can you, therefore, feel "lively," "awe-inspired," "expansive?"

At this point there emerge understanding people who will make a pool from a basin, with stones forming islands, and fish swimming around them in a circle, representing any number of thousands of *li.* There are also talented gentlemen who will mark out the boundaries of a garden, piling up soil and stones to form miniature mountains, and planting therein various plants, so that as a man twists and turns his way through the winding paths, he does not realize that he is in a space no greater than that beneath a desk! All who need to experience gradually in this way, can suddenly experience liveliness. But it cannot make people expansive, nor can it make them awe-inspired. And thus such gardens are utterly lacking in the element of "dangerousness."

Now, in the case of an area of thirty thousand acres, encompassing beautiful wonders innumerable in profusion, if one climbs to the surging ridges, all the feelings will compete to present themselves. It is lively. It is expansive. But one thing still lacks: it cannot make someone awe-inspired.

The ninefold layers of the Wu'yi Mountains are another case; these are all minor dangers, and without fully exhausting one's effort, one can garner them all. Inspiration to awe and liveliness are both complete here. But, alas! since the mountains are not *vast*, they cannot cause one to feel expansive! What is more, one regrets the fact that the Heavenly [natural] and man-made elements here are half and half; it is not completely Heavenly [natural].

The Yellow Mountains bring together peaks carved sheer, of thousands or several hundreds of fathoms, thousands of them all within one vast panoramic view. It is as if the Son of Heaven were holding state in the midst of surrounding mountains and vast lakes, while an Imperial Guard of the Feathered Forest, spears in hand, formed his entourage. It is as if a garden filled with tall bamboo one day had suffered the ignominy of being cut down, and new groves of wild bamboo had angrily sprung up everywhere. Or it is like a vast regatta of merchant vessels gathered day and night on the Hsiao and Hsiang Rivers, clustered together, with their masts spiking upwards towards heaven. The bases of these peaks cannot be even an inch apart, and their shoulders rub against each other so tightly that not even a single crenellated wall could interpose between.

The waterfalls plunging down from these mountains are perhaps three thousand fathoms in height, and they appear to the eye to be the Silvery River [Milky Way] falling from Heaven. The peaks themselves are a thousand fathoms high; gazing down from them, it is impossible to penetrate to their outer limit. All one can do is sit in a state of "neither thought nor non-thought," the realm of Jambudvīpa [one of seven islands surrounding the cosmic Mount Meru], as if on the brink of falling. There is no greater "dangerousness," there is no greater "vastness," there is no greater "suddenness," and anyone who does not here experience inspiration to awe, liveliness, and expansiveness, must be lacking in human feeling.

And then, after a single rainfall, the vapors from streams and springs merge together, forming the so-called Ocean of Cloud. Where it is thick in accumulation, like deep snow sparkling in sunlight, and of the thousands of peaks, some hide half their forms, while others are sunk in the clouds to their shoulders, and still others reveal only their conch-shell hairdos and darkened eyebrows bathing in the silvery sea! Where it is shallow in accumulation, then it only reaches to the feet of the mountains and there stops, leaving innumerable green bamboo-like forms jutting upwards both tall and sparse, or short and thick, all presenting to the utmost their great beauty, while the green colors and green luminosity, white colors and white luminosity are such that no treasures known in the world can possibly compare.

Of old it has been said simply that the pines here were born in High Antiquity, and that they do not have a single layer of soil in which to sink their "claws," but that they have grown to the height of a man, while the length of their "manes" [needles] reaches only that of eyelashes! The clustered blue-green of their colors is comparable to that of an emerald oil-paper canopy. There are tens of thousands of them in wondrous array, taller and shorter ones mixed in formation amongst the cliff faces, linking one to the next without end, while others grab hold with a fist or finger, just like human figures.

As for the elements that allow these mountains to usurp the title of Most Beautiful from all other mountains, there is nothing to choose between the rocks and the trees. With these together, one must praise the place as unique. Who would have thought there could be mountains and streams of such wondrous transformative beauty, which have never failed to complement each other? Examining them, if one selects the time when dawn winds die down, then moist clouds will be seen to dry out, arising in the formation of waves from the Mermaids' Palace; one does not then see ripples as calm as the surface of a mirror. Although they churn and shake in a hundred different formations, suddenly they will change shape and greenish and white lights will intermingle, which must slightly yield to the former scintillatingly brilliant configuration.

Also worthwhile are times of complete clearing, when nevertheless a wispy haze forms, and the ten thousand mountains turn a pure dark color, projecting the appearance of human eyebrows and hair, all dark blue-green. And at some dawns, all is clear and void, and ochre-colored markings appear in sequence, exactly as if ten thousand ships were sinking in water, or incense was spreading high and becoming paths for the partridges, suddenly narrowing into horses' hoofs in midair, then sharpening further into chicken bones! Although these mists rise to Heaven, spreading their fantastic hallucinations, whenever they are seen, they amaze one's eyes, but because of the pervasive darkness they are not easy to encounter, which can be cause for lingering disappointment.

Of the sharply protuberant mountains I have seen in the Guangdong-Guangxi regions, the phenomena of transforming clouds were not lacking in marvelousness. But if one speaks of them in relation to the Yellow Mountains, to say the difference is enormous is not to flatter the

Yellow Mountains. Although those other mountains may be "sharp," their configuration towards front and back is most awkward, and would not make for a painterly composition. And though their clouds do transform, they are banked up in such a manner that they easily disperse, which leads to few displays. And so they must yield in beauty to those of the Yellow Mountains.

For human life is like that of a louse living in somebody's pants. Few are the good aspects of it. There are only the liveliness, expansiveness, and inspiration to awe here described which a man can achieve by putting palm to earth, arriving at the place, and thus finding his blindness cured, and the dust swept off his lapels. Now, in the hundreds of thousands of *li* in the world, there is not one inch of territory which Anhui natives have not visited. But these mountains they do *not* come to! And in the hundreds of thousands of *li* in the world, those governing in Anhui do not find it easy to add to their number of servitors, and so they alone begrudge a journey of a hundred or so *li* to reach these mountains. And though they may not come, occasionally there may be one who does make it here, then they call it "sightseeing in the mountains," limiting their feelings to that. So even though this "host of the place" has finally gone there, there has been no benefit to his soul.

When the situation is made as obvious as this, one might as well yell it out loudly—there will be no response. Or to put it differently, one may say that there is a pathway to liveliness, expansiveness, and inspiration to awe hidden away here, taking the form of the mountains. But these people gaze with their eyes and see nothing, cock their ears and hear nothing. And yet they could *get there* with not even a single step!

Sirs, if you do not love the place, then either simply cover your mouths and mock, or, if not, hang your heads in shame and depart! Ah, one wishes they could put aside their petty-mindedness, like suppurating ulcers, and halt the carriages with which they attempt to undertake excursions! What difference, indeed, is there between what they do and exchanging the Black Dragon's Precious Pearl for a dung-beetle's dung-pellet!

For all antiquity, not a single man has gone to the Yellow Mountains for self-cultivation: I am not regretful on behalf of the mountains, but rather on behalf of all those men! But if I thought that merely by saying this, I could thereby fulfill the promise of the Yellow Mountains, it would be like gazing *westward* to see the Fu-sang Tree [the cosmic tree in the east, from which the sun rises]. The wonders of the Yellow Mountains can only be experienced by going there yourself; they cannot be approximated by anything the tongue utters or the writer's brush composes. And so how could I *not* feel regretful?

Vol. II [下/6b–7b]

逍遙溪
Xiaoyao xi, Stream of Free and Easy Wandering

Behind Cloud Valley one crosses two ridges, the path penetrating the ruins of the old Source Retreat. Another *li* or more, and one is up to one's shins in scrabble, while bamboo clumps brush against one's head. One must aim at the open, bright space ahead to know how to proceed. When the path ends, there is a sheer cliff, so one turns to follow a stream, the current strewn with rocks, and emerging between sheer embankments. As one proceeds, these gradually broaden out, until one reaches a wide-open space, and here the stream becomes the Stream of Free and Easy Wandering, also known as the Stream of Patterned Fish.

Following this stream, water and rock seem to be equally distributed, the rocks craggy and multiformed in strange shapes. Crouching ones, rearing ones, sheerly cut ones, roundly spiralling ones, each of them full of piercings and penetrations. Each rock has a unique shape of its own. One walks on top of these, while the water flows at their bases, and it is as if the stream's gurgling and one's breathing are responding to each other.

Then, abruptly, one deserts the stream and ascends precipitously, along a route where gibbons and birds would hardly be able to advance. There is a bridge of rotten wood; halfway across one must turn and, clutching the cliff face, creep forward like a snail, inching ahead then standing upright and stepping with great caution so as to avoid the worst of it.

The stream has three sources. One of these is central, and the other two flank it to left and right. That to the east, as it grows strongest, merges with the central and western ones in a great clash of currents, as if they were struggling with each other among the rocks. Mr. Tang Binyin [see above] has named this Fighting Jade.

Along the eastern defile, there is a pool, as if a mirror had been sandwiched in between the cliffs, whose steepness adds to the power of the scene. Below this is a series of pools, almost innumerable. The particularly wonderful ones are Signet Pool, Moon Pool, Sword Pool,

Rhinocerous Horn Pool, and Flower Pool—all of these named in accordance with their shapes, whether square, round, elongated, twisting, hornlike, or like a woven pattern of petals. The shapes are fantastic, and the colors too are fantastic. If the pool is shallow, the color is pale azure; if it is deep, it is deep blue. If the rocks in the pools are white, their color is pristine. If the rocks are ochre-tinted, their color is a rich vermilion like that of seal-paste. If the rocks are tinted like inlaid metal, the color is dazzlingly golden.

In the depths of these pools, there seem to be divine creatures hidden in hibernation. But these depths are such that they cannot be plumbed.

Proceeding along this stream, two thirds of the way one must tread upon rocks, while one third of the way the rocks block passage along the stream itself, and one must push through clustered brush on shore. Going further in this manner, one comes to a place where the two cliff faces on either side seem to struggle to contain a single peak which arises as if the guardian of the riverbank. It is capped by old pine trees. Now follows a *li* or more along which the water and the rock are disconnected: one can gaze down at the stream but cannot approach it.

Mr. Fang Gongqian [see Bridge of the Immortals, p. 96] says, "The pools are stacked one above the other, easily distinguishable one from the next. The eleventh pool is particularly green, with the radiance of emerald-tinted jade, a radiance which intermingles with reflected sunbeams to produce fantastical patterns. If one strikes this pool with one's walking staff, green raindrops seem to fly about even under clear skies. I am intimately familiar with this pool, and I know that it is only during times when autumn vapors are pure and limpid—times when moonlit nights are white, times of frost—that one gets the full effect. And even then these phenomena only appear from time to time, uncertainly. It must result from the reflected image of the peak, rather than because of some property innate in the stream-water."

The gazetteer states that there was once a party which traveled as far as seven or eight *li* in search of the ultimate source of this stream, but towards sunset they got lost. Sitting as a group on a rock, they saw torchlight blazing up towards heaven like candles in several spots. Becoming extremely frightened, they clambered hurriedly over the mountain and went over ten *li* until they finally reached Stone Bamboo Shoot Steps.

Vol. II [下/7b–8a]

散花塢,
Sanhua wu, Embankment of Scattered Blossoms

In the great gully to the northwest, the famous sights are impossible to exhaust; they are denominated in general the Embankment of Scattered Blossoms. In this area the forms of the rocks jaggedly and in zigzag fashion brush up against heaven. Every rock will inevitably have its own pine tree, roots penetrating downwards into the crevices, and these grow out sideways or hanging down, in a myriad different postures.

Whenever clouds are born from the depths of this gully, those rocks which are not completely hidden are half-visible above the clouds, like the Eight Types of Heavenly Creatures or the Humanoid Non-Humans:[139] as if riding in carriages pulled by foxes, or straddling tigers, stepping with their hooves or thrusting with their horns, rubbing shoulders, touching toes, crashing through cliffs or straddling oceans as they come, weirdly and frighteningly displaying all their hallucinatory transformations!

Pine branches catch and reflect brilliant beams of hazy light in profusion, filling the entire gully and rising to the sky, as if flowers were flying up and soaring down throughout the void, bluish, purplish in gorgeous profusion, now thick, now sparse, each presenting its marvelous attractions.

Men of the past have said that if you do not come to the Embankment of Scattered Blossoms, then you will never realize that the rest of the world utterly lacks pines and rocks! Thus the phrase Scattered Blossoms would actually refer to the pines and rocks. The gazetteer, however, claims that in the late spring season, the varieties of colorful flowers here number in the hundreds of thousands, all of them vying in displays of wondrous beauty and filling the gully, almost to the point of rising level with the peaks—and hence the name. Here we record both theories in hope of some future determination as to which is correct.

Vol. II [下/8b–10a]

皮篷
Pipeng, Bark-Roof

There was once a monk who resided at Scattered Blossom Embankment. He stripped branches and trunks to make a house, roofing it over with tree-bark. Passers-by frequently availed themselves of his hospitality, so that they could get to observe the wonders of pines and rocks in gullies, flower and birds. And they all called the place Bark-Roof. My disciple Hung Yunxing has said that the peaks of the Yellow Mountains are all of the "root-and-up" variety, so that in all cases, one gazes from above towards below. But this residence alone occupies the center of convergence of numerous gullies, so that in gazing at the peaks, one is looking from below upwards. Thus this monk has opened an entirely new perspective on the mountains.

If from Cloud Valley one takes a right-hand turn and ascends for several *li*, the peaks are connected and the ridges linked in such a manner that no path can get through. There is a rock there shaped like a person extending his hand and pointing to the west, with what appears to be a sleeve fluttering below. This is called the Peak Pointing the Road. Travelers by following the direction it indicates are able to carry on. There was a monk of Szechwan named Xin'yi who constructed a hermitage over the remains of the old Bark-Roof. This he called the Tusita Heaven Buddha-Hut, with three rooms. Here he would sit to welcome distant gullies. Recently, only ruins of this place have remained.

On three sides are peaks encircling; only the southeastern side is open, allowing clouds to float in. When these clouds first arise, from afar one sees as if a scarf of silk trembling and entering through the crack. After a few moments, it expands and fills the cliffs and gullies of the peaks, looking like an ocean of cloud.

And that is why Chan Master Xuezhuang[140] has changed the name of his residence to Cloud Boat [Yunfang]. The Master is a man of Huai'yin, in the lineage of the Caodong [Japn. Sōtō] school. Loving fine landscape, he let his hair down and undertook a journey to the Yellow Mountains. Reaching this spot, he "hung up his gourd and hat" among the pines. Alongside the ancient caves he perched, using branches from the area to construct a residence and roofing it over with bark just like his predecessor in antiquity, unbeknownst to anybody. Provisions being inadequate, he gathered roots and leaves and ate them. Daily facing wondrous peaks, he played music and sang, enjoying himself. Somehow or other, his name spread eventually all about, and some desired to present him at the capital. Messengers three times he sent away, but eventually, responding to pressure, he did go to the capital. In less than one month there, he firmly petitioned to return to the mountains. When people heard of his conduct, they admired him greatly, and from time to time would send him clothing and provisions. Upon this, he would take brush in hand and paint several varieties of mountain flowers to thank them. These were of a thousand varieties, hundreds of forms never seen before by human eye. My friend, Wu Song[141] compiled these into a *Manual of Mountain Flowers* [*Shanhua pu*].

The various peaks faced by the Bark-Roof and resembling actual objects are innumerable. Most extraordinary of them all are the Screen of Engraved Embroidery,[142] Presenting Offerings, Heavenly Music, Heavenly Physician, Dancing Dragon, and Incense Burner. Those resembling actual people include Guanyin with Fishbasket, Boyang Lao Zi [full name for Lao Zi the Daoist sage], Monk Facing Wall, Monk Listening to Waterfall, as well as Momma Carrying Baby on Back, Boy Gazing Upwards. If somebody stands, head erect, high above the sky, then sometimes he may be able to catch sight of one of these, sometimes two or three. Those who get to see all of them are very few indeed. This is because the cloud-vapors cover and eat into them.

The moon emerges for three seasons from the southeastern crevice, but the summer moon alone emerges partially obscured from behind Heavenly Music Peak. At this time the moon rises relatively late. Now, Cloud Boat has its back to this section, and so on the cliffs to left and right a pure radiance first scintillates. The Master then climbs by degrees until he can see the moon emerge from ten thousand pine trees. Between the pine needles there shoot forth single darts or manes of moonlight, and no longer can it hide. Therefore he built a structure of several beams, inscribing it with the title Pavilion Where You Get the Moon.

On Incense Burner Peak, there is a swath of ancient moss on the rock which, on moonlit nights, looks precisely like a huge man in white robe, standing bare-headed and leaning against the rock. If you approach nearer to him, he gradually disappears. If you look for him once the sun has come out, you will not find him. But at night, once again he will appear. This man is called, Moonlight Immortal. After he was discovered, every spring in the second month, and every autumn in the eighth month, at the times of the moon's greatest brilliance, people point towards him and announce to each other, "The Moonlight Immortal is coming! The Moonlight Immortal is coming!" The Master says that when he first came to the Yellow Mountains, he was sleeping on a spring night bundled up in his blankets, when he woke to the sound of what seemed to be string and wind instruments playing and Sanskrit chanting from beyond the sky, and intermingled with these sounds, the playing of cymbals, horns, and trumpets. As it became really loud and intense, he finally realized that this was the first breaking up of the springtime ice, thawing and flowing down among all the various crevices. As this struck here and dashed there, it formed this musical symphony! But softer, louder, faster, slower, as if with a rhythm of its own—the more he listened, the more magical it became. On the next day, when he went out to investigate what could have made sounds so like cymbals and horns and trumpets, he found that the ice breaking up in the stone-cracks was like water flowing through a vast tube; the hollower the inside, the louder the sound would echo.

In Cloud Boat, empty pavilions and winding chambers were constructed one after another. After a while, though, he ran out of roof tiles. Libationer of Wine Wu Yüan and myself went to visit the Master. He bowed us in, and we sat and stayed together in the wind-blown dew. The Libationer made for him a roof of bamboo and bark, covering the spots still left uncovered.

Far and near, all have heard of Cloud Boat. But they still call this place Bark-Roof just as before.

Vol. II [下/10a–11a]

師子林
Shizi lin, Lion Forest[143]

Lion Forest in a first general view into the far distance appears to be laid out as a garden in plots high and low; one does not sense that it is positioned above a thousand peaks and ten thousand gullies of the Rear Ocean. In the year *renzi* of the Wanli period [1612], the monk Yi'cheng[144] from Wutai [Five Terraces] Mountain visited here, and he said, "These peaks and gullies can provide places for wandering, while a plotted garden could be formed by strenuously hoeing and irrigating. What more could I ask?" And so he constructed a house of several bays, joining forces with a group of laborers to carry soil and lay foundations. In less than a month the retreat was completed. Donors of clothing and provisions came from far and near on a daily basis. But there were also some thieves who snuck into the house and hid there, at night stealing and divvying up all the contributed items. As they were about to open the door and leave, a beam of brilliant light suddenly flooded in through the edges of the door, illuminating the place as if in bright daylight. The workmen, startled awake, grabbed the thieves and held them. The Master simply laughed and sent them away.

The mountains on all four sides here are covered with thousands of crab apple blossom trees, and along the garden are planted everywhere with day lilies; when they blossom, the whole area is brilliant with ochre-yellow coloring.

The retreat faces Lion Peak straight on, and the peak is like an altar to the forest. If from the forest one gazes at the peak, this latter is extremely precipitous, while on the side it enfolds a slope where there is a huge boulder, level and flat. Seated on this is an image of the Master himself, with his long beard and elongated forehead. The image is fully remarkable in the round, not a mere approximation but a precise image of the Master!

Towards the outer perimeter there juts up a solitary peak which acts as the locked gate to the forest. Here many rocks have been clustered together, forming a whole group of images of the Master, hence the name Forest.

The retreat has been deserted for a long time now; below it was another retreat known as Lion Pennant, and this too later came to be deserted. At the start of the Kangxi period [1662], a certain magistrate of Taiping reconstructed the ruined Pennant below the peak, and installed a plaque across the entrance which had inscribed upon it Lion Forest, thus preserving the old name.

Vol. II [下/11a–b]

飛光岫

Feiguang xiu, Flying Radiance Peak

On the right flank of Lion Garden, there is a boulder several hundreds of fathoms tall. When the monk Yi'cheng resided in the Forest, at any frosty dawn, or on any misty evening he would ascend to the summit of this rock and gaze about at the view. One day, when he rose at dawn, he saw from amongst the clouds the sun emitting multicolored rays of most unusual aspect, and he immediately cried out to the other people to climb the rock and see this spectacle. The residual fog from the previous night had not yet dispersed, and the reddish radiance was pulsating there. The center was glittering, like a mirror with five different colors radiating in a nimbus around it. Every man saw his own form therein, and the Master realized that this was the Body-Reflecting Radiance.

On another occasion, he saw the moon pass on high; at midnight, as the moon set, suddenly all was as bright as if in daylight. When the Master looked at his own body, it glowed entirely with purplish-golden light! And now he recalled that while he had been residing in the Forest, he had seen unusual lights on several occasions. Thus it appeared as it this particular peak must have a special radiance that fitfully appears and disappears. Hence he named it Flying Radiance Peak. Mr. Zhao Huanguang, Hanshan[145] in large seal characters cut the three words Flying Radiance Peak [*Fei guang xiu*] on the cliff face.

Vol. II [下/11b–12a]

煉丹臺
Liandan tai, Terrace for Refining Elixir

[Notes in text are the author's own]

The Creator is in fact a great Painter. When it comes to the Yellow Mountains in particular, there is no respect in which the wrinkle-texture strokes[146] are not completely utilized. The "spread-hemp" strokes, "iron line" strokes, "unraveled rope" strokes, "mouse-footstep" strokes, "crab-claw" strokes (all of these the texture strokes of the various masters) are all deployed in accordance with the different locations. When the mountain's posture is heroic and abrupt, the texture strokes employed to a large extent are the "great axe-cut" strokes (one of the stroke techniques).

As for the Terrace for Refining Elixir, it is particularly unusual. The Terrace is positioned below the Peak for Refining Elixir. The slanting shadows of all the other Yellow Mountain peaks are scattered about to the sides, displaying their flowery lotus blossom-like beauty, while the Terrace is concealed in their midst. It is like a lotus seed within its capsule, and yet in expanse it can accomodate ten thousand people! On three fronts, abrupt escarpments hover, as if without ground beneath them; suddenly, one peak surges up from the ground and stands there, embracing the Terrace: this is called "Purple Jade Screen." At the summit of this Screen, as if pasted onto nothing, are overhanging rocks in the forms of brush-holders and inkstones; the mountain itself is like the desk on which they are arranged. Interspersed among the peaks to either side are stones clustered in bunches, seemingly attempting to rise from the gully to contest height with the peaks themselves, but falling short.

As for the substance of all these, they are gaunt. As for their color, they are all moistly rich. As for their markings, they are all vigorous in their delicacy, with hidden darknesses, windingly and coilingly lovely and seductive. It is as if everything had been painted and dyed using the texture strokes employed to draw in lines of eyebrows.

If you sit upon the Terrace and look around, it seems one is looking upon a young maiden who has not yet left her chambers, or a skein of silk not yet removed from its box. It is as if [the famous swords] Zhanlu and Chungou were glittering brightly, about to be unsheathed. The spectacle dazzles one's vision with its multicolors, and yet one is not frightened.

Towards the end of the Wanli period [1615 or slightly earlier], there was a monk who built a thatched residence in front of this Terrace, only large enough to accomodate one desk and one mat, and he erected a plaque naming it the Forest of Ten Thousand Official Tablets.[147]

This later fell into disrepair. The Wu monk, Yanhuang, rebuilt it. If one proceeds downwards from the Terrace, the cliff face is perforated with cinnabar caves, and these overlook a hidden stream below. There is a stone formation shaped like a lotus blossom blocking the entrance to each cave.

Mr. Wu Shiquan[148] eulogized this place as follows:[149]

> Penetrating clouds with a pair of sandals,
> Crossing seas in a single cup,
> Wildly shouting—about to burst!
> Rising to this Terrace of Immortals!
> Sparkling, glittering on this vast journey,
> Sinking deep, then rising high,
> Peaks all linked in brilliant display,
> Fragmented calyxes, broken mists!

Servant and clerk of the K'un-lun Mountains,
Potsherd amongst the Isles of Paradise!
Purple mists—soul expands!
Emerald-jade—awake from dream!
Here, ah, here both dawn and eve
How excellent! May I journey on!

Vol. II [下/12b–13b]

光明頂
Guangming ding, Radiant Brilliance Summit

Of the peaks of the Rear Ocean which might compete for preeminence with Heavenly Capital and Lotus Blossom Peaks, Radiant Brilliance Summit stands supreme, which is the same as the Peak for Refining Elixir. It is the first of the Thirty-six Peaks to be named in the illustrated gazetteer.

The first possible route is: starting from Lion Forest, passing the Stone Drums and circling around Flew-Here Rock, and climbing to Heavenly Ocean. The second possible route would be: starting from Cloud-Boat, asking the way to Pearl Forest Embankment, then ascending to White Sand Stone-Steps, and passing the Three Ocean Gates and the Stone-Bridge Even with Heaven. Either of these will get you through. Having arrived at this point, one climbs slanting steps, clutching the bending pine trees, until the monk-guide pulls you up to the topmost summit.

The summit is entirely barren, although horn-like formations thrust up imposingly on the eastern side. The drop is most difficult to plumb. If one playfully drops a stone down to plumb it, one will hear clinking, bumping sounds, suddenly bursting out loudly, then suddenly muffled in effect, thousands in sequence and never reaching a discernible end.

The left-hand side of the summit is extremely narrow, but right in front of it is a huge boulder like a tiger clutching a mat. If one gazes downwards on this side, close by one discerns the Five Elders Peaks, rubbing shoulders and touching heels to toes, jutting upwards in a circle, while in the distance, one discerns various peaks of both Rear and Front Oceans, each weighted with its own unique shape and not yielding to each other, but all as if prostrating themselves as they come to pay court.

For the rest, covering the mountains are fantastic rocks none of which fail to struggle to descend into the gully below, as if they were ten thousand horses escaped from the reins, flying or rearing back as they tred the clouds! Or they are like an army of hundreds of thousands of bears and tigers, silencers [held in mouth by troops so that they will not make any sound] in teeth and galloping along, lowering their war banners, wardrums silenced, and bursting through the passes and gateways!

Just as a visitor gazing down at this spectacle finds himself becoming intoxicated, the monk will take his hand and point beyond the mountains where there are layered tiers of peaks like waves in a sea crashing and swirling, and he says that these are all the various mountain ranges of the Yü-chang, Min, and Yüeh regions [i.e., the provinces to the southeast]. And what appears to be a silken sash spread out and unstable, sometimes obscured the the clouds, is the Yangtze River. The clustered group of smaller peaks like lotus petals are the Nine Sons. And what seems a place of dark blue collapsing or sinking at the very edge of heaven is Mt. Lu.

The monk further points through the space between Heavenly Capital and Lotus Blossom Peaks to where the Yangtze River bends three times, and beyond this again, where one's view nearly expires, and there appears a single vastly expansive, vague haze, that, he says, is the ocean!

Once in the past, there was a traveler who came here, and sat on the summit until nighttime, during which he witnessed the sun *rise up again*, ten or more feet above the horizon line, giving off a most unusual radiance. After a while, it set again, but its setting was not, as usual, gradual, but rather like that of a fiery wheel dropping down! After this, it again popped up, and again dropped down, and indeed it continued thus numerous times. Finally, after its last fall, the sun arose for the normal dawn.

One who ascended this summit has explained that the sun's disc here is ten times greater than normal. When it breaks through the mists and rises straight up, there is a sudden sound. From this one realizes that, perhaps because of the spot's great height, overlooking the distant sea, upon the sun's falling, the seawater splits as the sun strikes down into it, and after this the waves crash back together again, embracing the sun as it sinks; and then, when it reemerges, the seawater, having come together again, once again parts, spitting forth the sun and exposing its brilliance, as if the seawater were *lifting* it up. As for the sound it makes when it comes up at dawn, this must be caused by the slapping and rushing of the sea waves.

That the place is very high, and overlooks the sea, there can be no question.

Vol. II [下/13b–14a]

平天矼

Pingtian gang, Stone Bridge Even with Heaven

In the name Stone Bridge Even with Heaven, the word *gang* [矼, for Stone Bridge] is pronounced by the locals as *jiang*; it is actually the same as the word *hong* [虹, for rainbow], and it refers to rock formations which stretch or reach across, like the rainbow arching across the sky. Along this formation there is a pathway, very narrow, with stones piled on both sides of it. All of these are sharply angled, and they all have pine trees growing on them. These pines do not make as if to go soaring off, but rather tense their muscles and ligaments to increase their strength in clutching and grabbing hold.

As a man proceeds across the formation, the protrusions from these rocks and the sharp pine needles tear and prick his clothing. With every few steps there is a sharp turn, one must pillow oneself on a pine or crouch on a rock for a good long rest, before proceeding. Amongst them there is a pine only two feet tall, whose thickly clustered needles spread sideways, producing a shaded area of several tens of feet. The crown of this tree is flat and level as a whetstone, the whiskers and mane tightly woven so that one would take it for a large meditation cushion. Whenever visitors come there, they put aside walking sticks and pull themselves up by the needles onto the top of the tree. The space can accomodate four men seated cross-legged, as they gesture and converse. From here is pointed out in the near distance a craggy mountain thrusting up in layers as if in a painting, and in the far distance, beyond the mountains, city walls and villages, creeks and streams and cultivated fields, all arranged and composed as if they had been embroidered there.

After sitting there for a long time, the wind starts whistling and blowing, and one fears that the pine will take off and fly! Then perhaps one could ride the pine tree to navigate the winds! It almost seems as if the pine has a will of its own, as if it wanted to take one on a voyage to the distant sights! And is it not possible that it was provided as an aid for those who are not capable of ascending on foot the summit of Lotus Blossom Peak?

Vol. II [下/14a–15a]

飛來石
Feilai shi, Flew-Here Rock

The mountains have three Flew-Here Rocks: one fell to earth in front of Writing-Brush Forest Retreat; one fell to earth alongside the western peak near Blue-Green Temple; and one to earth on Ocean Gate Peak. The places which became bases for these rocks all look just as if they had been prepared beforehand for the task, just waiting there for the rocks to come flying down from the void, upward facing to receive them and fit them to a T!

But when it comes to being toweringly high and precipitous, majestically surging, none can surpass the one on Ocean Gate Peak. If one climbs the Stone Bridge Even with Heaven for a *li* or more, a stone pillar abruptly blocks one's progress, but with an opening in the center like a door. This too is called Ocean Gate. On ascending this Ocean Gate, and gazing on towards the peak, it appears to be a mere round boulder. But when one reaches the side of the peak, towering mountains and clustered peaks of several tens of fathoms are all about. The very summit of this peak is level and flat, and on it there is a boulder as if leaning against the void, slanting upward to a height of 100 feet or more, and completely unlike the other rocks below. The monks say that there was once a man who used ropes to climb over it as an experiment. The posture of the rock was such that it seemed as if it had only just landed, its base as if still hanging in thin air, and the whole wobbling as if about to fall over. Pressing his body against the stone, the man crossed the surface, a few places just barely affording a toe-hold. He continued to feel as if the rock was about to come crashing down and thus to crush him underneath. So he hugged the surface as tightly as he could, and peered downwards, while still trembling in fear. He threw a small rock down to plumb the depths, and its sound continued ringing into the distance. Then he threw a larger rock to follow, upon which an explosive burst of dust shot up higher than the top of the peak by several tens of feet. The monks below warned him not to throw any more rocks.

Below this is Iron String Pool, where a dragon is said to hibernate. Mr. Feng Mengzhen (see above) states that if one follows the cliff face from Flew-Here Peak and heads north, all the various peaks will display their wonders, surging and receding, slanting and thrusting, numbering in the thousands upon thousands and brilliantly scintillating, as if a dragon grotto spread out below.

Mr. Xie Bozhen's [traveling companion of Feng Mengzhen to the Yellow Mountains in 1605] servant playfully threw a large rock which fell with thundering noise, waking up the dragon so that suddenly there was a huge downpour of rain and hailstones. Only by falling prostrate on the ground was he able to avoid being hit by these.

Vol. II [下/15a–b]

石牀峰
Shichuang feng, Stone Bed Peak

One particular peak has green cliffs surging sheerly upwards, and on top, a stone bench-like formation slanting across, as if of white jade, and as smooth as a whetstone. There is a single ancient pine tree shading it profusely, as if purposefully sheltering it with a canopy.

There are in addition three purple Stone Beds, and three emerald-green Stone Beds. According to age-old tradition, the country of Kucha had an amber pillow, and if one slept upon it, the Five Lakes, Four Oceans, Ten Islets and Three Islands [of paradise] will all enter into one's dreams. But here, in this place, all one needs to do is to lie down on this bench and pillow one's head—and without even falling asleep and dreaming, there are the Penglai Isles of Paradise spread out right before one's eyes!

Behind the pillow portion of this bed is a screen-like cliff. If one leans upon the pillow and peers down into the gully, there below lies Iron String Pool.

Vol. II [下/15b–16b]

鐵絃潭
Tiexian tan, Iron String Pool

Dragon lairs within these mountains are not a few—but the most spiritually efficacious is Iron String Pool. It has been transmitted through the ages that in old times, there was once a great drought. A hunter who happened to have captured a live tiger, whose life was now in his hands. He decapitated the tiger, and threw the head, dripping with blood, into the pool. This caused the hibernating dragon to be startled awake, and a windblown rain storm immediately occurred.

Whenever any nearby region encounters a season of drought, the citizens of the immediate area and beyond come here in crowds, beating gongs and kowtowing, to pray to [the dragon of] the Pool. When the prayers are done, a man wraps a well-rope around his waist so as to form a rope-seat to take his buttocks. He hangs a vase from his waist, and, holding an iron tablet and a stick of burning incense, he is lowered down towards the surface of the Pool, to a point where the rocks are all a deep greenish color and a remarkable chilliness pierces to the bone; this brings him near to the location of the dragon's lair. He now ties the tablet to the exposed base of the [ignited] incense stick, thrusting the latter into a crevice in the rock, while dipping his vase down to the surface and scooping up some water in it. He is now hurriedly pulled back up again, and he and the others run as fast as they can to get away. The idea is this: once the incense stick burns down, the iron tablet will fall into the Pool [and startle the dragon awake]. When the men have gotten some ten *li* or so from the Pool, they look back to see a mighty wind arise with thunder and lightning from the Pool, while the water that had been scooped up in the vase starts to bubble and froth, with a loud gurgling noise. Wherever this vase of water is now carried, a sweet rainfall will inevitably occur. For this reason, the men will always carry poles and other weapons to guard the rear of the procession, in fear that there might be highwaymen along the way aiming to cut them off and steal the vase. For in such a case, the rainfall would only reach to the immediate local area. The popular name for this practice is "robbing the Dragon's Pool" (with *zhao* 抄 ["robbing," usually read in the first, level tone] read in the fourth, falling tone).

On one occasion, just as the assembled people were praying at the Pool, one man lost his footing and *fell into the Pool,* sinking to the very bottom! The crowd, terrified, scattered and ran away. They concealed the truth from the man's family, lying that he would "come back later." But then, amazingly, he *did* come back! The crowd, astonished, asked him what had happened, and he answered that the interior of the mountain is in fact entirely hollow. When he first fell in, he felt a soughing wind, seemingly supporting him and carrying him down a well of thousands of feet in depth. But then he suddenly found himself in a stone grotto right beside the Pool. This grotto was hollowed out in a series of interconnected cells, and pitch black. Proceeding slowly, turning and cutting back dozens of times, he finally saw a glimmer of daylight seeping into the cave. With this, he continued forward towards the light, elbows and knees to the ground, and shoulders and back rubbing against rock. Proceeding through ancient lichens and a wild profusion of stones for he didn't know how many tens of *li*, he gradually began to hear faint sounds of human beings, chickens and dogs, upon which he finally emerged from the tunnel, finding himself in the territory of another county! He asked the way home, and returned.

Vol. II [下/16b–17a]

西海門
Xihai men, Gateway to the Western Ocean

Below Flew-Here Rock the path runs level for over a *li*, with tall ridges lining the way on either side. Here one can still encounter village residences and farmhouses. The monk Cimin once resided here, and the place is called, Cimin's Retreat. Behind this Retreat, one ascends in levels upward to the Hall of Bhaiṣajya-guru [Chin. Yaoshifo].[150] In front of this there is a little pond. On a clear night, when the moon is brilliant and there is no wind, the reflections of the mountains appear upside down in this pond as clearly as if seen in a mirror.

Proceeding through the Retreat garden to the west for a *li* or so, one abruptly comes upon two pillar-like peaks seemingly holding up the sky, something like the towers of the Imperial Palace: and, similarly, although the pavilions and galleries lie fully open, one feels that one dare not rashly enter. But when one is crouching upon the summit of the mountain, these stone peaks surge upwards, reaching right up to one's feet.

Beyond the Gateway, vast reaches of peaks and cinnabar-tinted mountains are arranged about like a screen composed of upright writing brushes. And alongside the Gateway, peaks as high as heaven, utterly stripped of "skin" and "hair," bearing their claws and fangs thrust their way upwards, like dragons and krakens displaying their forms, or tigers and bears battling. If from the Gateway one gazes downwards, one beholds broad peaks, narrow ones, sharp ones, balding ones, straight ones, ones like trailing robes, as if straining their necks to rise from the abyss; it is impossible to say how many tens of thousands of them there are, like new sprouts of a bamboo forest, wildly casting their bluegreen radiance, on the point of breaking into a dance!

If from the Gateway one gazes upwards, one sees Cloud Gate Peak, Bridge of the Immortals, and Hibiscus Peak, as well as others, all configured in a circle around one's span of vision, and all curtaining the sky above.

When the place is deserted, at noontime forms give rise to doubled forms, shadows give rise to layered shadows—and if one gazes at the scene for too long, one's eyes become dazzled and confused to a painful degree. One must close them for a while, and then slowly reopen them, and only then will the gateways to all three oceans fully and completely present their miraculous wonders, the layered cliffs entirely renewed, all of them beyond the achievement even of the workmanship of gods or the skill of demons. No place can compare with the Gateway to the Western Ocean!

Vol. II [下/17a–18a]

始信峰
Shixin feng, Start-to-Believe Peak

Start-to-Believe Peak arises from a high portion of Scattered Flower Embankment. It faces gullies below on three sides, while having its back towards the north. If one climbs from the southern side, following the stone ridge upwards, when one is about to reach the top, there is a crevice in the stone over ten feet wide; looking down, it appears as if there is no bottom. But suddenly from the cliff face on the other side one notices a pine tree, trailing a long branch downwards; this is known as the Welcoming Pine. Below this pine is a single wooden plank, serving as a bridge. The traveler must inch his body along this, not daring even to blink, until his hand can reach that pine branch; then, feet stepping carefully along the bridge, he crosses, trembling with terror. Once across, one further crosses a gorge, and in this gorge are three rocks surging upwards. It is impossible to climb them, but using cracks in the rocks as footholds one is able to proceed, though the way becomes ever more precipitous, and one's clogs seem to slip more easily. Gazing all about, one sees that there is no pathway, but taking a quick bend, one suddenly appears leading straight ahead. If one proceeds from here just a few bends more, one abruptly emerges on the peak.

To the left and right of this peak are pine trees with dragon-branches and ancient trunks clutching on to the cliffs and hanging from the stone walls, no two alike in posture. They stretch out or shrink back, bend, twist or straighten, hovering and expressing to the full an attitude of soaring or dancing. If you sit at the roots of one of them, leaning against the sheer cliff behind, you get the most extensive possible view. To the right is Scattered Flower Embankment, purplish-green and kingfisher bluish-green, just like a picture or an embroidery. To the left are the Two Immortals Playing Chess, while behind them stands one in a headcloth, hands behind his back and watching the game.

My younger brother, Yangdu,[151] says, "If from Lion Forest you gaze at this peak, it looks like a mere mound of earth. But if you manage to get to the extreme, bottom-most point and then peer at it, you find that its base is impossible to discern. Gazing around in all four directions, your eyes will peer endlessly, with nothing to hold them; and then you realize that Start-to-Believe is indeed a peak, with precipitous cliff-walls all around in a circle." In the midst of this is a solitary thatched hut named Chamber of Samadhi-in-Voidness. This was constructed by the monk, Yi'cheng. For three years he would often go through Lion Forest and then stay at this place for the evening. But he declined in health because of the snowfall. His successor was the Daoist "Birdnest," who came to the mountains to gather herbs, and he too resided in solitude in this hut.

On the stone cliff are cut five characters: "Cold River Master alone resides" (*Han jiang zi du zuo*). The "Cold River Master" was the martyr Jiang Tian'yi[152] of the town [i.e., Shexian]. He was a man of extraordinary spirit, who loved fine landscape. He would often climb to the top of the peak and sit there all day without moving. He inscribed his name thus on the stone cliff to demonstrate his commitment. He also authored a "Letter Written on Behalf of the Yellow Mountains and Sent to Scholar-Officials in Distant Places." His death led to his sharing an equal reputation with Jin Wen'yi[153] [Jin Sheng, 1589–1645] as a martyr for his dynasty.

The Great Master of the Herb-Ground, Yaodi dashi from Qingyuan[154] [Fang Yizhi 1611–71] once did a painting of this peak, and sent it to me and my younger brother, with an invitation to join him in reclusion in the mountains. Thus we planned to build a retreat on the old foundations of the Chamber of Samadhi-in-Voidness, so that we might age in this spot.

Vol. II [下/18a–b]

擾龍松
Raolong song, Pine of the Roiling Dragon

The line of rocks constituting the Embankment of Scattered Blossoms runs straight into a valley, then abruptly rises to form a peak several thousands of feet high. On the summit of this peak stands a square screen formation of stone, and on top of this there grows a pine tree, covering the whole, called the Pine of the Roiling Dragon. The trunk of this pine tree does not even reach three feet in height, while it is over ten feet in circumference. The tree looks as if it wanted to clutch the rock and go flying off, but finding that it cannot, it merely twists about as if dancing on the rock. The left branch juts out thirty or forty feet in length, but when the very "firm" reaches an extreme it turns "soft," and so the bluegreen mane of needles trembles and shakes, almost like a weeping willow.

A traveler who loved to explore for unusual sights once groped his way up out of the valley here, and reaching halfway up the peak, he caught sight of the roots of a pine tree, winding and twisting over a length of several hundreds of feet, but he could not tell where they led to until, turning right, he saw this pine jutting straight up out of a crevice in the peak, straight up, and emerging at the summit where it was blocked by a horizontal rock slab. Its force being thus blunted, it was compelled to bend, to curl and shrink back, forming a tree trunk at the very top. The left-thrusting branch proved to result from its residual angry power thickly gathering and angrily hurrying outwards.

In the valley are a thousand peaks on all sides facing this pine tree, like a group of imperial consorts, jade sceptres in hand, coming to pay court to it. The gorgeous beauty of this pine tree's form, and the dignity of its position, and without equal. It is also known as The Emperor of Pine Trees.

Vol. II [下/18b–20b]

石筍矼

Shisun gang, Stone Bamboo Shoots Bridge

The Stone Bamboo Shoots constitute a wonder among wonders. What is wonderful are the individual peaks; what is especially wonderful is the Stone Bridge. The wonder of the individual peaks is merely that of individual stones, some several tens of fathoms high, thick below and sharply pointed above, thrusting up like the sprouting of newly grown bamboo, utterly stripped barren, as if they had just shed their sheaths. Seen from afar, they appear to be a single unified cluster, but when one moves to a side perspective, then each clearly juts up beautifully, entirely separate from the next peak in the sequence.

The wonder of the Stone Bridge is that, covered as it is with such a profusion of Bamboo Shoots, beyond enumeration, is that at first, the whole ensemble must have formed a single mountain, and that some great spirit grabbed hold of it, broke up the bones and scattered them abroad, into innumerable reproductions of itself, propping up the void above, and thus forming the rear portion of the Yellow Mountains. And it is as if each and every peak just happened to occupy a position suited to it. Could it be that the Creator actually had the *intention* of making it thus? Or did he do it unwittingly?

Within the space of just a few *li*, they burgeon and ascend: casting one's glance around in all four directions, one seems to have lost control of one's vision, and one's mouth hangs open in astonishment. Here are the forms of all the implements of the human realm, completely represented in full detail, and on display halfway up to heaven! Gazing to the west, there is a standing Buddha; gazing to the east, there is a barbarian ambassador presenting tribute. And right along the main body of the Bridge, one sees wandering immortals. The Buddhas [including *bodhisattvas*], to whom crowns would be suited, are given crowns. Those barbarians to whom military caps would be suited are given military caps. Those immortals to whom swords would be suited are given swords—if waist-ornaments would be suited, they are given waist-ornaments. If raised hairdos would be suited, they are given raised hairdos. If headcloths would be suited, they are given headcloths. It seems precisely as if these were all arranged by intention!

What is more, every stone peak reaches an utmost, towering point as if built up from a foundation. Wherever fissures appear, it is as if there are dangling whiskers that are on the point of falling but never actually fall. Every such peak inevitably has pine trees on it, and the wonderousness of these pines expresses to the full what might be conjured up by a painting master's imagination when he is not necessarily going by what he has actually *seen*. He depicts their forms, wiedling his brush freely, to the point where even the painter himself is astonished at how *unlike* the results are to the usual pine tree—and yet if he takes them as representing the pines on the stone peaks along the Stone-Bridge, then there is none that does not correspond to an actual example!

There are single stone peaks ornamented with several pine trees; there are single pine trees which, on the contrary, overshadow several stone peaks. For mounting the Stone-Bridge and inspecting the panorama, no time is more wonderful than shortly after clearing from rain. The colors of each individual stone peak emerge freshly washed the the rain, as the accumulated haze withdraws, or some residual snow leaves just a few traces. They form as it were a mountainous curtain of light gauze, like flowers seen in a mirror, or a beautiful woman hiding behind the blinds, as if now here, now gone, now obscured, now revealed. In addition, the clouds can not only veil them, but can proceed to demarcate them in such a manner that one might have been taking two peaks to be one, but then the clouds demarcate them and one realizes for the first time that they are two! Or one might have been taking a peak as rounded, but then the clouds demarcate it and one realizes for the first time that it is sharply precipitous. With every turn, the aspect is renewed, and the beauties are seen in unending sequence.

If one follows the cliff face down for twenty *li* along a stream, one comes to Pine Valley. In the year *jiaxu* of the Tianqi period [Wang makes an error here; correct is Chongzhen period, year 1634], the townsman Shao Shusheng [see above] found the most spectacular spot along the Stone-Bridge, and built a retreat there called Writing-Brush Forest Retreat. Considering that the forms of the peaks here being so very tall, nothing but a tower would suffice to do justice to their beauty, he also built a tower thereon, and to the left, along the cliff, he added a wing to serve as kitchen and dormitory, while to the right adding a pavilion for people to rest in while climbing the mountains.

Of the wonders displayed in front of, behind, and to the left and right of the Retreat, recorded in various travel accounts, the one most highly praised is Peak-Gorge. Opening the window, one faces this directly, as if a gateway had been cut to reveal all the myriad peaks, marking off the blue sky above into several tens—up to a hundred—roadways. Here is the so-called Summoning the Recluse Peak, surging upwards from the gully below, and further splitting on top into smaller peaks.

To the south, the Retreat directly faces Immortal's Palm, five peaks aligned together looking exactly like the palm of a hand in the size and relative length of the fingers. Here too is Flew-Here Stone, a peak like a stone pillar. This stone rises section by section in layers, without the slightest sign of any space inbetween. On top stand two stones shaped like a pair of divination cups[155] placed together, but split down the middle, and with yet another stone which seems to have flown down on top of the cups, which looks as if it is still unstable, and this is called Cross-Legged Peak. Halfway up this stone suddenly levels out, as if it had been cut in half, and then a sliver of rock was left behind as a cliff, precisely suited for placing a meditation mat upon for sitting cross-legged in meditation.

Gazing downwards, one overhangs a deep gully below, and all around are ancient pines, their tops rising to the level of one's seat. It is as if they were climbing up, clothed in clouds, and with a few more paces they would be right beside one! Below these pines, ten thousand mountains rise and fall, undergoing their transformations right in front of one's seat. This is called Frozen Cloud Retreat. Across the stream, it is so extremely steep that it is unclimbable. As one gazes further out, there, leaning against the void and standing like trees in a forest are the Bamboo Shoots.

Vol. II [下/20b–21b]

松谷
Song gu, Pine Valley

Pine Valley is the *nom-de-plume* of Zhang Yinfu, the "Perfected Man." During the Baoyou period of the Song dynasty [1253–1258], he was viciously calumniated by the then Prefect of Tianshui and sent into exile, where he met a magical man and learned alchemical technique from him. Afterwards, he went into reclusion at Immortal Source. Arriving beneath the layered cliffs, and loving the spot, he built a thatched hut among the pine trees, and named the place Pine Valley. In the Ming dynasty, Mr. Luo Rufang[156] inscribed here the the four words "Eastern Terrain Snow Mountain" [*Tong tu xue shan*]. The Perfected Man's tomb-pagoda lies behind the main hall.

The temple[157] is on the brink of a little stream, and above this stream are mountains on all four sides, and these mountains on all four sides confront the retreat as well. It is said that if one enters Pine Valley at night, and sits upon one of the rocks there, gazing at Green Dragon Pool, there are no words to praise the beauty of the scene, and no colors to which it can be compared. People usually praise this spot alongside of Yellow Dragon Pool. Although Yellow Dragon Pool cannot compare with Green Dragon Pool, if one follows the rocks back upstream, or follows them downstream, while it is indeed greatly inferior to Green Dragon Pool, in its limpid emerald color it is no different from Green Dragon and in fact one simply cannot reckon between them. The colors of the world under heaven here reach their supreme level, not can there possibly exist any other that will surpass this one.

Men of our kind by nature dote upon bodies of water and rocks, and our hearts yearn to seek them out throughout the entire world, but having arrived at this place, one feels as if one could spend one's entire life beside this one particular pool. Travelers, relying on the guide's suggestions, upon arriving at Pine Valley are led above the two pools in question; they take one glance at them, and then set their walking sticks in a homeward direction! Thus most of them fail to realize the richness of the pools in Pine Valley.

Mr. Wu Zhantai [see Tortoise-Fish Grotto, p. 118] says, "Encircling the Valley on all four sides, towering peaks pierce the sky, and ten thousand tall bamboo jut upwards, reaching the clouds and the sunlight. When night comes and all human sounds are silenced, one hears only the sounds as of rushing wind and speeding rain, in their fullness splitting the cliff-rocks and making a great noise. Then at dawn, one notices that the expanse of heaven is pure and entirely clear, and the sounds have passed into the distance, where they are heard more faintly. If one proceeds in the direction of these sounds, one will discover that The Five Pools are located there."

At the same time, if one starts from the foothills and approaches the Valley, when one is perhaps one *li* or so away from it, there too there are many pools. From afar one can hear them, producing their gurgling sounds, but as one approaches, these sounds actually grow *fainter*. Gazing downwards towards one pool, one sees that it is absolutely crystal clear, and that one's reflection, including whiskers and eyebrows, appears therein. This is called Mirror Pool. And yet this Mirror Pool is *not* counted among the Five Pools. So it must be the case that crystalline pools near the temple which have not yet been investigated must be nearly innumerable.

Vol. II [下/21b–23a]

五潭
Wu tan, Five Pools

When one is about to reach Pine Valley, in the distance one perceives a stream with waterfalls, flowing wildly down, and this turns out to be the body of water that will embrace on both sides the pathway one is traveling upon. From amongst the layered peaks, it comes rushing down full-force, striking rock and roaring with fantastic loudness, forming as it goes deep pools—green, yellow, black, and white—just like their names. It then flows further on, becoming crystalline and forming a single flow.

The one which begins just beyond Lion Forest and flows to the area behind the temple is Black Dragon Pool. Yellow Dragon Pool is to the right of Green Dragon Pool, above and clearly separate from it. The stream and these three pools are all positioned beyond the temple, and above the lower temple down in the valley. As for the valley itself, it has a Little White Dragon Pool, which is located right beside the path. Here the traveler can first rest for a while. Thus it is proclaimed that Pine Valley has four pools, which, when Oil Pool is added, makes five. The pool for which Mr. Tang Binyin[158] inscribed the name Pearl Abyss is precisely Yellow Dragon Pool.

Since these pools *receive* water, they have sand and pepples on their bottoms, and fish and waterplants in the main body; whatever they happen to have in them is fully visible. Also the forms of the sky, the mountains, people who happen to be passing by—clouds, mists, plants, trees, nails and fingers, whiskers and hair—all are fully reflected in this realm of brilliant radiance, merged together into a great unity, without any distinction between what is above and what below!

The pool which Mr. Wu Boyu[159] describes in the following passage is Green Dragon Pool: "The pool is a profound abyss, limidly clear; a great stone bridge-like formation slants across it, covering all but one third of its surface. When the sun is reflected therein, it is like a gemstone; when the empty sky is reflected therein, it looks like emerald glass. When clouds are reflected therein, they are like silvery beams from a candle or flying waterfalls."

Above the large rock formation is Heaven-Formed Pond. In this Pond, the radiance of the white pebbles and the glittering of the emerald crystals sparkle and coruscate, as if some divine creature were puffing and spitting therein: it actually makes viewers tremble in fear.

As for the so-called Oil Pool, it gets its name from the resemblance of the seams of the rocks here being perfectly straight, something like the striations of an oil-press.[160]

Crossing and continuing past this for several paces, there is a large rock filling the void above, like a house. It is inscribed Dragon Abyss. Surging waters flow across beneath this "house," with a rumble as of carriages rolling or thunder. The rock has perforations in it, each competing with the others marvelousness of shape. The pool itself looks like a gigantic cauldron for cooking a meal for five thousand people.

The colors of other pools become profoundly dark, so that one is unable to see anything at the dead center. This pool alone, while it has dark and dim twirlings and movements, is sufficiently translucent that one is able to see the bottom. At the bottom, white pebbles glitter as if they were angry. When fish are poised as if to jump out, one can reach down and pluck them out. If one sinks a long well rope, it will only reach partway down, and then run out. Even if you throw in a rope of over one hundred feet in length, it will still run out, leaving the larger portion.

It may be noted that the reason these Pools are given names like Green, Yellow, Black, and White, is that is because of the colors they reflect upon the stone cliff faces above. And the reason they have the word Dragon appended to their names is simply to express their profound depth. But the residents of this mountain came to take the *colors* to be those of the *dragons*, and thus came to believe that dragons really reside in them. Mr. Pan Zhiheng[161] once proposed changing their names: The Black Pool he called Jetstone Lake-Pool; the White Pool he called Jade Seal Pool; the Yellow Pool he called Dark Cup Pool; the Green Pool he called Void-

Green Pool; and the color of the Oil Pool being deep green, he called it Deep Verdancy Pool.[162] But alas! he never had these names inscribed on the rocks above the Pools.

Vol. II [下/23a–b]

仙人榜
Xianren bang, Plaque of the Immortals[163]

From Pine Valley one follows the stream, seeking out the pathway again, over a steep gradient three *li* in length, the sound of flowing water never stopping. In the midst of the water are great boulders piled up, all pure white, like white jade. Another few *li,* and one comes to the foundation of an old retreat. This is in fact the foundation of the thatched hut first built here by the Pine Valley Perfected Man.[164] As the mountain gets higher, it also gets more pointy, and towards the tip of the point, amongst a cluster of escarpments, there is a stone standing there like a high official, complete with girdled robe and sceptre. Small pine trees take the place of his hat-pin, and hat-tassles. This is the Immortal Who Hung Up the Plaque; the Plaque itself is right beside the Immortal. It is also known as The Heavenly Tablet Rock. When dim dawnlight shines upon it, columns of archaic clerk script-like strokes appear, seeming like the ancient tadpole or scallion-leaf scripts, but ultimately no one has been able to decipher them. It is said that at one time, a Daoist built a scaffold right on the pathway here, so that he could examine it at leisure. But he was finally able to make out only one word, "Immortal" [*xian*]. That night, a lightning bolt suddenly blasted down and struck the rock, effacing that one character! The place where the bolt struck can still be seen today.

If one turns again, one comes to a sheer, unmarked cliff: halfway up this cliff there is an opening, shaped like a half-circle. Through it shines daylight from the other side of the mountain, and so it is popularly known as the Eye of Heaven.

Vol. II [下/23b–24b]

翡翠寺
Feicui si, Kingfisher-Bluegreen Temple

In the second year of the Zhonghe period of the Tang dynasty [882], there was a monk who traveled ten thousand miles to east from India.[165] He established a temple below Kingfisher-Bluegreen Peak, hence it was named, Kingfisher-Bluegreen Temple. This monk wore hempen robes whether summer or winter; he would beg a hank of hemp, and thus was able to avoid illness. He was therefore known as Master Hemp Robe. His sloughed-off shell is entombed in a pagoda outside the Temple. In the courtyard there is a well with exceptionally sweet-tasting water, which never floods over nor does it ever dry out. According to tradition, it emerged spontaneously when Master Hemp Robe stuck his walking staff into the ground here. Thus it is called Walking Staff Stream.

Those traveling to this place approach from Hot Springs Ridge, emerging to the south behind Double Scissors Peak. Bordering the stream here on both sides are black cliffs a thousand fathoms high, ancient pines casting their reflections into the waters below, the latter descending to form an emerald pool. If one reckons several tens of paces from here, one comes to Fishing Bridge Retreat. Further crossing the little bridge, one comes to the flowing waters of Swallow-Tail Creek, which is in fact a waterfall that has come rushing down from the Terrace for Refining the Elixir, here encountering the source, then joining forces with other streams from various points, crashing and pounding against the rocks. Emerald ponds form here, in three tiers, as if layered with stone slabs.

Going further towards the west, one crosses Floating Ridge, and below this comes to a level pathway, which twists and turns following the flank of the mountain, cutting finally to the north, and thus reaching the Temple. In front of the Temple are many old pine trees, one of which has a trunk several spans in circumference. A blast of wind happens to have snapped one branch, so that it dangles down; at the point where the branch meets the surface of the trunk, it looks as if the branch must surely fall right off. But after it had hung there for a long time, the main branches of the tree gradually withered, while the bent branch continued to display green scales and bluegreen manes, flourishing richly by comparison with the others! This is called Bent Branch Pine.

Among the pine trees runs a rocky stream, with a Monks' Bridge crossing over it. On this has been built a room where travelers may rest. Mr. Wang Zemin[166] of the Yüan dynasty erected a plaque here, which reads "Like Spreading Wings" [*Yi ran*]. The Temple grounds are open and expansive; after seeing wild peaks covered with clustered stones, piled high and circling about, circling one on all sides up to this point, here one can relax for a few moments, imbuing oneself with a pure, far-reaching sense of free-spiritedness. Mr. Tang Binyin of the Ming dynasty inscribed the refectory here with the words, "Secluded in the Bluegreen" [*Yin cui*].

It is said that once, a woodcutter saw beneath the peak here, an ox of extremely bizarre appearance: it was entirely green in color. As he attempted to corral the beast, it suddenly plunged into the stream and disappeared! Therefore, the place where the kingfisher-bluegreen colors are deepest is known as Green Ox Source.

Mr. Pan Zhiheng says, "Someone asked, 'Why is Kingfisher-Bluegreen considered to be such a superlative spot?' I replied, 'To be able to occupy a solitary peak in the midst of ten thousand peaks, renders it *superlative* in solitude. To occupy one realm in the midst of a hundred realms, is to be *superlative* in remoteness. Is not Kingfisher-Bluegreen's position in the Yellow Mountains comparable to that of a dragon in cloud-filled mountains and crane-haunted abysses?' And another person said to me, 'The various other peaks of the Yellow Ocean, and Kingfisher-Bluegreen Peak, cannot be compared in terms of size, or worthiness. When one is at Kingfisher-Bluegreen, all the peaks of the Yellow Ocean withdraw and are invisible. When one is viewing these other peaks, Kingfisher Bluegreen Peak likewise hides away. It is as if the larger and smaller, the more and less worthy, are mutually supporting one another, rather than taking advantage of one another, or as if they are mutually yielding to one another, rather than infringing upon one another.' And is it not indeed thus?"

West Peak Hall is about one half *li* or so from Kingfisher Bluegreen Peak. From the level ground, there arises abruptly a single peak, very lovely in form, and halfway up this peak has been built a hall. In front of the Hall, flowers and bamboo flourish, while in the valley, tea shrubs have been planted. When these flower, the fragrant snow-white bloom spreads abundantly. Alongside the Hall, is the Mountain House of Singing Rocks, the estate of the Qiao family.

Vol. II [下/24b–25a]

洋湖
Yang hu, Vast Lake

Over twenty *li* west of Taiping County, a mountain confronts one, with clustered fantastic rocks on its summit: this is Hibiscus Peak. Below this Peak is a lake called Vast Lake. The Lake is ten *qing* [about 150 acres] in area, surrounded by peaks and with mountain springs flowing into it. In the middle grow aquatic plants like individual hairs that can be numbered separately. Brilliant dawn mists and slanting evening sunlight reflect all the way to the lake-bottom, and nighttime vapors here look like trailing bolts of silk. When the reeds flower along the shore, they look like an autumn snowfall extending limitlessly as far as the eye can see.

The monk Pumen [see Heavenly Capital Peak, p. 99] planned to build a viewing terrace in the middle of the lake, and to spare no effort in the construction. Along the wings of the main hall, ten gates were to open, standing thirty feet above the water. He also intended to build a surrounding embankment, and on this to add ten further halls, connected with each other by bridges to facilitate the passage of travelers from one hall to the next. And behind these halls, rising above the overhanging eaves, there were to be "flying pavilions," circling the lake all around. To reach the central terrace, rafts were to be employed. But this project was never to be accomplished, and today, the entire panorama around the lake consists of nothing but overgrown fields. But wild geese do land here, finding a temporary home on this Lake.

NOTES

TRAVELERS, MING LOYALISTS, AND PILGRIMS

[1] For the concept of the sacred mountain in China, see Wu Hung, "Immortal Mountains in Chinese Art," in Wang Wusheng, *Celestial Realm: The Yellow Mountains of China* (New York: Abbeville Press, 2006), pp. 17–39, and notes on pp. 212–214. See also Kiyohiko Munakata, *Sacred Mountains in Chinese Art* (Urbana-Champaign, Illinois: Kranner Art Museum, 1990). For a thorough analysis of the "religious landscape" of the southern of the sacred mountains (or "marchmounts"), see James Robson, *Power of Place: The Religious Landscape of the Southern Sacred Peak* (Nanyue) *in Medieval China* (Cambridge, Mass.: Harvard University Asia Center, 2009).

[2] For the pilgrimage aspect of Yellow Mountains art, see James Cahill, "Huang Shan Paintings as Pilgrimage Pictures," in Susan Naquin and Chün-fang Yü, *Pilgrims and Sacred Sites in China* (Berkeley and Los Angeles: University of California, 1992).

[3] The Anhui Provincial Library, Hefei, holds a handwritten MS of the work, identical in all respects to the published version of 1775. This may well be the version written out by Wang Hongdu's great-great-grandnephew, Wang He'de 汪詥德, in preparation for printing, and described by himself in his colophon, dated 1775. (See pp. 74.)

[4] Dean MacCannell, *The Tourist: A New Theory of the Leisure Class* (University of California Press, 1999 new edition of 1976 publication), *passim*.

[5] Xu Xiake, *Xu Xiake youji* 徐霞客遊記 (Shanghai: Guji chubanshe, 1980, 3 vols.), 1:16–17. See also Li Chi, "Hsü Hsia-k'o's Huang Shan Travel Diaries" in Li Chi and Dale Johnson, *Two Studies in Chinese*

Literature (Ann Arbor: Michigan Papers in Chinese Studies, No. 3, 1968).

[6] For the Yellow Mountains itineraries he followed, see *Ibid.*, 3 (appendix of maps): maps 7–8.

[7] See Jonathan Chaves, "The Yellow Mountain Poems of Ch'ien Ch'ien-i (1582–1664): Poetry as *Yu-chi* [travel essay]," Harvard Journal of Asiatic Studies, Vol. 48, no.2, Dec., 1988.

[8] For Shi Runzhang as poet, with several examples of his poetry translated into English, see Irving Yucheng Lo and William Schultz, *Waiting for the Unicorn: Poems and Lyrics of China's Last Dynasty* (Bloomington and Indianapolis: Indiana University Press, 1986), pp. 90–94.

[9] See the newly published complete *shi* (詩) poetry of Shi Runzhang, *Shi Runzhang shi* 施閏章詩 (Yangzhou: Guangling shushe, 2006 2 vols.), 1:411.

[10] The *Siku quanshu* 四庫全書 edition of the complete works of Shi Runzhang erroneously reads *you* 友 for *ji* 及 in this name, an error perpetuated in *Shi Runzhang shi*. That Shi was in contact with Cao Fen, or Binji, is demonstrated by at least three other references to this man in his collected writings, all using the correct character, *ji: Shi Runzhang shi*, 2:916; 2:982; Shi Runzhang, *Xueyutang wenji* 學餘堂文集 (*Collected Writings from the Hall of Leisure after Study*, his collected prose writings), edition of the *Siku quanshu*, 28/6b–8a. *Xueyutang wenji*), 25:24b. At least one stone inscription by Cao Fen is still extant in the Yellow Mountains. See Wu Lunzhong 吳倫仲 *et al.*, *Huangshan moya shike* 黃山摩崖石刻 (*Stone Cut Inscriptions at the Yellow Mountains*, Shanghai: Xuelin chubanshe, 2006, p. 48).

[11] His younger paternal cousin, Cao Yin 曹寅 (1659–1712) would become in turn the grandfather of one of the giants of Chinese literature, Cao Xueqin 曹雪芹 (1715–1763), celebrated as the author of the classic Chinese novel, *Dream of the Red Chamber* (*Hong lou meng*, 紅樓夢, also titled *Shitou ji* 石頭記, or *Story of the Stone*).

[12] Zhu Yizun, *Pushuting xuba: Qiancaitang Song Yuan ren ji mulu: Zhucha xingji shumu* 曝書亭序跋: 潛采堂宋元人集目錄: 竹垞行笈書目 ("Collected prefaces and colophons of Zhu Yizun with two of his bibliographical catalogues," Shanghai: Guji chubanshe, 2010), p. 93.

Confucianism and the Yellow Mountains

[13] Frederic Wakeman, Jr., *The Great Enterprise,* 2 vols. (Berkeley: University of California Press, 1985), 2:1093–1094.

[14] In fact, while Zhu Xi was born in Fujian Province, his family originated in Wuyuan (婺源), located in the Song-dynasty province of Jiangdong (江東) that had covered most of what by the early Qing was divided into Anhui and Jiangxi 江西 Provinces, but regarded by early Qing scholars as belonging to the Huizhou (徽州) or southern Anhui region. The claim that the ancestors of the Cheng brothers were from Shexian (歙縣), one of the counties most closely associated with the Yellow Mountains, was more controversial, and did not go unchallenged.

[15] Wang Shizhen, *Chibei outan* 池北偶談 ("Casual Chats North of the Pond"), edition in 2 vols. (Beijing: Zhonghua shuju, 1982), 1:79.

[16] See the recently published complete *shi* poetry of Shi Runzhang, *Shi Runzhang shi* 施閏章詩(Yangzhou: Guangling shushe, 2006 2 vols), 1:411.

[17] Personal communication. I am most grateful to Zhao Hongwei for researching this matter, and for calling my attention to the letter by Shi mentioned below.

[18] Shi Runzhang, *Xueyutang wenji* 學餘堂文集 ("Collected Writings from the Hall of Leisure after Study," his collected prose writings), edition of the *Siku quanshu,* 28/6b–8a.

[19] Geoffrey Keynes, ed., *Blake: Complete Writings* (London: Oxford University Press, 1966 edition of 1957 Nonesuch Press publication), pp. 480–481. This is of course the poem from the preface to Blake's *Milton* (1804–1808).

[20] See Wang Shiqing 汪世清, *Ming Qing Huangshan xueren shi xuan* 明清黃山學人詩選 ("An Anthology of Poems by Scholars of the Ming and Qing Dynasties Associated with the Yellow Mountains," Shanghai: Shanghai guji chubanshe, 2008), pp. 35–41, especially pp. 40–41.

Indeed, all these men are closely connected in a number of ways. Shi Runzhang himself, as it happens, may have been a painter: a poem addressed to him by yet another cultural arbiter of the day, and a major poet, Gong Dingzi 龔鼎孳 (1615–1673) describes an album of landscape paintings which was presumably painted by Shi. For this, see the newly published complete edition of Gong's poetry, *Gong Dingzi shi* 龔鼎孳詩 (Yangzhou: Guangling shushe, 2006, 2 vols.), 2:796. Note the grammatically identical title to a poem on p. 1304 where the poem text definitely identifies the recipient as the *painter*, and not merely owner, of the album.

21 Wang Hongdu knew Zha Shibiao; in a colophon dated 1713 to an album by Zha currently in the Moss Collection, London, Wang recalls a conversation with Zha about the art of painting.

22 See Jonathan Chaves, "Moral Action in the Poetry of Wu Chia-chi," *Harvard Journal of Asiatic Studies* Vol. 46: No. 2 (Dec. 1986), pp. 387–469.

23 Wu Yuan, *Bei Yi shanren shi* 北黟山人詩 ("Poetry by the Mountain Man of the Northern Yi Mountains", Kangxi period edition as reprinted in *Siku quanshu huishu congkan* 四庫禁燬書叢刊 ("Collectanea of Books Banned and Burned in the Four Treasuries"), p. 640. The Yi ("Dark") Mountains was an ancient name for the Yellow Mountains. Note that the title is sometimes given as *Bei Qian* 北黔.

24 For Wang Shuqi, see Wang Shiqing, *op. cit.*, pp. 392–404. See also Deng Zhicheng 鄧之誠, *Qingshi jishi chubian* 清詩紀事初編 in 2 vols. (Shanghai: Guji chubanshe, 1984 reprint of 1965 edition), 2:579.

25 Wang Hongdu, *Xin'an nüshi zheng* (copy in Shanghai Library Rare Book Reading Room, 1706), [pp. 1a–2b]; there is no pagination.

26 Personal communication. She calls attention to p. 331 of this publication as it appears in the *Zhongguo fangzhi congshu* 中國方志叢書, No. 246, "Anhui."

27 *Qinglian yusong*, copy in Anhui Provinical Museum, 1a–2a.

28 I was able to examine a copy of the first two *juan* of this work, and a microfilm of the whole, in the Anhui Provincial Library, Hefei. I have not seen the supplement and remain uncertain as whether it simply repeated or added to the illustrations already in the 1690 gazetteer. See Wang Shiqin, *Juanhuai tiandi zi you zhen—Wang Shiqing Yiyuan cha'yi buzheng sankao* 卷懷天地自有真—汪世清藝苑查疑補證散考 ("'Yes, there are truths, rolled up and hidden between Heaven and Earth'—the scattered

studies of Wang Shiqing on his investigations of problems in the world of art, with additional evidence,") 2 vols. (Taipei: Rock Publishing International, 2006), 1:225–228 for Wu Yi and the confusion that has arisen between him and another man named Sun Yi 孫逸.

[29] Wang Qimin 王啓敏 *et al.*, *Huangshan zhenxi zhiwu* 黄山珍稀植物 ("Rare Flora of the Yellow Mountains," Beijing: Zhongguo linye chubanshe, 2006).

[30] For Xuezhuang, see Joseph Chang, "A Wild Man and His Cloud Boat on the Yellow Sea: The Monk Xuezhuang and His Huangshan Residence," *Orientations* (Volume 39, No. 4, May 2008), pp. 3–5. For the Song Luo poems, see his collected works, *Xipo leigao* 西陂類稿 ("MSS Arranged by Category from West Slope"), 14/17b–21b. We learn that the names of the flowers depicted by Xuezhuang were carefully written down by a certain Wu Song 吳菘, courtesy name Qiyuan 綺園, who turns out to be one of three younger brothers of Wu Yuan, all of whom were poets. Interestingly, Wu Song's name is inscribed by hand on the cover of the copy of *Qinglian yusong* in the Anhui Provincial Museum, along with that of Wu Zhanqi 吳瞻淇 (degree 1703), the son of Wu Yuan and thus nephew to Wu Song. It is clear that Wu Yuan and his family were central in these circles. As for Sung Lo, he also contributed a preface to Zha Shibiao's printed poetry collection of 1700. It should further be noted that according to Song's preface to his set of poems on Xuezhuang's flower paintings, some of the flowers did not even have recognized names, and therefore he decided not to write poems about them!

For Wu Yuan's linked-verse on Xuezhuang's flower paintings, see *Bei Yi shanren shi*, pp. 710–711 (or 10/8b–10a). Other participants in writing this linked-verse were Wu Song and Wu Zhantai 瞻泰 (1657–1735), the latter being the elder brother of Wu Zhanqi.

DAOISM, BUDDHISM, AND THE YELLOW MOUNTAINS

[31] For a useful introduction to the whole question of different modes of Daoist philosophy or religion, see Herrlee G. Creel's classic study, "What is Taoism?" in his book, *What is Taoism? and Other Studies in Chinese Cultural History* (Chicago and London: The University of Chicago Press, 1970), pp. 1–25. The tension to which Creel calls attention between

"philosophical" Daoism, with its serene acceptance of death as part of the cosmic cycle, and what he calls "Hsien" (Xian) Daoism, with its aspiration to conquer death, remains key.

[32] Bai Ju'yi, *Baishi changqingji* 白氏長慶集, edition of the *Siku quanshu*, 3/4a–b. These are the concluding lines of Bai's devastating attack on Xian Daoism, *Hai manman* 海漫漫, "The Ocean is So Vast," in Bai's words, "an injunction against seeking to become an Immortal" (*jie qiu xian ye* 戒求仙也), one of his great series of fifty protest poems, *Xin yuefu* 新樂府, "New Music Bureau Poems."

[33] Wu Jingzi, *Julin waishi* (Macau: Xinsheng chubanshe, n.d. in 2 vols.), 1:121 ff. For an English translation, see Yang Hsien-yi and Gladys Yang, trans., with a foreword by C.T. Hsia (New York: Columbia University Press, 1992), pp. 193 ff. The episode takes place in Ch. 15.

[34] Zhang Yong and Pan Zhongli, *Huangshan tujing di banben yanjiu* （黃山圖經）的版本研究 ("A Study of the Printed Editions of *Huangshan tujing*"), *Zhongguo difang zhi* 中國地方志 (the journal, "Chinese Gazetteers"), 2007, no. 10, pp. 57–62. I am indebted to James Hargett for calling to my attention this article, as well as the *Huang hai* (see below).

[35] *Siku quanshu cunmu congshu* (Jinan: Qilu shushe, 1996), Vol. 229, pp. 804–807 for the "Investigation," and Vol. 230, pp. 1–7 for the remaining fragments of the actual work.

[36] *Ibid.*, Vol. 230, p. 230, upper level.

[37] Wang Hongdu, *Xilu shi* 息廬詩 (printed 1772; copy in Anhui Provincial Museum, Hefei), section of seven-character quatrains, p. 2a.

[38] Philip Sherrard, *Athos—The Holy Mountain* (Woodstock, New York: The Overlook Press, 1985), p. 67 and *passim*.

[39] See Wang Shiqing, *Ming Qing, op. cit.*, p. 25.

[40] See the edition of the *Siku quanshu*, 71/18b–20a. See also Wang Shiqing, *Ming Qing, op.cit.*, p. 383. For further information and bibliography on Xiong, see *Mingren zhuanji ziliao suoyin* 明人傳記資料索引 ("An Index to Bibliographical Materials for Persons of the Ming Dynasty"), published by the National Central Library, Taipei (Taipei: Guoli zhongyang tushuguan, 1965–1966, 2 vols.), 2:771–772.

[41] Wu Weiye, *Wu Meicun shiji jianzhu* 吳梅村詩集淺注 (Shanghai: Guji chubanshe, 1983, 2 vols.), 2:674–676.

[42] For Cao as a *ci* poet, see Lo and Schultz, *op. cit.*, pp. 134–138.

[43] Shen Deqian, *Qingshi biecaiji* (Shanghai: Guji chubanshe, 1984, 2 vols.), 1: pp. 222–223.

[44] For Qian's poems on this subject, see Jonathan Chaves, "The Yellow Mountain Poems of Ch'ien Ch'ien-i (1582–1664): Poetry as *Yu-chi* [travel essay]," *Harvard Journal of Asiatic Studies*, Vol. 48, no.2, Dec., 1988. For his prose travel essays on the Yellow Mountains, see Stephen McDowall, *Qian Qianyi's Reflections on Yellow Mountain: Traces of a Late-Ming Hatchet and Chisel* (Hong Kong University Press, 1981). For more on Qian as a poet, see the superb recent study by Lawrence C.H. Yim, *The Poet-historian Qian Qianyi* (London and New York: Routledge, 2009).

[45] *Siku quanshu congmu congshu*, Vol. 240, pp. 363–490. The Yellow Mountains poems are on pp. 383–490.

[46] Wu Qi, *Linhuitang quanji* 林蕙堂全集 ("Complete Writings from the Tree-Orchid Hall", edition of the *Siku quanshu*), 1/15b. For more on Wu Qi, see Wang Shiqing, *Ming Qing, op. cit.*, pp. 118–121.

[47] In fact, the line is by the Yuan-dynasty poet, Yu Ji 虞集 (1272–1348).

[48] According to the colophon to *Huangshan lingyao lu*, Wang Hongdu (presumably joined by his brother for at least part of the time) resided there for a period of ten years, although it is not yet possible to detemine the precise years of residence. The colophon places the residence "at the top" of the peak, although Wang Shiqing states that is was "below" the peak, and has long since disappeared (*Ming Qing, op. cit.*, p. 286.)

[49] Yang Jiqing 楊積慶, ed., *Wu Jiaji shi jianjiao* 吳嘉紀詩箋校 (Shanghai: Guji chubanshe, 1980), pp. 220–221. For more on Wu Jiaji, see Jonathan Chaves, "Moral Action in the Poetry of Wu Chiachi," Harvard Journal of Asiatic Studies Vol. 46: No. 2 (Dec. 1986), pp. 387–469.

[50] See Wu Lunzhong 吳倫仲 *et al.*, *Huangshan moya shike* 黃山摩崖石刻 ("Stone Cut Inscriptions at the Yellow Mountains," Shanghai: Xuelin chubanshe, 2006), p. 92 for color reproduction and transcription

of text. For the practice of cutting inscriptions in the living rock, and other surfaces, see Robert E. Harrist, Jr., *The Landscape of Words: Stone Inscriptions from Early and Medieval China* (Seattle: University of Washington Press, 2008).

51 See Judith A. Berling, *The Syncretic Religion of Lin Chao-en* [1517–1598] (New York: Columbia University Press, 1980).

52 For a superb pictorial survey of surviving southern Chinese folk religious practice as found in Taiwan, see Ruan Changrui 阮昌銳, *Zhuangyan di shijie* 莊嚴的世界 (Taipei: Wenkai chuban shiye gufen youxian gongsi, 1982 2 vols.).

53 See Jonathan Chaves, "Gone With the Flow of Time: Lost Water Paintings of China," *Asian Art & Culture*, Spring/Summer, 1995, pp. 52–59.

54 For other instances, see Jonathan Chaves, "Moral Action in the Poetry of Wu Chia-chi," pp. 420 ff.

55 Shi Runzhang, *Juzhai zaji, bieji* 矩齋雜記，別集 (*Miscellaneous Records from the Carpenter's Square Studio*, supplementary collection), p. 3/10b; in *Shi Yushan xiansheng quanji* 施愚山先生全集 ("The Complete Works of Mr. Shi Yushan [Runzhang])," edition in Library of Congress dated 1765.

56 See the translation by Conrad Schirokauer (Yale Univerity Press, 1981), *passim*.

57 Maurice Freedman, "On the Sociological Study of Chinese Religion," in Arthur P. Wolf, ed., *Religion and Ritual in Chinese Society* (Stanford University Press, 1974), pp. 36–37. The entire article is an incisive presentation of this subject, pp. 19–41.

WANG HONGDU AS POET

58 Paul Moss, *This Single Feather of Auspicious Light—Old Chinese Painting and Calligraphy* (multivolume set; London: Sydney L. Moss, Ltd., 2010), Vol. III, pp. 726–743. Note that Wang Daokun is actually great grand-uncle of Wang Hongdu.

[59] Tan Zhengbi 譚正璧 (1901–1991), *Zhongguo wenxuejia da cidian* 中國文學家大辭典 (Taipei: Shijie shuju, 1971, 2 vols.), 2:1466, No. 5793. Tan says his birth and death dates are unknown, and that he "flourished around the year 1711."

[60] Wang Shizhen, *Gufuyuting za lu* 古夫于亭雜錄 ("Miscellaneous Records from the Gufuyu Pavilion," edition of the Siku quanshu), 1/9b.

[61] Paul Moss, *op. cit.*, Vol. III, p. 740.

[62] The edition I consulted inexplicably misprints the third character of his name—which should be *zhen* 禎—as *zheng* 正. (This may simply have been an error on the part of the craftsman who carved the blocks, as *zhen* and *zheng* sound even closer in fact than appears in romanization, with many pronouncing the first as if there was a light "g" at the end; what is more, the erroneous character would actually work perfectly well in this position as part of the name.) Nevertheless, the editor's courtesy name is correctly given on the cover: Wang Ruanting 王阮亭.

[63] For him, see Wang Shiqing, *Ming Qing, op. cit.*, pp. 232–235. A significant poet, he was a close friend of Wu Jiaji.

[64] For Lu You's colophon, see *Huang Tingjian he Jiangxi shipai juan* 黃庭堅和江西詩派卷 ("The Volume on Huang Tingjian and the Jiangxi School of Poetry") in the series, *Gudian wenxue yanjiu ziliao huibian* 古典文學研究資料彙編 ("Compilations of Research Materials on Classical Literature," Beijing: Zhonghua shuju, 1978, 2 vols.): 1:112. The name of "Cheng Zhengbo" has been silently corrected from the erroneous printing of "Chen Bozheng" 陳伯正 (*sic*) in the volume of Wang Hongdu's poetry, *Xilu shi*.

[65] Note that Wu Yuan is partially quoting and partially paraphrasing from the original colophon by Lu You.

[66] See Han Yu, *Wubaijia zhu Changli wenji* 五百家注昌黎文集 ("The Collected Writings of Changli as Annotated by Five Hundred Commentators"), edition of the *Siku quanshu*, 37/11b.

[67] Gongsun Hong 公孫弘 (d. 121 BC), a righteous man who rose from poverty to become a Privy Councilor of Emperor Wu of the Han dynasty, but continued to live extremely frugally; he was falsely accused by an envious official of doing so merely to "fish for fame."

[68] This refers to a passage in Mencius, *Gongsun Chou/shang* 公孫丑/上.
问曰：夫子当路于齐，管仲、晏子之功可复许乎？
孟子曰：子诚齐人也，知管仲、晏子而已矣。

Asked whether, given the reigns of power in the state of Qi, Mencius
could replicate the accomplishments of famed former Qi prime ministers,
Guan Zi and Yan Zi ["Master Guan" and "Master Yan," both famed as
philosophers], Mencius replied, "You, sir, are truly a man of Qi. Thus
you know *only* of Guan Zong [Master Guan] and Master Yan!" The
implication is that there are critics in the world who are only willing to
promote the reputations of writers from their own home provinces.

[69] See Wu Yuan, *Bei Yi shanren shi*, pp. 645–648 for Wu's set of
twenty such poems, entitled *Huangshan ji* 黄山集, "Yellow Mountains
Collection," with its own prose preface.

[70] *Xilu shii, Qiyan gu* 七言古 ("Seven character per line ancient-style
verse"), pp. 10b–11a.

[71] Wang Shiqing, *Juanhuai, op. cit.*, 1:343–353.

[72] Cited by Zheng Xizhen 鄭錫珍, *Hongren Kuncan* 弘仁髡殘
("Hungren and Kuncan," Shanghai: Renmin meishu chuban she, 1963),
p. 8. For a fine, complete study of Hongren's art, see Jason Kuo, *The
Austere Landscape: The Paintings of Hung-jen* (Taipei and New York: SMC
Publishing in cooperation with University of Washington Press, 1991).

[73] McDowall, *op. cit., passim.*

[74] See Wang Qimin *et al., op. cit.*, pp. 98–99, and for the surviving
"named" pines, pp. 128–139.

[75] *Shi Runzhang shi, op. cit.*, 1:409–410, and 433. Mei Qing was a
member of the ancient Mei clan of Xuancheng, a descendant of its most
famous representative, the great poet, Mei Yaochen 梅堯臣 (1002–
1060). His pride in his hometown was such that he produced an album
of no less than twenty-four views of the city and its environs, dated to
1680. This work, once divided into two albums but now reunited, is in
the Charles A. Drenowatz collection, currently housed in the Reitberg
Museum, Zurich. It has been thoroughly analyzed by Chu-tsing Li in
his catalogue of that collection, *A Thousand Peaks and Myriad Ravines:
Chinese Paintings in the Charles A. Drenowatz Collection* (Ascona: 1974,
2 vols.), 1:186–199; 2:Fig. 46, Plates LXII–LXX. Mei includes scenes

involving the place of study and the tomb of Mei Yaochen, whom he proudly refers to as his "ancestor," 1:191 and 194. This sense of local pride has been given new vitality in our time. In May of 2011, I visited the site of a commemorative park in Xuancheng, then under construction. This memorial monument at that stage of development displayed a huge, bronze statue of Mei Yaochen (absurdly transforming him into an icon of Proletarian Heroism), and a traditional-style stone gateway, inscribed with the name of the park: Meixi gongyuan 梅溪公園 (Mei Stream Park), in front, and Meishi guli 梅氏故里 (Hometown of the Mei Clan), on the other side (facing the statue of Mei Yaochen). The Municipal Museum of Xuancheng has a special hall dedicated to the memory of another famous Mei of Xuancheng, Mei Wending (1633–1721), contemporaneous with Mei Qing and the other men discussed here, and himself a scholar and poet, today best remembered as a mathematician, his contributions to mathematics having been honored by a conference held in Xuancheng to mark the building of the hall, and the three hundred fifty-fifth anniversary of Mei Wending's birth, in 1988. See Cheng Sibao 程思寶, *Mei Wending: Qingchao diyiliu shuxuejia* 梅文鼎: 清朝第一流數學家 ("Mei Wending: A First-Class Mathemetician of the Qing dynasty," Xuancheng: Mei Wending Commemorative Hall, 2005). This includes the preface to Mei Wending's collected writings, by none other than Shi Runzhang (pp. 99–100). Shi opens his preface by putting Mei Wending in the line of poets originating from Mei Yaochen. He speaks of "the Mei clan of this, our Wanling," Wanling 宛陵 ("sloping banks of the Wan River") being an ancient alternative name for Xuancheng, as well as the name of Mei Yaochen's collected writings, *Wanling ji* 集. Mei Wending, it might be added, in 1688 and in the city of Hangzhou, paid a call on one of the leading Jesuit missionaries in China at the time, Prospero Intorcetta, S.J. (1642–1696), requesting his instruction in Western mathematics! (*Ibid.*, p. 81, where reference is also briefly made to a painting done by Mei Wending while visiting West Lake). Intorcetta is best known today for collaborating with the great Belgian missionary, Philippe Couplet, S. J. (1623–1693) on the publication of *Confucius Sinarum Philosophus* (1687), one of the most influential early books for Western knowledge of Chinese civilization. For Intorcetta's role in this project, and his importance in general, see Jerome Heyndrickx, ed., *Philippe Couplet, S.J.: The Man Who Brought China to Europe* (Nettetal: Steyler Verlag, 1990), *sub voce*. In addition, in 1690, Mei Wending discussed mathematics and astronomy (it should be kept in mind that his interests covered both, as they were seen to very closely related, both by the Chinese and by the Jesuits) with a Belgian Jesuit, Antoine Thomas, S.J. (1644–1709), who, prior to coming to China, had consulted with leading astronomers in France. What is more, Thomas functioned as personal instructor of the Kangxi Emperor in arithmetic and other aspects of mathematics and science. For all of this, see Cheng Sibao, *op. cit.*, p. 82 (where Thomas is wrongly identified as "French"); John Witek, S. J., "Philippe Couplet: A Belgian Connection to the Beginning of the Seventeenth-Century French Jesuit Mission in China," in Heyndrickx, *op. cit.*, pp. 148 and 151; and Catherine Jami's recent detailed discussion of Mei Wending's "efforts to integrate Chinese and Western mathematics" in her book, *The Emperor's New Mathematics: Western Learning and Imperial Authority During the Kangxi Reign*, 1662–1722, (Oxford University Press, 2012). Jami also gives details about Antoine Thomas and his mentorship of the Emperor. For a useful summary and critique of her book, see the review by Joseph W. Dauben in *Sino-Western Cultural Relations Journal* XXXIV (2012), pp. 70–81.

[76] Zhang Changhong, *Pinjian yu jingying: Mingmo Qingchu Huishang yishu zanzhu yanjiu* 品鑒與經營：明末清初徽商藝術贊助研究 ("Connoisseurship and Business: A Study of Artistic Patronage by Anhui Merchants in the Late Ming to Early Qing," Peking University Press, 2010), *passim*. See also Joseph McDermott, "The Making of a Chinese Mountain: Huangshan: Politics and Wealth in Chinese Art," *Asian Cultural Studies (Tokyo)* 17 (March 1989).

[77] Wu Yuan, *Bei Yi shanren shi*, p. 648.

[78] *Loc. cit.*, where Wang's poem is also appended; and *Xilu shi, Wuyan lü*, p. 9b. The text is identical in the two sources.

[79] *Xilu shi, wuyan lü*, pp. 6a–8b.

[80] See Arthur W. Hummel, *Eminent Chinese of the Ch'ing Period* (Taipei: Ch'eng Wen Publishing Company reprint of 1943 publication, 1975), pp. 415–416, 877–878.

[81] Wu Yuan, *Bei Yi shanren shi*, p. 633: the preface dated 1702 by Huang Liuhong 黃六鴻 (degree, 1651; fl. second half 17th c.– early 18th c.).

[82] For an excellent study of this poem, with full bibliographical citations, see David K. Schneider, *Confucian Prophet: Political Thought in Du Fu's*

Poetry (752–757), (Amherst, NY: Cambria Press, 2012), *passim*, especially Ch. 3, pp. 83 ff. I am grateful to Professor Schneider for the opportunity to consult this volume prior to publication.

[83] Yim, *op. cit.*, p. 148.

[84] Li Zhengchun 李正春, *Tangdai zushi yanjiu* 唐代組詩研究 ("A Study of Tang-dynasty Poem Sequences [or Cycles]," Nanjing: Fenghuang chubanshe, 2011), p. 166. I am grateful to Tao Feiya of Shanghai University for calling this work to my attention.

[85] Bai, *op. cit.*, 2/3b–8b, and chapters 3 and 4. For a seminal study of the Neo-Music Bureau cycle, see Chen Yinke 陳寅恪 (1890–1969), *Yuan Bai shi jianzheng gao* 元白詩淺證稿 ("Annotations and Evidentiary Material on the Poetry of Yuan [Zhen 稹 (779–831)] and Bai Ju'yi," Hong Kong: Shangwu yinshuguan, 1962), pp. 110–285.

[86] For the exchange of poems between these two men, see Yang Jiqing, *op. cit.*, pp. 141–142, 188 (for a poem by Wu to Wang's younger brother, Wenye), 220–221, 246, 541 (a poem from Wang to Wu).

[87] Shen, *op. cit.*, 1:607.

[88] Wang Yuqi and Wen Guoxin, *Lidai xushishi xuan* 歷代敘事詩選 (Guiyang: Guizhou renmin chubanshe, 1984), pp. 344–5.

[89] See the classic article by David T. Roy, "The Theme of the Neglected Wife in the Poetry of Ts'ao Chih," *The Journal of Asian Studies*, Vol. 19, No. 1 (Nov. 1959), pp. 25–31.

[90] Shen Deqian, *op. cit.*, 1:608.

[91] Qiu Zhao'ao 仇兆鰲 (1638–1717), *Dushi xiangzhu* 杜詩詳註 (edition of the *Siku quanshu*), 7/6b–9b.

[92] See the translation by Cyril Birch in his *Stories from a Ming Collection* (New York: Grove Press, 1958), pp. 45 ff.

[93] Edward Schafer, *The Divine Woman* (Berkeley: University of California Press, 1973, pp. 7–8.

[94] Zhang Yingchang, *Qingshi tuo* (Beijing: Zhonghua shuju, 2 vols.), 2:964.

[95] *Xilu shi, Qiyan gu*, 7b.

[96] *Ibid.*, *Qiyan gu*, 4a.

[97] See the meticulous annotated translation by Chung-wen Shih, *Injustice to Tou O (Tou O Yüan)* in the series, Studies in Chinese Linguistics (Cambridge University Press, 1972).

[98] See Chaves, *Moral Action*, pp. 397–8 and *passim*.

[99] *Xilu shi*, *Qiyan gu*, 4a–b.

[100] A particularly significant example is that of the highly innovative scholar, proto-anthropologist, and poet from Guangdong, Qu Dajun 屈大均 (1630–1696), to whom Wang Hongdu sent at least two poems that are recorded in *Xilu shi*. (Unfortunately the page numbers for these poems are unavailable. One is given, however, by Wang Shiqing, *Ming Qing, op. cit.*, p. 288.) Wang also contributed a colophon to an album of paintings for him, with leaves by such artists as Xuezhuang and Mei Qing; see Moss, *This Single Feather…*, III:742. Qu has poems of his own on no less than four of the cases that moved Wang Hongdu to verse (in the order in which they appear in Qu's works): the "pine-embracing woman;" the "calendar pearls;" the "human food market (see below);" and the old man who fell through the ice with his grandson. The first and fourth of these are designated *cao* 操, that is, songs to be accompanied by the *qin* 琴 (zither), again, a genre associated with antiquity and vaguely with both the *Shi jing* and *Li sao* traditions. In general, Qu seems to have mythologized the themes to a far greater extent than Wang, even bringing in supernatural elements such as the River God who puts in an appearance in the poem on the old man and his grandson. Although it is impossible to say which poet addressed the themes first, one gets the impression that Wang was closer to the actual events—especially given the Xuancheng venue of one of them—and he certainly presents them in a more "journalistic," realistic manner. In these cases and in others, several writers of the circles under consideration would be inspired to write on the same incidents; they may have shared information about them, or simply have been influenced by each others' poems. Qu's poems will be found in his *Daoyuantang ji* 道援堂集 ("Collected Writings from the Hall Where the Way is of Help"), preface dated 1704 (copy consulted in Library of Congress), 10/31a–33a.

[101] Wang Shizhen, *Chibei outan*, 1:166–167.

[102] *Shi Runzhang shi*, 1:25.

[103] *Xilu shi, Qiyan gu,* 4b–5a.

[104] *Ibid.*, *Qiyan* lü, pp. 8a–b.

[105] See Jonathan Chaves, *Mei Yao-ch'en and the Development of Early Sung Poetry* (New York and London: Columbia University Press, 1976), pp. 160–163. See also Ann Barrott Wicks, ed., *Children in Chinese Art* (Honolulu: University of Hawaii Press, 2002), for articles on the depiction of children in art, with literary references.

[106] For this, see Chaves, *Singing of the Source,* pp. 14–16, and *Gathering Tea for God, loc. cit.*

[107] *Ibid.*, *Qiyan jueju,* pp. 1a–b.

[108] See Chaves, *Gathering Tea for God,* pp. 19–23. For Gu, see Laurence Schneider, *Ku Chieh-kang and China's New History: Nationalism and the Quest for New Traditions* (Berkeley: University of California Press, 1971).

[109] In May, 2011, I had an opportunity to visit a workshop for the making of Xuan paper (i.e., paper from Xuanzhou 宣州), in the village of Shanglingkeng 雙嶺坑 (Twin Peak Gulley), not far from the town of Jingxian 涇縣，Anhui. The primary ingredient is the stripped-off bark of the wingceltis tree (*tanshu* 檀樹, or *qingtanshu* 青檀樹)，a variety found only in southern Anhui, and used for paper manufacture from at least the early Tang dynasty. For the development of paper making in Anhui, see Mu Xiaotian 穆孝天, *Anhui wenfang sibao shi* 安徽文房四寶史 (*A History of the Four Treasures of the Scholar's Studio in Anhui,* Shanghai: Shanghai renmin meishu chubanshe, 1962), pp. 1–12.

[110] For this famous story, see Richard Mather, trans., *Shih-shuo hsin-yü: A New Account of Tales of the World* by Liu I-ch'ing (Minneapolis: University of Minnesota Press, 1976), p. 389.

COMPREHENDING THE ESSENTIALS OF THE YELLOW MOUNTAINS

[111] Zhao Fang actually lived only one year into the Ming dynasty. Wang is referring to his "Preface to the Poems on Seeing Off the Great Scholar, Chen, as He Returns to the Yellow Mountains." This is found

in Zhao's collected writings, *Dongshan cungao* 東山存稿, Siku quanshu, 2/38a. The poems themselves are recorded in *Xin'an wenxian zhi* 新安文獻志 compiled by Anhui scholar, Cheng Minzheng 程敏政(1445–1500), *Siku quanshu,* 51xia/11a–12a. This is a set of five poems on specific spots in the mountains. The title of the set is *Fenti song Chen Zishan boshi you Huangshan* 分題送陳子山博士遊黃山, "Being Allotted Titles, Seeing Off Scholar Chen Zishan on His Excursion to the Yellow Mountains." The names of specific places were allotted to the various poets participating in the farewell gathering.

[112] Zhu Lu (1553–1632). A bamboo painter, represented by a folding fan mounted as an album leaf in the Metropolitan Museum of Art, of a bamboo with poem. Four poems of his are recorded by Zhu Yizun in his anthology of Ming poetry, *Mingshi zong* 明詩综, *Siku quanshu,* 72/16b ff. According to the latter, he traveled by himself to the Yellow Mountains, and to the sacred peaks Song and Hua, supporting himself wherever he went by painting bamboo. Eventually retired below Lotus Peak at Mount Hua.

[113] Hong Zong (1620–85). For more on him, see Wang Shiqing *Ming Qing, op. cit.*, pp. 140–142.

[114] Min Linsi (1628–1704). A major figure in Yellow Mountains literature; a poet himself, and the chief editor of the major Yellow Mountains gazetteer, *Huangshan zhi dingben* 黃山志定本.

[115] Wu Yuan (1638–1700), himself a leading poet of the Yellow Mountains. See references to him throughout this book.

[116] See below.

[117] Shao Shusheng, a man of Shexian, is recorded in Wan Shiqing, *Ming Qing, op. cit.*, p. 4.

[118] Chen Jiru 陳繼儒 (1558–1639), a major literatus of the day.

[119] Cao Fen 曹鈖 was a close friend and relative of the much more famous Cao Yin 曹寅 (1658–1712) who was, in turn, grandfather of Cao Xueqin 曹雪芹, see note 11.

[120] Gibbons are a standard trope in Chinese bestiary lore, according to which several of the creatures will reach drinking water by linking arms,

the first gibbon holding on to a tree above and the last one reaching the water to drink.

[121] Bao Yuanze, from She, also Zhengyuan 正元, Yuanze his courtesy name. Recorded in Wang Shiqing, *Ming Qing, op. cit.*, p. 4.

[122] The *qu* (簴) is a specially constructed frame for hanging bells, drums or chime-stones, here a single hanging chime.

[123] A square *gui* (簋) is a type of ancient Chinese ritual bronze vessel.

[124] This would appear to be a natural bridge.

[125] Pan Zhiheng 潘之恆 (c. 1536–1621), an associate of the writer's great grand-uncle, Wang Daokun, already discussed above. His lengthy work, *Huang hai* 黃海 (*Yellow Ocean*), is a compilation of passages from the classics and other sources referring to the Yellow Emperor. This includes a "Study of the Illustrated Classic of the Yellow Mountains" (*Huangshan tujing kao* 黃山圖經考) including several prefaces and colophons from the Song-dynasty text of this, the earliest gazetteer of the Yellow Mountains, as well as descriptions from the latter of the thirty-six chief peaks, thirty-six chief streams, and other features, the largest fragment of the apparently lost original to survive. (I am grateful to James Hargett for calling this work to my attention.)

[126] Fang Gongqian 方拱乾 is an important poet and scholar of the period.

[127] Yang Pu 楊補 (1598–1657), a painter.

[128] There is a three-character hiatus where the name should be.

[129] Wu Song 吳菘, the younger brother of Wu Yuan (see note 115), already mentioned in the text.

[130] For monk Pumen 普門, see Wang Shiqing, *Ming Qing, op. cit.*, p. 25. Pumen founded Compassionate Light Temple, and was the individual most responsible for the opening of the Yellow Mountains in this period.

[131] No longer exists; this is confirmed in Wang Longzhong *et al.*, p. 49.

[132] Wu Zhilu 吳之騄 (1644–1715), a poet from Shexian; see Wang Shiqing, *Ming Qing, op. cit.*, pp. 269–274. His collected poetry no longer survives.

[133] The tortoise-fish is a mythological creature with elements of both the carp and the tortoise, often used to decorate the roofs of shrine buildings.

[134] Wu Zhantai 吳瞻泰 (1657–1735), son of Wu Yuan (see note 115); see Wang Shiqing, *Ming Qing, op. cit.*, pp. 325–6. He was a poet himself, and also co-edited, with Wang Shizhen and Wang Hongdu, the collected poetry of poet and painter Cheng Jiasui 程嘉燧 (c. 1565–1643).

[135] Tang Binyin 湯賓尹 (degree 1595). A Hanlin Scholar from Anhui.

[136] Master Hong, Yunqi 雲棲紅公, also called Zhuhong 袾宏 (1535–1615), was the greatest monk of the age, famous for attempting a synthesis of Pure Land and Chan practices. He had many literati followers. See Kristin Yü Greenblatt, "Chu Hung and Lay Buddhism in Late Ming Thought," in William Theodore deBary, ed., *Self and Society in Ming Thought* (New York and London: Columbia University Press, 1970), pp. 188–225.

[137] Master Bo'an 檗菴, or Xiong Kaiyuan 熊開元, *jinshi* degree 1624, was a native of Shexian and a famous figure. As indicated in the text, his punishment resulted from his memorializing against a favorite of the last Ming Emperor. The "Ming loyalists" also included those who stood bravely against the acknowledged debauchery and decadence of the last Ming emperors. Wu Weiye has a pair of poems inspired by a portrait of him, with a lengthy, informative preface *Wu Meicun shiji jianzhu* (Wu's collected poetry), 2:674–676. See also Wang Shiqing, *Ming Qing, op. cit.*, p. 383 top.

[138] Master Tiefu 鐵夫師 is an elusive figure. Zhu Yizun knew him and has two poems involving him in his own collected works. The first is about a painting of magnolias by a certain Fang Qian 方乾, which the artist did for a "Monk Tiefu" 鐵夫上人. In the text, Zhu refers to this Fang Qian as associated with Heavenly Capital Peak, but nothing else about him is recorded. Immediately following this poem, in Ch. 21 of Zhu's collected works, is this delightful one:

題黃山鐵公小像

鐵公黃海至； 曾占最高峰
山後一茅屋； 階前萬壑松
禪心離怖畏； 詩卷閱春冬
不信巖居樂； 君看冰雪容

Inscribed on a Portrait of Master Tie of the Yellow Mountains

Master Tie, arrived at the Yellow Ocean
Chose for himself the very highest peak.
Behind that mountain, his one thatched hut;
Before its stairs, ten thousand gullies of pines.
His heart of Zen has left all fear behind;
His book of poems records each winter, spring.
If you don't believe the joy of cliff-top living,
Just look at his face, so pure!—Like ice, like snow.

See Zhu Yizun, *Pushuting ji* 曝書亭集 ("Collected Writings from the Pavilion for Airing Books"), edition of the *Siku quanshu,* 21/15a–16a.

[139] Eight Types of Heavenly Creatures; Humanoid Non-Humans: These are both Buddhist categories of fantastical creatures. The first consists of (1) Devas or deities like Indra and other celestial beings; (2) Nāgas or

divine serpents, assimilated by the Chinese to their own *long* or "dragons"; (3) yakṣas or demons; (4) gandharvas; (5) asuras; (6) garuḍ as or magical bird-like creatures; (7) kinnaras or bird-like creatures with human heads; (8) mahoragas. The second is a general category including those of these creatures that have humanoid features, like the kinnaras.

[140] Chan Master Xuezhuang 雪莊 (fl. late seventeenth century), one of the leading painters of the Yellow Mountains, whose work has only recently been rediscovered. Already discussed above; see note 30.

[141] See note 30.

[142] The characters for "embroidery" 縷 and "[in]numerable" 數 mistakenly reversed by woodblock cutter.

[143] Throughout this text, and in several other sources as well, the character *shi* 師 appears for *shi* 獅. Were it meant to be read as usual, the name of the locale would be "Forest of the Master," actually consistent with the fact that the place was founded for a Buddhist Master. But it is more likely that the character is simply an alternate version of the usual *shih* for lion, with the animal radical to the left.

[144] Monk Yi'cheng 一乘 was said to have founded the locale in 1612, upon arriving at the Yellow Mountains from the sacred Buddhist peaks of Five Terraces Mountain (Wutai shan).

[145] Zhao Huanguang, Hanshan 趙宦光, 寒山 (1559–1625), famed for his seal calligraphy.

[146] "Texture strokes," *cunfa* (皴法), a key term in Chinese painting, refers to the wrinkle-like brushstrokes used to articulate the surfaces of rocks and cliffs. The other kinds of brush-strokes mentioned by Wang are special variations of these.

[147] *Hu* (笏) are scepter-like objects of wood, bamboo, ivory, etc., used as emblems of office.

[148] Wu Shiquan 吳士權 was the Ming author of a book of six eulogies, or *sung* (頌), on the Yellow Mountains.

[149] In four-character metre, rhymed.

[150] I am grateful to Robert Gimello for a personal communication in which he speaks thus of Bhaiṣajya-guru, the "Medicine Teacher": "He's definitely a buddha, not a bodhisattva. His *buddhakṣetra* (buddha Land/ Field) is in the East (like Akṣobhya's), is made of *vaidurya* (lapis lazuli/ beryl?), and rivals Amityābha's Sukhāvatī in its splendor. There's another, lesser deity with a somewhat similar name— Bhaiṣajyarāja (藥王)— who is a bodhisattva, but he's rarer and not nearly as important."

[151] Wang Yangdu 汪洋度 (1647–?), was Wang Hongdu's younger brother, also a fine poet, who shared with him ten years of residence at this location, and figures in the discussion above.

[152] Jiang Tian'yi 江天一 (1602–45), is a revered Ming loyalist martyr. Although the inscription has long since disappeared, it is recalled and discussed in an inscription at more or less the same spot by the famed scholar, Li Yi'meng 李一氓 (1903–1990); see p. 34 for a discussion of this.

[153] Jin Wen'yi 金文毅, or Jin Sheng 金聲 (1589–1645), is another revered martyr for the Ming dynasty.

[154] "The Great Master of the Herb-Ground," Yaodi dashi 藥地大師, given name Fang Yizhi 方以智 (1611–71), is one of the most intriguing figures of the period, and the subject of Willard Peterson's classic study, *Bitter Gourd: Fang I-chih and the Impetus for Intellectual Change* (Yale University Press, 1979). He was also an esteemed painter; see Moss, *This Single Feather…*, 2:442–457.

[155] Divination blocks, *jiao* (珓 or 筊), also called moonblocks after their shape, are wooden fortune-telling tools typically used in pairs to request yes-no answers for questions asked of the spirits.

[156] Luo Rufang 羅汝芳 (1515–1588) was an important Neo-Confucian thinker of the "School of Mind," and disciple of Wang Ji 王畿 (1498–1583). At least one stone inscription of his still survives at the Yellow Mountains (see Wu Lunzhong *et al.*, p. 117), and other stone-cut calligraphy of his can be seen in the Xuancheng Municipal Museum. He also wrote poems about the Yellow Mountains.

[157] Presumably the previously mentioned "hut" was later developed into a Buddhist temple.

[158] See note 135.

[159] Wu Boyu 吳伯與 (*jinshi* degree 1613) was from Xuancheng. Also known as Fusheng 福生, or Suwen素雯, he authored an unpublished book on the Daoist thinker Zhuangzi.

[160] An old Chinese oil press and modern equivalent.

[161] See note 125.

[162] "Deep Verdancy," *xuanli* (懸黎), was the name of a dark-green jadestone of antiquity.

[163] As discussed in the first chapter, tradition claims that the name of every traveler who visits this spot will appear among the "inscriptions" (natural markings that look like archaic writing) on the "plaque." For an album leaf by painter Jiang Zhu depicting this spot, accompanied by an original poem by Wang Hongdu, pp. 4–5.

[164] See pp. 152–153.

[165] Shenduguo 身毒國, the earliest Chinese name for India, occurs in the *Shiji* (*Records of the Historian*, second century BC).

[166] Wang Zemin 汪澤民 (1273–1355), is a relatively rare example of a pre-Ming writer involved with the Yellow Mountains.

Bibliography

As the relevant literature is immense this bibliography does not aspire to comprehensiveness, but is limited to works most directly related to the themes explored in this book.

Bai Juyi 白居易. *Baishi changqingji* 白氏長慶集. Edition of the Siku quanshu.

Berling, Judith A. *The Syncretic Religion of Lin Chao-en* [1517–1598]. New York: Columbia University Press, 1980.

Birch, Cyril. *Stories from a Ming Collection*. New York: Grove Press,1958.

Cahill, James. "Huang Shan Paintings as Pilgrimage Pictures," in Susan Naquin and Chün-fang Yü, *Pilgrims and Sacred Sites in China*. Berkeley and Los Angeles: University of California Press, 1992.

_____. *Shadows of Mount Huang: Chinese painting and printing of the Anhui School*. Berkeley: University of California Art Museum, 1981.

Cao Zhenji 曹貞吉. *Huangshan jiyou shi* 黄山記游詩 ("Poems on Travels Through the Yellow Mountains"), edition of the Siku quanshu congmu congshu.

Chang, Joseph. "A Wild Man and His Cloud Boat on the Yellow Sea: The Monk Xuezhuang and His Huangshan Residence," *Orientations*, Volume 39, No. 4, May 2008, pp. 3–5.

Chaves, Jonathan. "Gathering Tea for God," *Sino-Western Cultural Relations Journal* XXIV (2002), pp. 6–23.

_____. "Gone With the Flow of Time: Lost Water Paintings of China," *Asian Art & Culture*, Spring/Summer, 1995, pp. 52–59.

_____. *Mei Yao-ch'en and the Development of Early Sung Poetry*. New York and London: Columbia University Press, 1976.

_____. "Moral Action in the Poetry of Wu Chia-chi," *Harvard Journal of Asiatic Studies*, Vol. 46: No. 2 (Dec. 1986), pp. 387–469.

_____. *Singing of the Source: Nature and God in the Poetry of the Chinese Painter, Wu Li* [1632–1718]. Honolulu: University of Hawaii Press, 1993.

_____. "The Yellow Mountain Poems of Ch'ien Ch'ien-i (1582–1664): Poetry as *Yu-chi* [travel essay]," *Harvard Journal of Asiatic Studies*, Vol. 48: no. 2 (Dec., 1988), pp. 465–492.

Chen Yinke 陳寅恪. *Yuan Bai shi jianzheng gao* 元白詩淺證稿 ("Annotations and Evidentiary Material on the Poetry of Yuan [Zhen 稹 (779–831)] and Bai [Ju'yi].") Hong Kong: Shangwu yinshuguan, 1962.

Cheng Mingzheng 程敏政. *Xin'an wenxian zhi* 新安文獻志 ("A Record of Literary Contributions from Xin'an"), edition of the Siku quanshu.

Cheng Sibao 程思寶. *Mei Wending: Qingchao diyiliu shuxuejia* 梅文鼎: 清朝第一流數學家 ("Mei Wending: A First-Class Mathemetician of the Qing dynasty.") Xuancheng: Mei Wending Commemorative Hall, 2005.

Creel, Herrlee G. "What is Taoism?" in his book, *What is Taoism? and Other Studies in Chinese Cultural History*. Chicago and London: The University of Chicago Press, 1970, pp. 1–25.

Deng Zhicheng 鄧之誠. *Qingshi jishi chubian* 清詩紀事初編. 2 vols. Shanghai: Guji chubanshe, 1984.

Du Fu. See under Qiu Zhao'ao.

Freedman, Maurice. "On the Sociological Study of Chinese Religion," in Arthur P. Wolf, ed., *Religion and Ritual in Chinese Society*. Stanford University Press, 1974, pp. 19–41.

Gong Dingzi. *Gong Dingzi shi* 龔鼎孳詩. 2 vols. Yangzhou: Guangling Shushe, 2006.

Greenblatt, Kristin Yü. "Chu Hung and Lay Buddhism in Late Ming Thought," in William Theodore deBary, ed., *Self and Society in Ming Thought*. New York and London: Columbia University Press, 1970, pp. 188–225.

Han Yu 韓愈. *Wubaijia zhu Chengli wenji* 五百家注昌黎文集 ("The Collected Writings of Changli [Han Yu] as Annotated by Five Hundred Commentators."). Edition of the Siku quanshu.

Harrist, Jr., Robert E. *The Landscape of Words: Stone Inscriptions from Early and Medieval China.* Seattle: University of Washington Press, 2008.

Heyndrickx, Jerome, ed., *Philippe Couplet, S.J.: The Man Who Brought China to Europe. Nettetal:* Steyler Verlag, 1990.

Huang Tingjian he Jiangxi shipai juan 黃庭堅和江西詩派卷. ("The Volume on Huang Tingjian and the Jiangxi School of Poetry"). 2 vols. In the series, *Gudian wenxue yanjiu ziliao huibian* 古典文學研究資料彙編 ("Compilations of Research Materials on Classical Literature"). Beijing: Zhonghua shuju, 1978.

Hummel Arthur W., *Eminent Chinese of the Ch'ing Period.* Taipei: Ch'eng Wen Publishing Company reprint of 1943 publication, 1975.

Kuo, Jason. *The Austere Landscape: Paintings of Hung-jen.* Taipei: SMC Publishing Co., 1998.

Li, Chu-tsing. *A Thousand Peaks and Myriad Ravines: Chinese Paintings in the Charles A. Drenowatz Collection.* 2 vols. Ascona, 1974.

Li Zhengchun 李正春. *Tangdai zushi yanjiu* 唐代組詩研究 ("A Study of Tang-dynasty Poem Sequences [or Cycles].") Nanjing: Fenghuang chubanshe, 2011.

Lo, Irving Yucheng and William Schultz. *Waiting for the Unicorn: Poems and Lyrics of China's Last dynasty.* Bloomington and Indianapolis: Indiana University Press, 1986.

Mather, Richard B., trans. *Shih-shuo Hsin-yü* [世說新語]—*A New Account of Tales of the World.* Minneapolis: University of Minnesota Press, 1976.

McDermott, Joseph. "The Making of a Chinese Mountain: Huangshan: Politics and Wealth in Chinese Art," *Asian Cultural Studies (Tokyo)* 17, March 1989.

McDowall, Stephen. *Qian Qianyi's Reflections on Yellow Mountain: Traces of a Late-Ming Hatchet and Chisel.* Hong Kong University Press, 2009.

Min Linsi閔麟嗣. *Huangshan zhi dingben* 黃山志定本. In *Anhui Congshu* 安徽叢書, 1935.

Mingren zhuanji ziliao suoyin 明人傳記資料索引 ("An Index to Bibliographical Materials for Persons of the Ming dynasty"). 2 vols. National Central Library, Taipei, 1965–1966.

Miyazaki Ichisada. *China's Examination Hell*. Translation by Conrad Schirokauer. Yale Univerity Press, 1981.

Moss, Paul. *This Single Feather of Auspicious Light—Old Chinese Painting and Calligraphy*. 4 vols. and 3 foldout portfolios. London: Sydney L. Moss, Ltd., 2010.

Mu Xiaotian 穆孝天. *Anhui wenfang sibao shi* 安徽文房四寶史 ("A History of the Four Treasures of the Scholar's Studio in Anhui.") Shanghai: Shanghai renmin meishu chubanshe, 1962.

Munakata, Kiyohiko. *Sacred Mountains in Chinese Art*. Urbana-Champaign, Illinois: Kranner Art Museum, 1990.

Pan Zhiheng 潘之恒 *Huang hai* 黃海 ("The Yellow [Cloud]Ocean"), 1612. Reprinted in Siku quanshu cunmu,1996.

Peterson, Willard. *Bitter Gourd: Fang I-chih and the Impetus for Intellectual Change*. Yale University Press, 1979.

Qiu Zhao'ao 仇兆鼇. *Dushi xiangzhu* 杜詩詳註 ("The Poetry of Du [Fu] with Detailed Annotations.") Edition of the Siku quanshu.

Qu Dajun 屈大均. *Daoyuantang ji* 道援堂集（"Collected Writings from the Hall Where the Way is of Help."）Preface dated 1704; copy consulted in Library of Congress.

Robson, James. *Power of Place: The Religious Landscape of the Southern Sacred Peak (Nanyue) in Medieval China*. Cambridge, Mass.: Harvard University Asia Center, 2009.

Roy, David T. "The Theme of the Neglected Wife in the Poetry of Ts'ao Chih." *The Journal of Asian Studies*, Vol. 19, No. 1 (Nov. 1959), pp. 25–31.

Ruan Changrui 阮昌銳. *Zhuangyan di shijie* 莊嚴的世界 ("A World of Solemn Beauty.") 2 vols. Taipei: Wenkai chuban shiye gufen youxian gongsi, 1982.

Schafer, Edward. *The Divine Woman.* Berkeley: University of California Press, 1973.

Schneider, Laurence. *Ku Chieh-kang and China's New History: Nationalism and the Quest for New Traditions.* Berkeley: University of California Press, 1971.

Schneider, David K. *Confucian Prophet: Political Thought in Du Fu's Poetry (752–757).* Amherst, New York: Cambria Press, 2012.

She xian zhi 歙縣志 or "Gazetteer of She Prefecture"of 1690. First two chapters, and microfilm of the whole, in the Anhui Provincial Library, Hefei.

She xian zhi 歙縣志 or "Gazetteer of She Prefecture" of 1937, in *Zhongguo fangzhi congshu* 中國方志叢書, No. 246, "Anhui."

Shen Deqian沈德潛 *Qing shi biecai ji* 清詩別裁集 ("A Separate [or Special] Selection of Qing dynasty Poetry.") 2 vols. Shanghai: Guji chubanshe, 1984.

Sherrard, Philip. *Athos—The Holy Mountain.* (Woodstock, New York: The Overlook Press, 1985.

Shi Runzhang 施閏章. *Juzhai zaji, bieji* 矩齋雜記，別集 ("Miscellaneous Records from the Carpenter's Square Studio, supplementary collection) in *Shi Yushan xiansheng quanji* 施愚山先生全集 ("The Complete Works of Mr. Shi Yushan [Runzhang]),"dated 1765, held by Library of Congress.

_____. *Shi Runzhang shi* 施閏章詩. 2 vols. Yangzhou: Guangling shushe, 2006.

_____. *Xueyutang wenji* 學餘堂文集 ("Collected Writings from the Hall of Leisure after Study," collected prose writings of Shi Runzhang), edition of the Siku quanshu.

Shishuo xinyu, see under Richard B. Mather

Shih, Chung-wen. *Injustice to Tou O (Tou O Yüan),* in the series, Studies in Chinese Linguistics, Cambridge University Press, 1972.

Song Luo 宋犖. *Xipo leigao* 西陂類稿 ("MSS Arranged by Category from West Slope"). Edition of the Siku quanshu.

Tan Zhengbi 譚正璧. *Zhongguo wenxuejia da cidian* 中國文學家大辭典 ("A Comprehensive Dictionary of Chinese Writers.") 2 vols. Taipei: Shijie shuju, 1971.

Wakeman, Jr., Frederic. *The Great Enterprise.* 2 vols. Berkeley: University of California Press, 1985.

Wang Hongdu. *Huangshan lingyao lu* 黃山領要錄 ("Comprehending the Essential of the Yellow Mountains"). Handwritten MS dated 1775, held by the Anhui Provincial Library, Hefei.

──────────. *Huangshan lingyao lu.* Printed edition in *Zhibuzuzhai congshu* 知不足齋叢書.

──────────. *Xilu shi.* 息廬詩. ("Poems from the Resting Hut.") Dated 1772, held by the Anhui Provincial Museum, Hefei.

──────────. *Xin'an nüshi zheng* 新安女史徵 ("Evidence for a History of Women in Xin'an.") Dated 1706, held by the Shanghai Library Rare Book Reading Room.

Wang Hongdu et al. *Qinglian yusong* 青蓮輿頌 ("Public Eulogies of the Blue Lotus"). Dated 1717, held by the Anhui Provinical Museum, Hefei.

Wang Qimin 王啓敏 et al. *Huangshan zhenxi zhiwu* 黃山珍稀植物 ("Rare Flora of the Yellow Mountains"). Beijing: Zhongguo linye chubanshe, 2006.

Wang Shihong 汪士鋐 (1632–1706). *Huangshan zhi xuji* 續集, in *Anhui congshu.*

Wang Shiqing 汪世清. *Juanhuai tiandi zi you zhen—Wang Shiqing Yiyuan cha'yi buzheng sankao* 卷懷天地自有真一汪世清藝苑查疑補證散考 (" 'Yes, there are truths, rolled up and hidden between Heaven and Earth'—the scattered studies of Wang Shiqing on his investigations of problems in the world of art, with additional evidence.") 2 vols. Taipei: Rock Publishing International, 2006.

──────────. *Ming Qing Huangshan xueren shi xuan* 明清黃山學人詩選 ("An Anthology of Poems by Scholars of the Ming and Qing Dynasties Associated with the Yellow Mountains.")Shanghai: Shanghai guji chubanshe, 2008.

Wang Shizhen 王士禎. *Chibei outan* 池北偶談 ("Casual Chats North of the Pond"). 2 vols. Beijing: Zhonghua shuju, 1982.

_____. *Gufuyuting za lu* 古夫于亭雜錄 （"Miscellaneous Records from the Gufuyu Pavilion."） Edition of the Siku quanshu.

Wang Wusheng. *Celestial Realm: The Yellow Mountains of China*. New York: Abbeville Press, 2006.

Wang Yuqi 王余杞 and Wen Guoxin 聞國新. *Lidai xushishi xuan* 歷代敍事詩選 ("An Anthology of Narrative Poems Down Through the Centuries.") Guiyang: Guizhou renmin chubanshe, 1984.

Wicks, Ann Barrott, ed. *Children in Chinese Art*. (Honolulu: University of Hawaii Press, 2002.

Wu Jiaji. See under Yang Jiqing.

Wu Jingzi 吳敬梓. *Julin waishi* 儒林外史 ("The Unofficial History of the World of the Scholars," or "The Scholars.") Macau: Xinsheng chubanshe, n.d., 2 vols.

_____. English translation of above: Yang Hsien-yi and Gladys Yang, trans., with a foreword by C.T. Hsia. New York: Columbia University Press, 1992.

Wu Lunzhong 吳倫仲 et al. *Huangshan moya shike* 黃山摩崖石刻 ("Stone Cut Inscriptions at the Yellow Mountains.") Shanghai: Xuelin chubanshe, 2006.

Wu Qi 吳綺. *Linhuitang quanji* 林蕙堂全集 ("Complete Writings from the Tree-Orchid Hall"). Edition of the Siku quanshu.

Wu Weiye 吳偉業. *Wu Meicun shiji jianzhu* 吳梅村詩集淺注. 2 vols. Shanghai: Guji chubanshe, 1983.

Wu Yuan 吳苑. *Bei Yi shanren shi* 北黟山人詩 ("Poetry by the Mountain Man of the Northern Yi Mountains.") Kangxi period edition as reprinted in Siku quanshu huishu congkan 四庫禁燬書叢刊 ("Collectanea of Books Banned and Burned in the Four Treasuries").

Xu Xiake. *Xu Xiake youji* 徐霞客遊記 ("The Travel Essays of Xu Xiake") 3 vols. Shanghai: Guji chubanshe.

Yang Jiqing 楊積慶, ed. *Wu Jiaji shi jianjiao* 吳嘉紀詩箋校. Shanghai: Guji chubanshe, 1980.

Yim, Lawrence C.H. *The Poet-historian Qian Qianyi*. London and New York: Routledge, 2009.

Zha Shibiao 查士標. *Meihe shanren yincao* 梅壑山人吟草 ("Draft MS of the Poetry of the Mountain Man of Plum Valley." Qing dynasty MS held by the Shanghai Library Rare Book Reading Room.

_____. *Zhongshutang yigao* 種書堂遺稿 ("Writings Preserved from the Hall for Planting Books"). Edition dated 1700, held by the Shanghai Library Rare Book Reading Room.

Zhang Changhong張長虹. *Mingmo Qingchu yishu Pinjian yu jingying: Mingmo Qingchu Huishang yishu zanzhu yanjiu* 品鑒與經營：明末清初徽商藝術贊助研究 ("Connoisseurship and Business: A Study of Artistic Patronage by Anhui Merchants in the Late Ming to Early Qing.") Peking University Press, 2010.

Zhang Yingchang 張應昌. *Qingshi tuo* 清詩鐸 ("The Tocsin Bell of Qing Poetry"), 1869. Modern edition, Beijing: Zhonghua shuju, 2 vols., 1960.

Zhang Yong and Pan Zhongli, "Huangshan tujing di banben yanjiu 黃山圖經 的版本研究 ("A Study of the Printed Editions of Huangshan tujing"), *Zhongguo difang zhi* 中國地方志 (the journal "Chinese Gazetteers"), 2007, no. 10, pp. 57–62.

Zheng Xizhen 鄭錫珍. *Hongren Kuncan* 弘仁髠殘 ("Hungren and Kuncan.") Shanghai: Renmin meishu chuban she, 1963.

Zhu Yizun 朱彝尊. *Pushuting ji* 曝書亭集 ("Collected Writings from the Pavilion for Airing Books"), edition of the Siku quanshu.

_____. *Pushuting xuba: Qiancaitang Song Yuan ren ji mulu: Zhucha xingji shumu* 曝書亭序跋: 潛采堂宋元人集目錄: 竹垞行笈書目 ("Collected prefaces and colophons of Zhu Yizun with two of his bibliographical catalogues"). Shanghai: Guji chubanshe, 2010.

Zhuang Mingjing 莊明景. *Huangshan zhi mei* 黃山之美 ("The Beauty of the Yellow Mountains," a book of photographs. Taipei: Jinxiu chubanshe, 1986.

Zurndorfer, Harriet T. *Change and Continuity in Chinese Local History: The Development of Hui-chou Prefecture 800–1800*. Leiden: Brill (Sinica Leidensia, No. 20), 1997.

CHARACTER LIST FOR CHINESE NAMES AND TERMS

Ai lian shuo 愛蓮説 *A Discourse on Cherishing the Lotus*

Bai Ju'yi (or Po Chü-i) 白居易 (772–846)

Bai yue 白岳 White Peaks

Bao Yuanze 鮑元則 (early-mid seventeenth century)

biji 筆記 brush notes

Bo'le 伯樂

Cao Dingwang 曹鼎望 (1618–1693)

Cao Fen 曹鈖 (b.c. 1655), courtesy name Binji 賓及

Cao Zhenji 曹貞吉 (1634–1698)

Cheng Chia-sui 程嘉燧 (1565–1643)

Cheng Hao 程顥 (1032–1085)

Cheng Sui 程邃 (1605–1691)

Cheng Yi 程頤 (1033–1107)

Cheng Zhengbo 程正伯 (late 12th century), courtesy name of Cheng
    Gai 程垓

Cheng Zhu queli zhi 程朱闕里志 *Gazetteer of the Ancestral Homes
    of the Chengs and Zhu Xi*

Chunqiu 春秋 *Spring and Autumn Annals*

Cimin 慈愍 uncertain dates

Dai Kui 戴逵 (d. 396)

dai 代 substitution

Dayong 大用 (late Ming dynasty)

Dongtu Xueshan 東土雪山 Eastern Terrain Snow Mountain

Dou E yuan 竇娥冤 *Injustice Done to Dou E*

Du Fu 杜甫 (712–770)

Emperor Lizong 理宗 (r. 1225–1264)

Fang Ye 方夜 (late Ming-early Qing dynasty)

Fang Yizhi 方以智 (1611–71), aka Yaodi dashi 藥地大師
    Great Master of the Herb-Ground

Fei bai 飛白 Flying White

Feiguang xiu 飛光岫 Flying Radiance Peak
Feng Menglong 馮夢龍 (1574–1646)
Feng Mengzhen 馮夢禎 (1548–1605)
Focheng 佛乘 (late Ming dynasty)
Geng Jingzhong 耿精忠 (1644–1682)
Gu Jiegang 顧頡剛 (1893–1980)
Guiji dianlu 會稽典錄 *Classic Records of Guiji*
Gu She shanchuan tu 古歙山川圖 *Illustrations of the Mountains and Rivers of Ancient She Prefecture*
Gu Zongbo 顧宗伯 (unidentifed), courtesy name, Xichou 錫疇
Guan Hanqing 關漢卿 (c.1240–c.1320)
Han jiang zi du zuo 寒江子獨坐 "Master Cold Stream [Jiang Tian'yi] Sits Alone"
Han Shan 寒山 (early 9th century)
Han Yu 韓愈 (768–824)
Hong Hanxian 洪憨仙 character in the novel *The Scholars*
Hongren 弘仁 (1610–1664), courtesy name Jian jiang 漸江
Huayan 華嚴 "Flower Garland" school of Buddhism; Skt. Avataṁsa
huang hai 黃海 cloud ocean
Huang Tingjian 黃庭堅 (1045–1105)
Huang Yigong 黃𡉉公, unidentified man referred to by Shi Runzhang
Huangdun 篁墩, placename in Anhui
Huangshan jiyou shi 黃山記遊詩 *Poems Recording Journeys to the Yellow Mountains*
Huangshan lingyao lu 黃山領要錄 *A Record of Comprehending the Essentials of the Yellow Mountains*
Huangshan tujing 黃山圖經 *Illustrated Classic of the Yellow Mountains*
Huangshan yin: zeng cao binji 黃山吟贈曹賓及, name of poem by Shi Runzhang
Huanyu zhi 寰宇志 *Gazetteer of the Entire Realm*
Hung Yunxing 洪雲行 disciple of Wang Hongdu
Jian jiang 漸江 a river in Anhui, also courtesy name of Hongren
Jiang Dong 江東 (Ming dynasty)
Jiang Tian'yi 江天一 (1602–1645), courtesy names Wenshi 文石, Chunchu 淳初, and Hanhao 涵灝
Jiang Zhenxian 蔣振先, also *She yihou Jiang gong* 歙邑侯蔣公 "Master Jiang, Magistrate of She City"
Jiang Zhu 江注 (fl. Kangxi period)
jie 節 chasteness

Jin Sheng 金聲 (1589–1645), courtesy name Wen'yi 文毅

Jin Wen'yi 金文毅 (see Jin Sheng)

Jin Zhijing 靳治荆 (Magistrate of She during the 1680's)

Jing xian 涇縣 Jing county

Jixi 績溪, a stream in Anhui

Jun'guo zhi 郡國志 *The Monograph on Commanderies and Kingdoms*

Juren 舉人 lower-level degree

Ke dao, ke dao 客到客到 "Guests come, guests come!"

Kong Shangren 孔尚任 (1648–1718)

Kuo'an 闊菴 (mid- or late-Ming dynasty)

Li Daoyuan 酈道元 (469–527)

Li Jingfang 李敬方 (ninth century)

Li Panlong 李攀龍 (1514–1570), courtesy name Yulin 于鱗

Li sao 離騷 *Encountering Sorrow*

Li Yimang (or meng) 李一氓 (1903–1990)

Lian dan feng 煉丹峯 Peak for Refining the Elixir

Lian shui 練水 Lian river, in Anhui

Lian xi 濂溪 Lian stream, associated with Zhou Dunyi

Liu Xie 劉勰 (c.465–c.520)

Liu Zhizhi 劉直指 (unidentified)

Lixue 理學 School of Principle

Luo Kai 羅愷 (unidentified)

Lu Ji 陸機 (261–303)

Lu You 陸游 (1125–121)

Lu Yun 陸雲 (262–303)

Luo Wengong 羅文恭 (1504–1564), courtesy name Hongxian 洪先

Master Fuqiu 浮丘公 legendary alchemist of high antiquity

Mei Qing 梅清 (1623–1697)

Meihe shanren yincao 梅壑山人吟草 *Draft MS of the Poetry of the Mountain Man of Plum Valley*

Min Linsi 閔麟嗣 (1628–1704)

Ming shi zong 明詩綜 *A Compilation of Ming Poetry*

Minjian zongjiao 民間宗教 folk religion (of the Yellow Mountains)

Pan Zhiheng 潘之恒 (c. 1536–1621)

Pumen 普門, a Buddhist monk

Qian Qian'yi 錢謙益 (1582–1664)

Qinglian yusong 青蓮輿頌 *Public Eulogies of the Blue Lotus*

qinglian 清廉 pure incorruptibility

Qingshi duo 清詩鐸 *The Tocsin Bell of Qing Poetry* [1869]

Qing shi biecai ji 清詩別裁集 *A Separate [or Special] Anthology of Qing dynasty Poetry*

qingtan 清談 pure discussion

Qinzhong yin 秦中吟 *Songs from the Qin Region* [ten poems]

Qu Yuan 屈原 (339–278 BC)

Rong Geng 容庚 (1894–1983)

Rulin wai shi 儒林外史 *Unofficial History of the Scholars*

Sanjiao wei yi 三教為一 "The Three Teachings are One"

Sanjue 三絕 the Three Perfections, i.e., poetry, painting, calligraphy

Shan 剡-stream paper

Shang shu 尚書 *Book of Historical Documents*

Shanhua pu 山花譜 *Manual of Mountain Flowers*

Shao Shusheng 佘書升 (early seventeenth century)

She xian zhi 歙縣志 *Gazetteer of She Prefecture*

Shen Deqian 沈德潛 (1673–1769)

Shen Jingxu 申清虛 alchemist of uncertain date, possibly Ming dynasty

Shexian 歙縣, Shexian, placename in Anhui

Shijing 詩經 *Book of Songs,* including sections titled *Daya* 大雅 and *Xiaoya* 小雅

Shi Li 施琜, courtesy name Zhicun 質存 (dates unknown)

Shi Runzhang 施閏章 (1618–1683)

shishi 詩史 poet-historian

Shi Xiansheng chang chui diao qi shang 石先生嘗垂釣其上 literally, "Mr. Shi [i.e., Zheng Yü] Once Fished Here" inscribed on a stone people call "Master Zheng's Fishing Rock"

Shuangzhi wu 雙枝塢, Twin Branch Embankment

Shui Guan 水官 Minister of Water

Shui jing zhu 水經注 *Water Classic with Annotations*

suisui 綏綏 "prowling back and forth"

Sung Luo 宋犖 (1634–1713)

Taohua shanji 桃花扇記 *The Peach Blossom Fan*

Tao Qian 陶潛 (365–427)

Tao Ya 陶雅 (early tenth century)

Tihua shi 題畫詩 poems inscribed on paintings

Wang Daokun 汪道昆 (1525–1593)

Wang Guanyu 王觀予, unidentified friend of Shi Runzhang

Wang He'de 汪詥德 (fl. Qianlong period)

Wang Hongdu 汪洪度 (1646–1721/22), courtesy name Yuding 于鼎

Wang Huizhi 王徽之 (d. 388)

Wang Ji 汪輯 (1636–1699), courtesy name Zhouci 舟次

Wang Shiduan 王石端 (dates unknown)

Wang Shizhen 王世貞 (1526–1590, courtesy name Yanzhou 弇州

Wang Shizhen 王士禎 (1634–1711)

Wang Shuqi 汪樹琪 (1683–1760), courtesy name Yu'yi 玉依

Wang Wenjie 汪文節 (fl. fourteenth century), courtesy name
  Zemin 澤民

Wang Xizhi 王羲之 (309–c. 365)

Wang Yangdu 汪洋度 (b. 1647), courtesy name Wenye 文冶

Wang 汪 of Yenzhen 嚴鎮 (unidentified)

Wei Zhongxian 魏忠賢 (1568–1627)

Wenxin diaolong 文心彫龍 *The Literary Mind and the
  Carving of Dragons*

Wu Jiaji 吳嘉紀 (1618–1684)

Wu Jingzi 吳敬梓 (1701–1754)

Wu Qi 吳綺 (1619–1693)

Wu Sangui 吳三桂 (1612–1678)

Wu shen xiang ji 侮神象記 *An Account of Defiling the Image of a Deity*

Wu Shiquan 吳士權 Ming Dynasty author (dates unknown)

Wu Tingjian 廷簡 uncle of Wu Zhilu

Wu Weiye 吳偉業 (1609–1671)

Wu Yi 吳逸 (fl. late seventeenth century)

Wu Yuan 吳苑 (1638–1700)

Wu Zhilu 吳之騄 (1644–1715)

Wushi dushuyuan cangban 五世讀書園藏版 "Published from the
  Collection of the Garden Where Books Have Been Read
  Through Five Generations"

Xi shan shi xu 西山詩序 "Preface to the Poems on the
  Western Mountains"

xian 仙 an immortal

Xian Yuan 仙源 Source of the Immortals

Xiang Xue 響雪 Sounding Snow

xiao 孝 filial piety

Xie Bozhen 謝伯貞 (late Ming dynasty)

Xilu shi 息廬詩 *Poems from the Resting Hut*

Xin Hun Bie 新婚別 Parting Newlyweds

Xin yuefu 新樂府 *Neo-Music Bureau Poems,* fifty poems

Xin'an nüshi zheng 新安女史徵 *Evidence for a History of Women
  in Xin'an*

Xin'an 新安 placename in Anhui, sometimes general term for
 southern Anhui

Xin'yi 心一 (possibly Ming dynasty)

xing hua chun yu jiangnan 杏花春雨江南 "Spring rain in the
 apricot blossoms South-of-the-River," a line of poetry

Xinghua chun yu lou 杏花春雨樓 Pavilion-Tower of Spring Rain in
 the Apricot Blossoms

Xiong Kaiyuan 熊開元 (degree 1625), religious name Bo'an 檗菴

Xiuning 休寧 placename in Anhui

Xu Chu 許楚 (1605–1676)

Xu Xiake 徐霞客 (1586–1641)

Xuancheng 宣城 city in Anhui

xue da xing tian 學達性天 "learning that penetrates Human Nature
 and Heaven"

Xue Yong 薛邕 (late eighth–early ninth century)

Xue'ye du yi tu 雪夜讀易圖 "Reading the *Yijing* on a Snowy Night"

Xuezhuang 雪莊 (c. 1646–1719)

Yangzhou zhuzhi ci 揚州竹枝詞 *Bamboo Branch Songs of Yangzhou*

Yanhuang 雁黃 late Ming-early Qing

Yaodi dashi 藥地大師 Great Master of the Herb-Ground,
 Fang Yizhi 方以智 (1611–71)

Yi'cheng 一乘 Buddhist monk, among those who opened the
 Yellow Mountains

Yi'she 黟歙 alternate name for the Yellow Mountains region

Yishan 黟山 Dark Mountains, old name for the Yellow Mountains

You hu 有狐 "There is a fox…"

Youxi 尤溪 Fujian

Yun fang 雲舫 Cloud Boat

Yu Yu 虞預 (c.285—340)

Yu'-an, Master Ji 寓安寄公 (late Ming dynasty)

Yuan Huang 袁黃 (unidentified)

Zha Shibiao 查士標 (1615–1698)

Zhang Yinfu, the "Perfected Man" 張真人尹甫
 (mid-thirteenth century)

Zhang Yingchang 張應昌 (1790–1874)

Zhao Fang 趙汸 (1319–1369)

Zhao Hongwei 趙紅衛 (contemporary)

zhen 貞 chastity

Zheng Yu 鄭玉 (fourteenth century)

Zhiman 志滿 (eighth century)

zhong 忠, loyalty

Zhongshutang yigao 種書堂遺稿 *Writings Preserved from the Hall for Planting Books*

Zhou Dunyi 周敦頤 (1017–1073)

Zhou Yanru 周延儒 (b. 1593)

Zhoushu yiji 周書異記 *Records of Strange Matters from the Book of the Zhou Dynasty*

Zhu Chang 祝昌 (*jinshi* degree, 1649)

Zhu Renyuan 朱人遠 (fl. Kangxi period)

Zhu Song 朱松 (1097–1143)

Zhu Xi 朱熹 (1130–1200)

Zhu Yizun 朱彝尊 (1629–1709)

Zhuzhi ci 竹枝詞 *Bamboo Branch Songs*

Zi jing fu Fengxianxian younghuai wubai zi 自京赴奉先縣詠懷五百字 *Five Hundred Words Singing of My Feelings, While Traveling from the Capital to Fengxian County*

Ziyang shuyuan 紫陽書院 Purple *yang*-force Academy

Zi yu 紫玉 Purple Jade

Zong Bing 宗炳 (375–443)

Floating World Editions

Floating World Editions publishes books that contribute to a deeper understanding of Asian cultures. Editorial supervision: Ray Furse. Book and cover design: Michelle Landry, Digital Dragon Designery. Production supervision: Elizabeth Kerry. Printing and binding: IBT/Hamilton, Troy NY. The typefaces used are Adobe Garamond Pro, Trajan Pro, Droid Sans, Droid Serif and SimSun.

Printed in the USA
CPSIA information can be obtained
at www.ICGtesting.com
JSHW010334190924
69888JS00009B/141

9 781891 640704